THE NATURE

OF

HISTORICAL

THINKING

THE NATURE

OF

HISTORICAL

THINKING

by

ROBERT STOVER

THE UNIVERSITY OF NORTH CAROLINA PRESS
CHAPEL HILL

Copyright © 1967 by
The University of North Carolina Press
Manufactured in the United States of America
By the Seeman Printery, Durham, N. C.
Library of Congress Catalog Card Number 67-17031

TABLE OF CONTENTS

Chapter IV. The Deterministic Intelligibility of Rational Action

Chapter V. Ordinary History Scrutinized: A Critique of Appearances

PART TWO. LIVING IN THE WORLD

Chapter VI. The Standpoint of Living in the World

INTRODUCTION

This is a study of historical thinking. In the main it deals with the thinking of professional historians, but inasmuch as the historian is merely a specialist in pursuits which, to a lesser or greater extent, engage us all, what we shall say pertains to the thinking of all of us.

Controversies about the nature of history and of historical knowledge persist. I am attempting here, as others have done before, to resolve some of these controversies by formulating a number of fundamental distinctions regarding historical thinking. These distinctions serve to make our notions of history at once clearer, more comprehensive, and more coherent; to illuminate misconceptions and misunderstandings; and to provide a basis for constructive criticism of historical works and judgments of all sorts. This study is not intended to be exhaustive, however, for it would be rash to assume that there are no fundamental distinctions pertinent to the nature of historical thinking other than those here treated.

The plan of this study and its relation to recent work in the field can be indicated by an outline of the argument, of the fundamental distinctions that are to be made and the major controversial issues that are to be dealt with.

We should first characterize the subject of our investigation somewhat more precisely. Historians are commonly looked upon as specialists in ascertaining and reconstructing particular happenings of the human past. This conception will guide our inquiry, but not in any rigid manner: we shall not assume that proper historical subject matter is limited to past happenings, and we shall pay little or no heed to the thinking that goes on in connection with fact-finding as such. Our major problem is the nature of historians' thinking about particular happenings—how particular happenings are made intelligible.

We shall also consider questions that arise about the significance of human life as a temporal affair in a temporal world—when we think of ourselves as having a past, present, and future in a world which was before us and will be after us. Whether these questions are the proper concern of the historical profession may be debatable, but there is no contesting the frequency with which opinions about the "meaning of history" crop up in historical literature; and we cannot afford simply to ignore the view that *any* historical intelligibility ultimately presupposes comprehension of the significance of man's "historicity" or of human history as a whole.

The underlying premise of this study is that an adequate conception of historical thinking must be *radically pluralistic*. This premise is a reflection of crosscurrents in contemporary philosophy of history.

A new and healthy emphasis has been placed on what historians actually do—healthy because philosophers in the past have been inclined to assume a lofty posture and to claim a special insight which entitled them to instruct historians as to what they ought to be doing. This contemporary emphasis has not eliminated controversy about the nature of history. It is increasingly apparent that philosophizing on "what historians actually do" is no simple matter, but certain results have been achieved. We can no longer doubt that there are relatively common, relatively distinctive features of conventional historiography in the Western world, and that the more familiar we are with these features the more we will know about the structure of historical thinking. Considerable attention has been given, for example, to the narrative form as typical of historical discourse. Illuminating as this has been, it is extravagant to claim this as a revelation of "history proper"—as the way all authentic historians today aim to make happenings intelligible. Yet the tendency to indulge in this kind of claim persists. Contemporary philosophers defend their quest for the essence of history as plain empiricism, sometimes with the admonition that for the fairest sampling of histories the philosopher should select the most ordinary works of the most acceptable authors. But it has proved impossible to discover one essential thing that *all* professional historians do. An investigator without bias is ultimately led to ask about the significance of allegedly distinctive or common features of ordinary historical writing; to ask whether the narrative form, where it is used, is an unambiguous, autonomous way of making sense out of worldly happenings or, as we shall maintain, a form that is compatible with fundamentally different ways of thinking about particular occurrences.

There is a contrasting strain in contemporary thinking about history. Its representatives maintain that the formula for success is *divide et impera;* that philosophical mastery of history depends on a breakdown of histories and historians into types. Pluralistic conceptions of historical intelligibility have become increasingly common. We hear it said on every side that there are "varieties of history"—different ways of conceiving and writing history. A growing literature is devoted to characterizing the different views of history peculiar to different cultures and periods: the classical Greek view of history, the Hindu view of history, the Chinese view of history, the Christian view of history, and so on. In a more analytic vein, it has been convincingly shown that historians provide satisfactory explanations of the most diverse sorts. We can no longer overlook that what counts as a satisfactory historical explanation depends largely on what is called for in a given problem-context.

But we must sooner or later get around to asking about the significance for the intelligibility of particular human occurrences of these cultural variants, of the various methodological approaches, and of the many kinds of explanation. For example, granting that the problem-context determines what in particular constitutes a satisfactory explanation, is it not possible that the *same* fundamental way of thinking underlies *diverse* particular requirements? A sound pluralistic conception of history must distinguish contextual—and cultural—diversity from fundamental diversity.

On the one hand, our discussion will, then, reflect insights derived from recent empirical concern with characteristics of history as actually written—but will not rashly depict "ordinary history" as "history proper"; and, on the other hand, it will be mindful of recent disclosures of "varieties of history"—but will not take all diversity in historical thinking at face value.

A pluralistic conception of historical thinking ultimately raises philosophical questions which cannot be slighted. In a novel way it obliges us to grapple with the old problem of the unity of historical thinking. We cannot be content simply to replace the discredited essence of history with any number of essential types and to disregard the philosophical consequences. Our own conclusion that critical philosophical analysis discloses two distinct, irreducible, universally human standpoints of thinking distinguishes the radical pluralism of this study from other pluralistic conceptions—a distinguishing trait not likely to prove immediately attractive. A less rigorous pluralism has obvious appeal: in repudiating reductive dogmatism, it licenses the pursuit of whatever type of thinking happens to be congenial. The disintegration of historical intelligibility and conscious tension between disparate human perspectives on the world—consequences of our radical pluralism—are probably less appealing, if not positively unsettling. A more receptive frame of mind might be encouraged by recalling that the nature of history is still being debated on all sides, that historians disagree about the aims of their own profession, and that there is no unanimity regarding such matters as the relevance of past history to present problems, the appropriateness of moral judgments in history, or man's ability to shape his own destiny. It seems reasonable to suppose that significant headway in thinking about history depends on our being prepared to look deeply into the nature of historical thinking, well beyond obvious characteristics of those books that most indisputably qualify as histories; possibly also, then, it depends on our entertaining seriously the thesis of radical pluralism.

Having stressed the novelty of this study of history, it should be added that no altogether new type of historical thinking will be disclosed here. In its analyses and descriptions of different types, this study draws heavily upon recent contributions to the philosophy of history from diverse philosophical approaches: *positivism* with its bold defense of the unity of science; *analytical philosophy* with its anti-systematic orientation and its respect for ordinary language; *pragmatism* with its emphasis on the practical function of thinking; *phenomenology* with its aspiration of providing penetrating descriptions of distinct types of experience and related cognitive "styles"; and Wilhelm Dilthey's sensitive exploration of the foundation of the *Geisteswissenschaften*. What is new here stems largely from juxtaposing ideas that to many readers will be familiar, from stressing differences which others seem to have slighted, from querying the definitive character of any one of the various notions of the nature of history, and from showing the often subtle but always significant transformations that any conception of history undergoes when it is made to pass for the whole truth. The approach is fruitful in the fresh insight it affords into a number of ancient perplexities.

Just how pluralistic is historical thinking? As indicated, we shall maintain that there are two fundamental lines of questioning, i.e., two ways in which we make occurrences intelligible, and, corresponding to them, two fundamentally distinct types of historical thinking: thinking *from the standpoint of natural order,* and thinking *from the standpoint of living in the world.* We leave open the possibility that there are others. In Part One, which deals with natural order intelligibility, we shall defend the thesis that historical knowledge is neither necessarily nor in fact fundamentally different from scientific knowledge, since the same standpoint of natural order can be and sometimes is shared by both alike. Objections to the concept of natural order intelligibility as such and objections to its applicability to history are taken up and answered in turn (chap. II, sec. 9 and chaps. III through V). We shall pay particular attention to the applicability of the natural order standpoint to rational action. Important distinctions are drawn (in chap. IV) between kinds of *meaning relations* (including agents' reasons) and between ways these can be treated in historical accounts: they can be described (*descriptive understanding*); they can be accounted for—in occurrences—from the standpoint of natural order; and they can be understood from the standpoint of the agent (*identifying understanding*). Alleged discrepancies between ordinary history and a "scientific" model are discussed in detail (chap. V).

Part Two, beginning with a description of the second standpoint of thinking, living in the world, examines various ways in which this is involved in historical thinking: in the historian's evaluations, in his reconstruction of rational actions from the standpoint of the agent, and in his criticisms of agents for their practical decisions.

Chapter IX deals, on the one hand, with the use of historical knowledge of the past in confronting contemporary problems or preparing for the future, and, on the other hand, with the dependence of thinking about the past upon our view of present and future.

The analysis of rational action begun in Part One is continued throughout Part Two. The thesis is developed that although deterministic intelligibility is consistent with the "indeterministic" requirements of practical reasoning and criticism from the standpoint of agency, there is nonetheless no possibility of total coherence, no possible integration of the two standpoints from which occurrences are thought about by human beings, historians included. The concluding sections of chapter IX trace the implications of this thesis for human responsibility (our own as well as that of past agents), historical inevitability, and the "meaning of history."

The philosophical assumptions of this study can be briefly summarized. Philosophers have long debated whether the ideas and conceptual structures in terms of which we think about the world are rooted in the object (i.e., the world and our activities *in themselves*) or in the subject (i.e., *in us as thinkers,* making sense out of things by thinking them). Neither alternative will do. What philosophical reflection discloses, *all* that it discloses, is how the world makes sense for us. This disclosure is gradual. Mankind began—as children begin—by being naive in its viewing of the world. It takes time and practice and experimentation and mutual criticism before reflection has the wherewithal to make discriminating judgments on how man makes sense out of the world. The very idea and standards of critical reflection are themselves an outgrowth of this process.

Viewed philosophically, the immensely rich and intricate course of human thought is marked by two related features: experimentation with and gradual refinement of distinct ways of thinking about the happenings of the world, and reflection on these ways of thinking. The history of thought—and, most pertinently, the history of historical thinking—is a progressive revelation of what might be called the nature of man. More precisely, what is disclosed is the way we, as human beings, look upon the world and upon our activities in the world and make sense out of these. *The* way? Rather, we should say, the *ways.*

What are some of the consequences of this view for a study of the nature of history? For one thing, no mere inspection of historical events as "given" can be expected to reveal how they are intelligible, nor can the philosopher limit himself to examining how historians have thought. Secondly, "the nature of history" and "the nature of historical thinking" are two sides of the same coin, or two ways of referring to the one thing that philosophical reflection on history aims to disclose. Thirdly, questions about the nature of history or of historical thinking are fundamental philosophical problems, not merely questions about special techniques of inquiry into a special kind or sector of phenomena.

Critical reflection, progressive refinement, and discrimination between fundamentally different ways of making sense out of the world come about through situations that call for re-examining accepted presuppositions.

Just as there are revolutions (such as the Copernican) within a natural science, so there are intellectual revolutions in which the very nature of science is at stake, and more besides. Thus the Cartesian Revolution, sparked by discoveries of quantified laws of nature, challenged the dominant conception of Western science and, in doing so, also challenged generally accepted presuppositions of valuation and normative judgment. Postulating the mechanical-mathematical intelligibility of everything in the world except mind and its activities, Descartes took issue with the idea that all of nature is intelligible in terms of final causes. Since the categories of moral science—good, bad, right, wrong, etc.—were thereby declared inappropriate for understanding any created thing other than man, Cartesianism envisioned the transformation both of science and of moral reflection.

Most philosophers would like to think that revolutions which shake up and reform our most fundamental ways of thinking are not simply historical occurrences. They yield, at least in the long run, a perfected awareness of how it is *appropriate* to think about the world, including, of course, man himself. Some philosophers have maintained that this process of developing awareness terminated with their own definitive insights. The trouble is that these definitive insights are continually becoming outdated, if we judge by the balance of philosophical opinion. It has proved extremely difficult even to formulate criteria permitting confident *comparative* judgments of ways of thinking about the world, permitting us to evaluate them as superior or inferior relative to one another. An acknowledged general method of proving that an intellectual innovation or critique represents a step forward, a perfected awareness, rather than a step backward, has eluded the philosophical profession at large.

This being the case, we must adjust our philosophical sights accordingly. We certainly cannot avoid the issue completely. At the root of controversies about the nature of history—and science—are conflicting general presuppositions as to how it is appropriate to think about the world.

I have proceeded on the basic premise that there can be objective insight into the intelligibility-of-the-world-for-man, insight that accrues and undergoes refinement in the course of the history of philosophical reflection, including reflection upon historical thinking. I thus postulate a crucial distinction between, on the one hand, how men have at any time actually thought of themselves and the world (including their historical thinking) and, on the other hand, critically sound thinking about man and world. At any given moment of intellectual history we find ourselves employing certain ways of thinking, encountering specific difficulties in using them, and trying, in consequence, to revise our intellectual presuppositions. The problems of revision are always concrete and specific. The way to attack the problem of history's relation to science, for example, is to treat the problem as we encounter it here and now. This approach, however, in no sense compromises the ultimate intent of re-examination and revision. That intent is to discern ways of thinking which are *definitively* appropriate in respect to all that is known about man and the world. I want only to emphasize that we ineluctably exercise that intention in a *specific situation.* Our ideas, then, must be judged in the first instance by ourselves and our contemporaries in the light of the problems experienced by us and of all relevant available data. The durability of conclusions judged to be sound here and now will depend upon the continuity of the specific philosophical problem-situation. The very terms of the problem can be altered by new knowledge about man and the world.

The affirmation that there are fundamentally different ways of thinking about the world—and, accordingly, different kinds of historical thinking—warrants our distinguishing philosophy from all thinking about the world: philosophy as a thinking about thinking. In the sense most pertinent to this study, this takes the form of *discriminating between kinds* of thinking about the world and *refining our conceptions* of these. Philosophy, so understood, is critical thinking.

I offer no proof of radical pluralism: the claim that it is human to think about the world in different fundamental ways. I only present a descriptive analysis of different ways in which we do think about the world. I focus this analysis on historical thinking. There are no simple rules for identifying or characterizing a critically conceived fundamental way of thinking. My own procedure has emphasized (a) an underlying line of questioning, including specification and description of the experiential context within which the questioning arises; (b) the requirements of adequate answers to questions of this kind; and (c) the scope of the line of questioning and points of contrast with other ways of thinking. I have referred loosely to these various characteristics as the *presuppositions* constituting the *scheme of intelligibility* peculiar to each way of thinking about the world. The principal difficulties confronting philosophy of history lie in clearly apprehending the presuppositions of fundamental ways in which we seek knowledge of the world, and in establishing the relevance of these ways to historical thinking. Neither in Part One nor in Part Two have I attempted a complete statement of presuppositions, aiming rather at a presentation responsive to the central problems in contemporary philosophical discussion of history.

Philosophers sharing the view that to understand history is ultimately to understand man himself have sometimes cast their reflections in the form of a theory of man: philosophical anthropology. They have often had little to say about historians, about works written by historians, or about other philosophical analyses of historical works. I have reversed this emphasis. Although mindful of the anthropological implications of a study of history, this inquiry centers upon the thinking of historians and deals at length with other philosophical opinions about what historians are doing.

The importance of understanding the nature of historical thinking transcends the immediate objectives of philosophical analysis. Vital interests are at stake. Although critical philosophy of history does not make human destiny—whether in grand design or in intimate detail—any less problematic, the self-knowledge it affords enters into practical reasoning, and he who has this insight correctly reckons himself the wiser for it.

PART ONE

NATURAL ORDER

Chapter I.

Natural Order Intelligibility

1. INTRODUCTION

In this Part we shall discuss one way in which men think about the happenings of the world with the aim of making them intelligible: namely, natural order thinking.

Our initial formulation of natural order intelligibility will seem disconcertingly remote from the subject of our study, the nature of historical thinking. A general account of natural order intelligibility is needed, however, if we are to get at the roots of the controversies between those who defend and those who attack the assimilation of history to science.[1]

Roughly speaking, natural order is an orderliness manifested in occurrences: under the same circumstances the same things happen, either always or with the same frequency. To think about the world, to observe it, to form concepts, and to reason with a view to making judgments about the orderliness of happenings, is what we call thinking from the standpoint of natural order, and the

1. Expert logical analyses of scientific thought are available and constitute an invaluable resource. Unfortunately, however, we cannot refer to any of them as authoritative for our purposes. Even though some of these analyses treat historical thinking extensively, one looks in vain for a competent general analysis of science readily applicable to history and sensitive throughout to the controversial issues surrounding historical thinking. As might be expected, taking history seriously from the outset influences the resultant conception of science. This is reason enough for our providing in chapters I and II a brief but precise delineation of natural order intelligibility. The originality of this delineation should not be exaggerated. With some major and some minor modifications, it derives from the work of Carl G. Hempel and Ernest Nagel, a debt that is obvious but deserves nonetheless to be explicitly acknowledged.

objective of thinking from this standpoint is natural order intelligibility.

This standpoint characterizes much of what we call scientific thinking. The quest for valid empirical generalizations, for unifying theories, for systematic knowledge, all *can* be carried on from this standpoint. Scientific thinking, however, is not always from the standpoint of natural order, and even when it is, specific objectives of the scientist are likely to be selective, narrower in scope than those of the standpoint itself. For this and other reasons we shall not equate natural order intelligibility with science.

The standpoint of natural order also characterizes much historical thinking. The most striking manifestation of this is the interest shown by historians in the causes and effects of human events and actions. Even Trevelyan in his rededication of history to the muses, although insisting that the historian's "interpretation of the cause and effect of any one particular event cannot rightly be called 'scientific,'" conceded that guessing about such things was part of the business of the historian.[2] In so far as both the thinking called scientific and that called historical are done from the same standpoint, we are about to give an affirmative answer to the old question: Is history a science? More precisely, we are about to formulate a scheme of intelligibility that is relevant to some of the thinking done by scientists and historians alike. With important qualifications, we are affirming the "unity of science": it *can* make sense to speak of a fundamental affinity between history and science. Little wonder, then, that some historians and philosophers have so stubbornly defended this point of view.

But this also should be made quite plain: we are not saying that natural order thinking constitutes the main line of questioning of *every* historian in at least *some* of his investigations, or even that it is the main line of questioning of *some* historians in *all* of their investigations. Rather, we say that natural order intelligibility is a plausible objective of thinking about particular occurrences of the human past; that it is the *principal* objective of *some* historians on *some* occasions; and that it is *among* the objectives of *many* historians on *many* occasions. It constitutes one very common idea of what historical inquiry is all about: a quest for the order exhibited in world happenings.

Natural order intelligibility, as we shall formulate it, is not

2. G. M. Trevelyan, *Clio, A Muse* (2d ed.; London: Longmans, Green and Co., 1930), pp. 144, 148.

restricted to accounts of events that have already happened: it extends to thinking about present and future occurrences as well. Correspondingly, natural order generalizations are not by definition exclusively about what has already happened; they are not essentially restricted to past events. Yet much of our discussion will focus on accounts of past occurrences because most historians, in thinking from the standpoint of natural order, have been engaged in explaining past happenings. For the same reason, we shall concentrate on the intelligibility of particular occurrences.

We shall not begin by scrutinizing a sampling of historical works. Such a beginning, although apparently in keeping with sound empiricism, actually would obscure rather than disclose what we are looking for. The scheme of intelligibility that we are here concerned with cannot be found by leafing through the pages of any history book that unquestionably contains explanations of events. We are looking for a scheme or framework taken for granted by the historian, indeed so far taken for granted that he would probably be unable to expound it satisfactorily if requested to do so. Our endeavor here is to formulate adequately this scheme confusedly and imperfectly implicit in the thought and work of many historians.

We shall largely disregard, especially at the outset, any incidental peculiarities of historical explanations that do not shed light upon the nature of natural order intelligibility. Indeed, our thesis is that there are essential presuppositions and requirements which define *what it is for an occurrence to be intelligible to us* and that one set of such presuppositions and requirements defines natural order intelligibility. Many so-called distinctive features of historical explanation do not go to the heart of the matter. They often reflect common modes of simplification or expository shortcuts, which are perfectly acceptable but which nonetheless leave *un*intelligibility in their wake. Such residual unintelligibility can be traced to conventional expectations, professional custom, selectivity of interest on the part of author or reader, the usual gaps in available information, and so on. The historian may tell us all that we want to know about why certain events happened, or all that can be told, and tell us in just the way that appeals to us— but it does not follow that he has thereby fully met the intelligibility requirements of a standpoint of thinking.

The question: "Why did this happen?" is familiar enough. But how shall we discern a fundamental scheme of intelligibility presupposed in answering it? What we are looking for is rooted in the very ordinary idea that events, happenings, actions, etc. depend for their occurrence upon specific circumstances. To account for something that happened, in this sense, is to show upon which specific circumstances it depended; to show what were the determining conditions; or to single out the circumstances in relation to which its occurrence was "likely." This idea—which we shall have to refine through further discussion—gives us our clue to one type of historical intelligibility. Following out this clue we can reformulate the issues of historical explanation in such a way as to undercut controversy.

Let us for the time being waive the question of whether or in what sense it is a presupposition of natural order thinking that *everything* that exists or happens is bound to happen. Our immediate objective is to define the *natural order intelligibility of a particular occurrence*, a concept whose applicability to any particular occurrence is independent of its applicability to all. This definition will be normative in the sense that it could serve as a basis for criticism of the adequacy of an historian's account and as a model for an historian aspiring to think plausibly and express himself unequivocally. Its sanction is not opinion or convention. Its status as defining a plausible objective of thinking, its suitability to function as a critical norm or model, derives from the fact that it is a definition representing a critical tradition of continuous questioning, a process through which there has gradually been refined and differentiated a way of thinking about the world.

For a particular occurrence e to be intelligible in natural order terms the following requirements must be fulfilled:

There must be a confirmed regular relation between occurrences of this kind (E) and certain other kinds of occurrences referred to collectively as the sufficient conditions. This natural order relation (as we shall call it) between a particular occurrence e and its sufficient conditions $c_1, \ldots, c_n$ can be more formally expressed as follows: "Whenever occurrences of kinds $C_1, \ldots, C_n$ occur then an instance of kind E occurs in a specified spatio-temporal relationship to $C_1, \ldots, C_n$."[3] This formulation of the regular relation we shall call a nomological universal. (secs. 2 and 3)

3. We shall use the expression "determining conditions" to refer to one or more of the sufficient conditions. A particular occurrence e that has sufficient conditions will be called "conditioned." Whether nomological relations are "deterministic" is a question we shall consider later (chap. II, sec. 7). Capital letters are used throughout to stand for *kinds*, lower case letters for *particulars*.

A nomological universal refers to an indefinite number of instances. (sec. 4)

A nomological universal must be partially confirmed by indirect evidence. (sec. 5)

A nomological universal is characterized by unrestricted universality. (sec. 6)

Our definition of natural order intelligibility will take form as we proceed to discuss these requirements. *What* is intelligible are occurrences and we shall first consider what these are.

2. Occurrences

We use the term "occurrence" to refer to any discriminable trait or set of traits (qualities, relations, or combinations thereof) coming into existence, enduring unchanged, changing in some repects, or ceasing to exist (or some combination thereof) at or during some specifiable time and at some specifiable place or places in the unique and all-inclusive system of temporal-spatial order which we call "the world."

The term "occurrence" recommends itself as a familiar one in discussions of history. It readily suggests both a content (i.e., traits): that which came into existence, changed, etc., and the existential condition: that it came into existence, that it changed, etc.[4] It is not usually associated with enduring unchanged but, on the whole, is probably less restricted in reference than the term "event." "Happening" would serve equally well, and we shall sometimes use it as equivalent in meaning to "occurrence."

We should emphasize that our concept "occurrence" does not entail a restrictive commitment as to what sorts of things exist, nor a commitment as to the intrinsic propriety of treating or not treating any discriminable trait or set of traits as occurrences. The class of occurrences can include bodies in motion, electromagnetic phenomena, social structures and processes, relations of meaning, and all manner of subjective experiences.

An occurrence can be considered in respect to its differences from other occurrences or its resemblances to them. Irrespective of how it is considered, an occurrence is essentially unique in the sense of non-duplicable. Oftentimes, even in differentiating one occurrence from others, essential non-duplicability is not made explicit. Occasionally, however, it is important to distinguish be-

4. For convenience we shall use "trait"—or "state of affairs"—as including existential conditions, i.e., coming into existence, enduring, etc.

tween occurrences or to identify an occurrence by characteristics that do set it apart from all others, actual or possible, including, therefore, all those that could be said to be like it in some respect. Mindful of the controversy over the alleged uniqueness of historical events and the implications of this uniqueness, we shall frequently use the expression "particular occurrence" in order to stress essential non-duplicability, and it is appropriate that we clarify the latter concept.

When I differentiate between two presently existing writing-desks, identifying one as style Louis XV and the other as Second Empire, I have differentiated two particular occurrences (two desks now actually existing) by traits which do not disclose the essential non-duplicability of these occurrences. All Louis XV writing-desks differ from all those whose style is Second Empire. Contextually my stylistic differentiation may be convenient and sufficient; if these are the only two writing-desks in a certain room I can unambiguously designate one of them to a connoisseur of furniture by calling it "the Louis XV writing-desk." But were there two Louis XV writing-desks in the room I would have to specify, for example, "the Louis XV writing-desk with the missing leg." Were there two Louis XV desks with missing legs, I would have to specify further, and so on. We are led to ask: What makes the desks in question not only different from each other but essentially non-duplicable? Can we state what distinguishes a particular occurrence from *any* other, irrespective of what others there might be or might have been?

Ultimately the ground of essential particularity is the existence of a certain discriminable kind of trait (or traits) at a particular time and place. What particularizes occurrences specified as being at the same time and place are *differences in the traits*. (For example, the heat, the din, and the smell of a battlefield might be discriminated as three different occurrences at the same time and place.) On the other hand, two occurrences of the *same* trait or set of traits are essentially particular by virtue either of their existing at a different time or in a different place (or both). It is axiomatic that no two time locations on the world time scale are identical and that no two places in world space are identical. In combination, spatio-temporal co-ordinates "fix" an occurrence of the same trait or traits, constituting its non-duplicability. This way of putting the matter vastly simplifies the way dating and placing are sometimes done. We do not need to take into account all the complexities involved, however, providing we make clear our assumption that, in principle, objective agreement can always be reached as to the identity of any particular occurrence. There is no insuperable relativity of spatio-temporal co-ordinate systems.

We should note that a particular occurrence is not to be confused with a particular value of the variables in laws containing variables. The reason for this is simply that particular values of variables are temporally and spatially duplicable; there can be multiple instances of the same value of a variable at different times in the same place, or at the same time in different places, or at different times in different places.

With suitable refinements these considerations apply to such common historical subject matters as particular persons, particular countries, particular revolutions, particular battles, particular elections, particular cases of industrial development, population growth, imperialistic expansion, and so on. Most important, this conception of an occurrence as essentially non-duplicable is precise enough to serve as a basis for subsequent analysis of judgments which assert that a certain actual occurrence—essentially unlike all other occurrences actual or possible—was necessary or probable under the circumstances.

3. Nomological Universals

We shall subsequently maintain that most "causal" accounts of events to be found in historical works are a special form of natural order intelligibility. In holding that natural order intelligibility presupposes as an essential requirement a confirmed *regular* relation, we are implicitly taking a stand on the meaning of causality in history. We are subscribing to a "generality" interpretation of causality: causal accounts of occurrences are essentially general in the sense that they imply a general proposition (or imply that there is one), namely, a general proposition of the sort which we are calling a nomological universal.

In one respect our statement of the generality requirement may be misleading. In saying that the intelligibility of an occurrence in natural order terms presupposes a regular relation we have suggested that it presupposes but one nomological universal. Our requirement can stand as formulated, but we should stress that it is intended to allow for cases in which the one required law (nomological universal) is derived from a set of laws (nomological universals). The distinction between natural order accounts involving one law and those involving many is in no case absolute because of the "indirect evidence" requirement. It is a useful distinction, however, and we shall have occasion to clarify it and to assess its significance.[5]

In calling $c_1, \ldots, c_n$ "sufficient conditions" we mean to indicate that when more than one factor (trait and existential condition) is specified as a determining condition of an occurrence, every factor specified is a necessary member of the set, i.e., the nomological universal would be falsified by the omission of any one. In other words, no superfluous traits are included among the determining conditions constituting the sufficient conditions.

We do not assume that occurrences of kind E have only one set of sufficient conditions. In other words, our concept of sufficient conditions allows for "plurality of causes." Sometimes we may have reason to assert that "E if and only if $C_1, \ldots, C_n$." Only in such cases does knowledge of an occurrence e permit us to infer the occurrence of $c_1, \ldots, c_n$.

There is an important difference between nomological universals and universals as interpreted in modern symbolic logic. It is customary in symbolic logic to transcribe universals as conditionals, e.g., "All pieces of copper when heated under normal circumstances expand" becomes "For any x, if x is a piece of copper heated under normal circumstances then x expands." Universal conditionals—and this is the crucial point—are held to be true providing there are no instances at all of the kind described in the antecedent clause. Any nomological universal can, indeed, be transcribed as a universal conditional but, by contrast with the stated interpretation, "the mere fact that nothing happens to exist (in the omnitemporal sense) which satisfies the antecedent clause . . . is not sufficient to establish its truth."[6]

4. Indefinite Scope of Predication

The nomological universals presupposed as a requirement of natural order intelligibility are distinguished from some universals by the following feature: a nomological universal must not

5. See chap. V, sec. 6.
6. Ernest Nagel, *The Structure of Science* (New York: Harcourt, Brace and World, 1961), pp. 51-52. Another example of a nomological universal, one more closely associated with human events—and therefore with history— but cumbersome for purposes of illustration, is the following: "In an economy characterized by 'perfect competition,' a rise in the price of any one good is, under normal circumstances, followed by a decline in demand for that good."

be formulated so as to restrict to a definite number the occurrences to which it applies. The following universal, for example, fails to meet this requirement: "All the planets known to astronomers in 1967 have elliptical orbits." This failing is apparent even when the universal is stated in conditional form: "If e is the orbit of any planet known to astronomers in 1967, then e has an elliptical orbit." Of course there might be *independent* evidence supporting the judgment that there cannot actually be more than some definite number of occurrences of the kind specified. All that is required is that this fact "not be inferable from the term in the universal conditional which formulates the scope of predication."[7]

This requirement signifies, in effect, that relations of natural order are independent of the number of actual instances of the kind specified in the relevant nomological universal.

5. INDIRECT EVIDENCE

We face the problem of distinguishing a nomological universal from a so-called universal of fact which is not finite in scope of predication. Consider, for example, the universal "All matriculated students at the University of Paris are less than 100 years of age." The terms of the description—"matriculated students at the University of Paris"—do not set any definite limit on the number of students who fit the description. Let us assume, moreover, that the University regulations specify no maximum age limit for matriculation. Even if we inspected the University records and were able to find out the age of every student up to the present, we could not base the assertion about the age of "all matriculated students" *solely upon these data*. It is entirely consistent with these data (i.e., direct evidence) that next year a person matriculates whose age is 100 or more. Were this actually to happen it would be obvious that the stated generalization was an accidental universal, a mere universal of fact, one that happened to be valid up to a certain time but was false thereafter.

What requirement serves to distinguish a nomological universal from true universals of fact? The requirement is indirect evidence. A nomological universal can be indirectly confirmed in one of two ways: "by instances that directly confirm more general hypotheses from which it follows or less general statements that follow from it."[8]

7. *Ibid.*, p. 59.
8. Arthur Pap, *An Introduction to the Philosophy of Science* (New York:

The generalizations (variously referred to as general hypotheses, general statements, and general laws) that appear in argumentation indirectly confirming nomological universals are also nomological universals.[9] Which nomological universals are cited as indirect evidence and which as making the particular occurrence under discussion intelligible will, of course, depend. Our point is simply that any natural order account presupposes evidence for a "covering" universal, and that in part this evidence is indirect in character.

The concept of indirect evidence incidentally sheds light upon the possibility of confirming a nomological universal even without knowledge of *any* directly-confirming occurrences.

6. Unrestricted Universality

Our second requirement was that a nomological universal not be formulated in terms that entail a scope of predication restricted to a definite number of occurrences. This is not to be confused with the requirement now to be considered: unrestricted universality. The latter we interpret to mean that the descriptions of the kind of occurrence and kinds of determining conditions include no restrictions as to specific time or place, nor even any specific segment of time or region of space, and no restriction as to particular objects.[10] Restricted universality can be compatible with fulfilment of the second requirement. For example, "Every time a resident of Philadelphia, Pennsylvania, in the seventeenth century suffers from double pneumonia, the attack is fatal." Although the description of the kind of occurrence is not unrestrictedly universal, for it includes restrictions as to a specific period and place, one cannot deduce from the description "resident of Philadelphia, Pennsylvania, in the seventeenth century and suffers from double pneumonia" that any definite number of instances of death from double pneumonia occurred then and there.[11]

The Free Press, 1962), p. 302. Cf. Nagel, *Structure of Science,* pp. 64-65; R. B. Braithwaite, *Scientific Explanation* (London: Cambridge University Press, 1953), pp. 301 ff.

9. Generalizations (such as pure mathematical expressions) that do not explicitly refer to empirical content of any kind must be unequivocally interpretable in terms of empirical content if they are to have a confirming function.

10. See Nagel, *Structure of Science,* p. 57; Carl G. Hempel, "Studies in the Logic of Explanation," in *Aspects of Scientific Explanation* (New York: The Free Press, 1965), pp. 266 ff.; Karl Popper, *The Logic of Scientific Discovery* (London: Hutchinson, 1959), secs. 13-15.

11. We shall postpone discussion of the significance of this requirement. See chap. II, sec. 6 below.

At this point we can elucidate the sense in which an occurrence can be said to be "necessary" in regard to natural order. The necessity of an occurrence relative to a covering nomological universal (1) is to be distinguished from logical necessity and (2) contrasts with the contingent correlation of traits formulated in an accidental universal.

(1): There is one class of universal statements, i.e., statements without any formulated restriction on scope of predication, in regard to which we speak of necessity but which is distinct from the class of nomological universals. The mere form of a statement can be misleading. We have tried to differentiate nomological universals by the following characteristics: A nomological universal of the form "All cases of A are cases of B" implies that "There is no case of A which is not a case of B" and that "if anything were a case of A it would be a case of B," where A is a non-finite class. But consider the statement "All divorcees are persons formerly married and subsequently legally separated from their spouses": it implies that "There is no divorcee who is not legally separated from his (or her) spouse," and the class of divorcees is non-finite. We might very well say, as logicians have said, that what we have here is a *necessary* relation. But if we interpret these statements about divorcees in the most natural way they exemplify a kind of necessary relationship which is different from that of a nomological universal. We are dealing here with a relation, often called "analytic," between a word and the meaning of the word. These statements assert nothing informative about matters of fact. The necessity in this case, called "logical" or "analytic," is to be distinguished from nomological necessity.

To avoid ambiguity, then, we must further specify that a nomological universal is not analytic. It does not stipulate the meaning of a word or words nor does it formulate conventional or customary meanings. A nomological universal is an informative assertion about matters of fact, often called a "synthetic" proposition. It is an essential characteristic of nomological universals that they "can be established only by induction, not by analysis of meanings and formal deduction alone." Accordingly, whereas it would make no sense to speak of "confirming" an analytic proposition, we have specified that natural order intelligibility presupposes *confirmed* general propositions. We shall be content here to note that this requirement presupposes generally accepted "rules of critical inductive generalization in accordance with which the acceptance" of a nomological universal "is justified by 'confirming' empirical evidence"; also that it presupposes comparable rules for asserting that a particular occurrence is an instance of a nomological relation.[12]

(2): We have noted that our concept of natural order intelligibility incorporates a "generality" interpretation of causal relations. It is evident from what has been said that our analysis also incorporates a "regularity" interpretation of causality, namely, the view that causal propositions can be analyzed without employing notions of logical or physical necessity.[13] Yet it seems natural to us to restate a nomological universal ("Whenever C_1 , . . . , C_n, then E") in the following way: "If C_1 , . . . , C_n, then *necessarily E*." The "necessarily" in this restatement reflects the difference between assertions of *de facto* constant conjunction (accidental universals or universals of fact) and assertions of natural order (nomological universals): the latter require indirect evidence. Applying this to causality, we can say that the necessity of the causal relation is "nothing but" regularity *providing* that we have clearly in mind that the requirement of indirect evidence differentiates nomological and, therefore, causal regularity from mere *de facto* regularity.

12. Pap, *Philosophy of Science*, pp. 304-5. We intentionally by-pass this potential trouble spot in natural order thinking. As Nagel observes: ". . . in sharp contrast to what has been accomplished in codifying the principles of demonstrative inference, there is at present no generally accepted, explicitly formulated, and fully comprehensive system of logical rules for performing these crucially important tasks" (*Structure of Science*, p. 591).

13. Pap, *Philosophy of Science*, pp. 315-16. Cf. Bernard Berofsky, "Determinism" (Ph.D. dissertation, Columbia University, 1963), pp. 169-70.

Chapter II.

Natural Order Intelligibility
as an Ideal

1. INTRODUCTION

Having stated some principal requirements of natural order intelligibility we pass to a consideration of these requirements as constituting an ideal. Many accounts of particular occurrences that do not satisfy the stated requirements are correctly judged satisfactory relative to contextual requirements. It suffices that an account tells us just what we wanted to know—no more and no less. If we did not want an account of a particular state of affairs in natural order terms there can be no objection when something else is provided. But some natural order accounts of particular states of affairs, even though they satisfy contextual requirements, are plausibly regarded as imperfect accounts *relative* to natural order thinking as a line of questioning about the world which, when completely and successfully pursued and its results fully formulated, issues in what we have called natural order intelligibility. The accounts we wish to focus upon are those which do not provide something *else* than natural order intelligibility, but something *less*.

Why precisely this occurrence at precisely this time and place? Just what occurrence will take place there next? These are questions that can be plausibly answered in terms of regular relations among states of affairs. Adequate answers to these questions must meet the requirements we have formulated. As will be shown in the following sections, accounts of occurrences which fall within the natural order line of questioning, but which fail to meet the requirements, constitute only partial or sketchy answers to these questions.

2. Ceteris Paribus or Quasi-General Accounts

By a *ceteris paribus* account we mean an account stating that an occurrence *e* together with the circumstances of its occurrence are in accord with a generalization of the form "Whenever C_1 , . . . , C_n then E, other things being equal," there being no specification of these relevant "other things" or of their traits when they are "equal." The *ceteris paribus* proviso itself need not be explicitly stated; for example, "Better educated men drafted into the armed forces of a nation show fewer psychosomatic symptoms than those with less education."

The generalization in a *ceteris paribus* account differs from a nomological universal in not specifying the sufficient conditions. Such accounts do respond to the question "Why did this happen?" by answers in terms of regular relations among states of affairs; they obviously do not suffice, however, as accounts of why precisely this state of affairs happened at precisely this time and place. The generalization that is invoked in giving the account would not be rejected as false, in some situations, even though the specified determining conditions occurred and an instance of E did not. As Nagel comments in reference to the above example: "For it is unlikely that the generalization would be rejected as false should some particular group of college-educated draftees display a larger number of such symptoms than a group of draftees with only primary grade schooling, if it should also turn out, for example, that the commanding officer of the two groups had a special animus against college men and enjoyed making life miserable for them."[1]

It would simply be said that other things were not equal. Allowance for exceptions to the C_1 , . . . , C_n to E relationship, exceptions due to the unspecified other things, is built into *ceteris paribus* accounts. We must therefore hold that no *ceteris paribus* account as such adequately informs us why *e* did occur, why it did not *not* occur. A *ceteris paribus* account may satisfy a limited curiosity on our part, but it clearly leaves questions unanswered relative to the notion of making particular occurrences intelligible in terms of

1. Ernest Nagel, *The Structure of Science* (New York: Harcourt, Brace and World, 1961) p. 465.

regular relations among states of affairs, the very mode of intelligibility presupposed in *ceteris paribus* accounts.

3. STATISTICAL ACCOUNTS

Let us next consider accounts of particular occurrences in which the implicit generalization asserts an invariable statistical or probabilistic relation between states of affairs. The probability here in question has nothing to do with the degree of certainty with which a law is asserted. We do distinguish between generalizations that are probably true and those about which we are certain. But these degrees of certainty or degrees of confirmation characterize *all* empirical generalizations of indefinite scope of predication. In this sense of probability *any* warranted nomological universal can appropriately be termed probabilistic.

What interests us here, rather, are accounts of particular occurrences involving laws of the form "Under conditions $C_1, \ldots, C_n$, occurrences of kind E happen with a statistical probability greater than one-half but less than one."[2] For example, suppose we are asking why John Doe's hay fever attack subsided. A statistical account in response to this question might take the following form: "That John Doe's hay fever attack subsided was a very likely occurrence in view of (a) the fact that he took 8 milligrams of chlor-trimeton and (b) the confirmed general regularity that the probability for subsidence of a hay fever attack upon administration of 8 milligrams of chlor-trimeton is high."[3] Such statistical accounts are inadequate relative to the line of questioning we are discussing for exactly the same reason that *ceteris paribus* accounts are inadequate: they fail to account for particular instances of the kind of occurrence referred to in the law. Statistical laws, like *ceteris paribus* generalizations, do not assert that certain specified conditions are invariably accompanied by a particular occurrence of a certain kind. The non-occurrence of an instance of the kind is perfectly compatible with the law cited in statistical accounts

2. Statistical laws, of course, do not always assert a relative frequency greater than one-half. E.g., "If a geometrically and physically symmetrical cube is repeatedly tossed, the probability (or relative frequency) that the cube will come to rest with a given face uppermost is 1/6" (Nagel, *Structure of Science*, p. 76). Such laws might be relevant were we investigating the determining conditions of the *in*frequency of traits or of their non-occurrence, but to deal with these cases would needlessly complicate our analysis.

3. See Carl G. Hempel, "Explanation in Science and in History," in *Frontiers of Science and Philosophy*, ed. R. G. Colodny (Pittsburgh: University of Pittsburgh Press, 1962), p. 13.

of particular occurrences. All such accounts leave us with the question: Why in fact in this case did the particular occurrence take place?[4]

Another type of statistical account should be noted, namely that in which particular instances of statistically described properties are accounted for in terms of regular relations between them and other states of affairs. Thus an increase in the frequency of suicide in a certain community might be accounted for by citing a dependence of frequency of suicide upon the strength of social bonds. The generalization implied in such an account might be formulated as follows: "In any community displaying a difference in the strength of social bonds at any two different times, the frequency of suicide will be greater at the time the social bonds are weaker."

Certainly unanswered questions remain in all such accounts. The statistical descriptions refer to a non-statistical state of affairs— to that which occurs with such and such a frequency; in the above example the reference is to acts of suicide. Now although this second type of statistical account tells us why a certain state of affairs (a relatively greater frequency of suicide) occurred just there and then, it does not adequately account for any particular non-statistical state of affairs (any act of suicide). The above generalization cannot account for the fact that a particular person did or did not commit suicide at one or the other of the times mentioned. It would be quite compatible with this generalization and with the account utilizing it if the diminished strength of social bonds were not even one of the determining conditions of a particular suicide occurring at the time this state of affairs prevailed. In general, non-statistically described properties are not adequately accounted for by generalizations about statistical properties. These statistical accounts do, then, leave questions unanswered. But it would seem arbitrarily restrictive to hold that descriptions of the type "*E*'s occurring with a certain frequency" do not themselves describe occurrences. If we concede that they do describe occurrences, then statistical accounts of this second type, by contrast

4. See Nagel, *Structure of Science*, p. 559; also pp. 18 (example 7) and 20 (example 10). Our allegation as to the inadequacy of statistical accounts of the sort just discussed must be defended against two critical reservations: Is the ideal of natural order intelligibility appropriate in the light of the objectives of current scientific inquiry? and: Is it not possible, or even probable, that some occurrences are not intelligible other than in terms of statistical accounts? We shall deal with these in sec. 9 (iii) and sec. 11 respectively.

with the first, are not inherently inadequate. They can complete a line of natural order questioning.

4. CAUSAL ACCOUNTS

Some features ascribed to causal accounts are compatible with the requirements of adequate natural order accounts. This applies, for example, to the following features, which are often cited as characteristic of the relation specified in the generalizations ("causal laws") implicit in causal accounts: (1) the specified relation between determining condition (cause) and conditioned occurrence (effect) is invariable in the sense that whenever the alleged cause occurs so does the alleged effect; (2) the relation holds between events that are spatially contiguous; (3) the relation has a temporal character in the sense that the cause precedes the effect and is also continuous with the latter; and (4) the relation is asymmetrical in the sense that the occurrence called the effect is not also a cause of the event called the cause.[5]

Other common characteristics of causal accounts, however, *do* render them inadequate as natural order accounts. It will be helpful if we distinguish two types of causal accounts. In one type, "c_1 caused e" means that "c_1 made e possible." In the second type, "c_1 caused e" means that "given c_1, e necessarily occurred." In regard to the first of these we may observe that no assumption is implied to the effect that the occurrence is intelligible in natural order terms. Happenings of the world could conceivably be orderly only in the sense that they happen in accordance with generalizations of this sort: "Never E unless $C_1 , \ldots , C_n$." The order of the world, so conceived, would be an order in which conditions made occurrences possible but not necessary. Assertions of this sort of order would adequately answer the question "Under what conditions is E possible?" Moreover, the plausibility of the question "Under what conditions is E possible?" does not presuppose the plausibility of the question "Under what conditions is E necessary?" But answers to the question about possibility obviously do not suffice as answers to the latter natural order question. They leave partially unanswered the question: "Why did precisely this occurrence actually take place just then and there?" If the latter *is* a plausible question, if the natural order line of questioning is plausible, then it makes sense to say that relative

5. Cf. Nagel, *Structure of Science*, p. 74.

to *this* line of questioning, questioning that is limited to possibility-conditions is incomplete and corresponding answers are inadequate. Even if it turns out that conditions of possibility can be established without reference to natural order and even if we are sometimes curious to know only what conditions made a particular occurrence possible, accounts which merely state that "c_1 made e possible" nonetheless do fall short of providing intelligibility relative to a fundamental line of questioning about world happenings.

Accounts of the second type (to which we shall henceforth restrict the designation "causal accounts") do, by contrast with those of the first type, essentially presuppose natural order intelligibility. The only plausible analysis of an assertion of necessary occurrence is in terms of a rule of occurrence of the sort we have called nomological universals. An assertion that "c_1 caused e" meaning that "given c_1, e necessarily occurred" implies that there are kinds of conditions under which events of the kind E would always occur. Those conditions are sufficient. In practice causal accounts seldom specify the sufficient conditions. More commonly there is a tacit assumption or explicit qualification to the effect that what is asserted is only one or some of the sufficient conditions; e.g., "c_1 was among the causes of e," or "given c_1 together with other circumstances e necessarily occurred." Causal accounts that do specify the sufficient conditions afford complete natural order intelligibility. But if, as is usually the case, they do not, they are obviously inadequate relative to the ideal requirements of the line of questioning which they themselves presuppose.[6] They leave unanswered the question: "Were there other causes and, if so, what?" In short, causal accounts do not merely *suggest* natural order intelligibility as an ideal that *might* be attainable in regard to the phenomena in question; they *presuppose* that the particular

6. Their deficiency is not always that they fail to specify an entire set of sufficient conditions. As recent analyses have made clear, a confirmed causal explanation need not and often does not even imply that the cause *as described* in the explanation would figure in the description of the determining conditions appearing in an adequate deterministic account of the occurrence in question. This makes it doubly important to distinguish between saying that "Every singular causal statement implies a general law" (which is not the case) and saying that "Every singular causal statement implies *that there is* a law" (which still needs refinement to save it from triviality but comes closer to being a correct analysis). See Morton White, *Foundations of Historical Knowledge* (New York and London: Harper and Row, 1965), pp. 62-63. Also: Donald Davidson, "Actions, Reasons, and Causes," *The Journal of Philosophy*, LX (1963), 698; and Bernard Berofsky, "Determinism" (Ph.D. dissertation, Columbia University, 1963), pp. 91-95.

occurrences of which they are an account *are* intelligible in natural order terms.

Most causal accounts resemble *ceteris paribus* accounts; in fact they could be classified (for present purposes, at least) as a sub-type of the latter. Like *ceteris paribus* accounts causal accounts do make actual occurrences intelligible in terms of regular relations among traits or states of affairs; they fall within the natural order line of questioning. But, like *ceteris paribus* accounts, they usually do not fulfill this line of questioning; specifying only some of an assumed set of necessary conditions, they leave partially unresolved the problem: Why did precisely this occurrence take place just then and there?

5. DISPOSITIONAL STATEMENTS

Philosophers have sometimes distinguished dispositional statements from laws and, correspondingly, dispositional accounts of occurrences from lawful accounts of occurrences. Our interest lies in whether dispositional statements are nomological universals and whether, as such, they provide natural order intelligibility of particular occurrences.

We can begin by quoting Ryle's conclusions as to the distinctions between dispositional statements and laws. Dispositional statements he defines as statements "to the effect that a mentioned thing, beast or person, has a certain capacity, tendency or propensity, or is subject to a certain liability."

It is clear that such statements are not laws, for they mention particular things or persons. On the other hand they resemble laws in being partly 'variable' or 'open.' To say that this lump of sugar is soluble is to say that it would dissolve, if submerged anywhere, at any time and in any parcel of water. To say that this sleeper knows French, is to say that if, for example, he is ever addressed in French, or shown any French newspaper, he responds pertinently in French, acts appropriately or translates it correctly into his own tongue. This is, of course, too precise. We should not withdraw our statement that he knows French on finding that he did not respond pertinently when asleep, absent-minded, drunk or in a panic; or on finding that he did not correctly translate highly technical treatises. We expect no more than that he will ordinarily cope pretty well with the majority of ordinary French-using and French-following tasks. 'Knows French' is a vague expression and, for most purposes, none the less useful for being vague.[7]

7. Gilbert Ryle, *The Concept of Mind* (New York: Barnes and Noble, 1949), pp. 123-24.

Ryle distinguishes among the dispositions attributed to individuals in dispositional statements. Some dispositions are highly specific, "single-track" (e.g., the brittleness of glass or a man's habit of smoking), others are "highly generic or determinable" (e.g., greed or elasticity). "There are several different reactions which we expect of an elastic object, while there is, roughly, only one sort of behavior that we expect of a creature that is described to us as a ruminant. Similarly there is a wide range of different actions and reactions predictable from the description of someone as 'greedy,' while there is, roughly, only one sort of action predictable from the description of someone as 'a cigarette smoker.' "[8]

Can any disposition statement, in Ryle's sense of the term, be said to make an occurrence intelligible? Ryle says they are used in explaining, predicting, and retrodicting.[9] It would seem correct to say that in being so used a disposition statement does fall within the framework of the questioning and answering about occurrences which we have associated with natural order thinking. In other words, in dispositional accounts questions about particular occurrences such as "Why did this happen then and there?" are being answered in terms of regular relations among states of affairs. But answers to these questions in the form of disposition statements do not fulfill the requirements of natural order intelligibility. These statements—even those with highly specific, "single-track" disposition terms—fail to specify the sufficient conditions of the kinds of occurrences they are used to explain, predict, or retrodict. In this respect disposition statements resemble *ceteris paribus* generalizations and causal laws. By means of a dispositional statement we know all we want to know, if all we wanted to know was that a particular occurrence fits into a pattern of behavior of a particular thing or person and is therefore what could have been expected or what we can expect on some future occasion, but we will not have the answer to why just that occurrence did happen at some specific time and place. As Ryle himself says, in effect, disposition terms—and thereby disposition statements—are "vague" expressions describing "ordinary" situations. And although they are, "for most purposes, none the less useful for being vague," this utility is not a substitute for the natural order intelligibility which they do not, indeed cannot, afford us.

Our comments thus far on disposition statements have empha-

8. *Ibid.*, pp. 43, 118.
9. *Ibid.*, p. 124.

sized that they do not specify the sufficient conditions of occurrences. Ryle (like William Dray)[10] delimits the class of disposition statements to statements which, although "open" in one sense, are restricted in that they ascribe dispositions only to particular things or persons. Their openness corresponds roughly to one of our requirements for nomological universals, namely, indefiniteness in scope of predication. But we also specified that a nomological universal must be unrestrictedly universal. In mentioning particular things or persons, disposition statements fail to meet this requirement. This is another reason for denying that dispositional accounts of occurrences provide natural order intelligibility. Disposition statements are by no means the only general statements which are not unrestrictedly universal; the following section deals with *all* accounts that are inadequate relative to the ideal of natural order intelligibility by virtue of their comprising generalizations of restricted universality.

6. RESTRICTED UNIVERSALITY

Why is it plausible to require unrestricted universality? Why judge inadequate any account that fulfills all of the other requirements mentioned in chapter I? Is it not enough to assert of a particular occurrence that it is related to certain states of affairs as its determining conditions by a confirmed regular relation between specified sufficient conditions and a specified class of occurrences which can be formulated, which "covers" the occurrence to be accounted for, which is indefinite in scope of predication, and which is partially confirmed by indirect evidence?

Let us first consider unrestricted universality in respect to space and time. Universal conditionals with descriptions specifying absolutely the time and place of traits and existential conditions could have only one instance, and are ruled out by the requirement that nomological universals be indefinite in scope of predication. But why do we reject as a nomological universal any universal conditional in which the description of traits and existential conditions includes predicates specifying a certain segment of the unique spatio-temporal order? Our requirement of unrestricted universality would exclude a universal conditional about the determining conditions of political revolutions which was restricted in scope of predication to "political revolutions occurring during the

10. William Dray, *Laws and Explanation in History* (London: Oxford University Press, 1957), p. 146.

nineteenth century in the spatial region called 'Europe.'" Doubts
about the plausibility of our unrestricted universality requirement
are raised by noting how many generalizations actually used in
accounting for particular occurrences of all sorts are formulated
so as to apply only to occurrences in certain places at certain times.

To clarify the point at issue we must suppose that such generalizations specify the sufficient conditions, and that the direct and
indirect evidence confirming them includes no general knowledge
revealing why an occurrence of kind E occurs under the specified
determining conditions *only* at the designated time and place.

What lies behind the plausibility of our requirement is a rule
derived from past inquiry, namely, that natural order is to be
presumed invariant with respect to time and place. This rule
derives from the generalization, repeatedly supported by experience, that specific periods of time or regions of space are not
themselves determining factors; that, instead, there are determining traits which happen to obtain during specified periods in
specified regions. We consider it a sound presumption that if we
knew more we could replace reference to a specific period of time
and spatial region by a description of the relevant traits. When we
cannot make this substitution we presume that we are ignorant of
the "real" reason for the occurrences.

Finding out what we do not know in such cases is not like accounting for some regularity of phenomena in terms of regularity
at a different level of description (e.g., accounting for laws of
light refraction in terms of a wave-theory of optical phenomena).
What we find out is not that the place and time, as a "particular"
manifestation of a more "general" correlation, are determining
factors, but rather that place and time as such make no difference
at all, i.e., they are not themselves determining conditions. Once
we can describe the hitherto unspecified conditioning traits we
can assert that the regularity—reformulated by substituting "purely
qualitative" terms for the terms designating a specific temporal
period and spatial region—is invariant with respect to uniquely
specified times and places.[11]

11. "Thus, the terms 'soft,' 'green,' 'warmer than,' 'as long as,' 'liquid,'
'electrically charged,' 'female,' 'father of,' are purely qualitative predicates,
while 'taller than the Eiffel Tower,' 'medieval,' 'lunar,' 'arctic,' 'Ming' are
not" (Carl G. Hempel, "Studies in the Logic of Explanation," in *Aspects of
Scientific Explanation* [New York: The Free Press, 1965], pp. 268-69). Cf.
Karl Popper, *The Logic of Scientific Discovery* (London: Hutchinson, 1959),
pp. 68-70.

On the basis of the aforementioned presumption of ignorance, then, we plausibly deem ourselves not to have given an adequate account of an occurrence in terms of regular relations between states of affairs when we cannot remove restrictive specifications of time and place from our universal conditional. In adequately accounting for occurrences in terms of regular relations between states of affairs, we impose the requirement that universal conditionals must be of unrestricted universality with respect to time and place.

The idea that "laws of nature" change in the course of time therefore runs counter to our formulated ideal of natural order intelligibility. To account for an occurrence in terms of a regular relation which is itself unaccountably subject to modification in the course of time (past or future)—as contrasted with modifications in our formulations of laws as we refine our knowledge of natural order—is to concede that we do not know the sufficient conditions of the occurrence, for we are then unable to state why the regularity assumed to obtain at the time of the occurrence obtains at that time and not at some other time. Conceivably, cumulative evidence could lead us to qualify the generalization that "when" and "where" are not themselves determining conditions; at the present stage of inquiry there is no area in which the existence of such evidence is generally acknowledged. Hence the plausibility of presuming that recourse to the concept of evolving "laws of nature" is an indication of our ignorance, of our inability to attain a plausible ideal of natural order intelligibility.

We come now to a consideration of unrestricted universality with respect to particular objects, the point raised at the conclusion of the preceding section. Inclusion in a universal conditional of a proper name or of equivalent signs designating but one object always raises a question: Why does the stated regularity apply to just this one thing? A similar question is posed by restrictions of the regularity to a finite number of objects designated by proper names or equivalent signs. And we note that the question is posed irrespective of whether the regularity is statistical or non-statistical and whether or not it specifies the entire set of sufficient conditions. Universal conditionals with a *ceteris paribus* proviso, causal laws, dispositional statements—all of these can be formulated so as to apply to an indefinite number of occurrences and yet be restricted in that they pertain to a particular designated thing or things.

The question arises because a proper name identifies objects to which the regularity applies but does not disclose why the regularity is restricted to just this or these particular things. We presume that certain traits of these designated particulars are determining conditions and that certain other traits are irrelevant. Thus it might be stated that wherever in space the earth and its moon might be located and at whatever time, the earth pulls the moon with a force of a certain magnitude when they are at a specified distance from each other. This universal conditional might be cited in accounting for any number of particular occurrences. But it would not be an adequate account of these occurrences unless we knew what traits (qualities and relations) of the earth and moon were relevant to this regularity, relevant as determining conditions—the relevant traits being, in this case, their respective masses. Once we do know this we know that, for example, the chemical make-up of these objects, their circumferences, or their physiographical surface features are irrelevant to the occurrences in question. What we know is that whenever *any* two objects with masses of specific magnitudes are at a specific distance from each other each exerts on the other a force of a certain magnitude, and that the earth and moon are two such objects.

We may find it convenient to employ "irrelevant" traits in *identifying* particular objects falling within the scope of predication of a nomological universal, but we cannot be said to give adequate accounts of occurrences in terms of regularities between states of affairs when we are unable to distinguish between identifying traits and determining conditions. Designations by proper names presumably function by means of trait identification. Being able to identify the objects named in a universal conditional is not the same as being able to distinguish identifying traits from determining conditions.

Once again we note that the inadequacy here under discussion is not due to ignorance of a more fundamental uniformity underlying a regularity of phenomena; it is rather due to our presumed inability to specify a regularity.

It is now apparent why we deem inadequate those accounts of occurrences in which the universal conditional refers to particular things. We presume that there are sufficient conditions for the occurrences.[12] The concept of sufficient conditions, as we noted

12. By contrast, we found that the requirement of unrestricted universality with respect to time and place stems from a generalization, based on past

earlier, excludes superfluous factors. When we are not able to distinguish merely identifying traits (i.e., superfluous factors) from determining conditions, we are unable to specify the sufficient conditions. On the presumption that an occurrence has sufficient conditions, it is appropriate to maintain that ideal intelligibility in terms of regular relations among states of affairs—natural order intelligibility—requires unrestricted universality with respect to particular things. The plausibility of the presumption that an occurrence *has* sufficient conditions will be discussed in section 11.

7. NATURAL ORDER AND DETERMINISTIC RELATIONS

A "natural order relation" is the relation between a *kind* of occurrence and certain *kinds* of traits formulated in nomological universals, or the relation between *particular* conditions and a *particular* conditioned occurrence, i.e., an instance of the relation formulated in a nomological universal. An occurrence is often said to be "determined" when what happened could not have happened otherwise—when it was bound to happen as it did, when it did, where it did. An occurrence standing in a nomological relation to certain states of affairs is determined in this sense. The nomological relation, accordingly, can be described as "deterministic."[13] Viewing our analysis of nomological relations as an explication of "could not have happened otherwise," we shall use the designation "deterministic (I)" to refer to that sense of "deterministic" which is equivalent to natural order (or nomological).

"Deterministic" is sometimes defined more narrowly. One restriction is exemplified in Nagel's definition of a deterministic system: A deterministic system comprises two or more determinable traits or variables of which there are one or more determinate instances or values (depending upon how many "members" the system has) at specific times and places. The variables "stand to each other in definite relations of interdependence, so that the value of a variable at any given time may be said to be 'determined' by the values of the other variables at that time."[14] This definition requires

experience and inquiry, as to the sort of thing that is a determining factor of occurrences, the generalization, namely, that uniquely specified temporal periods and spatial regions are not determining factors.

13. The relations we have called "natural order" or "nomological" might therefore have been called "deterministic" from the outset. We preferred to avoid using so treacherous a term until the requirements of the scheme of intelligibility had been set forth and their status clarified.

14. Nagel, *Structure of Science*, p. 595.

that all terms (i.e., a determinate value of each of the variables) of a deterministic relation exist at the same time. Some familiar nomological universals do have this form: Nagel cites as an example the relation of the amount of water in a gaseous state to the amount of water in a solid and a liquid state respectively in a given closed container. However, it is obvious that not all nomological universals have this form, and it is not clear on what grounds the designation "deterministic" is restricted so that it applies to some and not to others.

Elsewhere Nagel defines "deterministic system" in an even more restrictive fashion, presupposing what is often called a "closed system": the relations of interdependence are such that "when the state of a system is given for some initial time (in whatever manner the state may be defined), the theory for it must determine a unique state of the system for any other time."[15] But it is once again not clear why only such accounts are to be considered adequate answers to the question: "Why precisely this occurrence there and then?" There seems to be no good reason for defining "deterministic relation" with the "at any time" restriction or with the requirement (also stipulated) that the description of the determining conditions and determined occurrence be instantaneous state descriptions (i.e., not making references to different times).

Finally, often coupled with the foregoing restrictions is the requirement that the values of the determinables among which the deterministic relation holds must be numerical magnitudes. Such a restriction would require that nomological universals be numerical laws, laws, e.g., of the two sorts mentioned by Nagel:

(a) *Numerical laws stating an interdependence between magnitudes such that a variation in any of them is concurrent with variations in the others.* (E.g., the Boyle-Charles' law for ideal gases, that $pV = aT$.) Note that the relation stated by the law must be distinguished from the sequential order of the events that may occur when the law is being tested or used for making predictions.

(b) *Numerical laws asserting in what manner a magnitude varies with the time, and more generally how a change in a magni-*

15. *Ibid.*, p. 320. This definition is more restrictive because the "closed container" referred to in the paragraph above is not a "closed system." For example, the application of heat to the container will change the proportion of gas to solid and liquid. The amount of gas at t_1 (before heating) and at t_2 (after heating) does depend on the amount of liquid and solid at t_1 and t_2 respectively; but the proportion of gas to liquid and solid at t_2 is not determined by the proportion at t_1. Regarding "closed systems" in historical explanations, see below, chap. V, sec. 6.

tude per unit of time is related to other magnitudes. (E.g., Galileo's law, that the distance travelled by a freely falling body is equal to $gt^2/2$ where g is constant and t is the duration of the fall.)[16]

Again there seems to be no warrant for making this an essential requirement.

One unhappy consequence of incorporating *these* narrower requirements into a definition of "deterministic" is that it becomes difficult to do justice to the feeling of many historians that their fundamental objectives are those of the scientist. The historian who senses this kinship rarely aims to give accounts of particular occurrences in the human past in terms of the aforementioned requirements; yet, as likely as not, he finds himself typed as a determinist. Confusion is likely on the part of both proponents and critics of historical determinism when "deterministic" is defined in terms of relations of functional dependence between numerical magnitudes in closed, dynamic systems; for whether history is or is not deterministic in this sense is seldom if ever a point at issue between them.

We might well ask, however, whether the concept which figures in controversies over historical determinism is identical with deterministic (I) (i.e, natural order). I think we must agree that it is not identical. It is a narrower concept than deterministic (I), and to distinguish it we shall use the designation deterministic (II).

It is narrower by virtue of at least one additional requirement: An occurrence *e* can only be in a deterministic relation to (or "be determined by") a sufficient condition or set of sufficient conditions which is *contemporaneous with or antecedent to* itself. If the sufficient condition is a set of factors, the requirement must be satisfied by all factors in the set. In other words, discussions about determinism in history incorporate the assumption that the determining conditions of an occurrence are not subsequent to the occurrence itself. To ask whether an historical occurrence was determined is to ask whether it was necessary relative to certain concurrent or antecedent states of affairs. (It is sometimes supposed that the determining conditions must *all* be *antecedent* to the conditioned occurrence, but this is readily shown to be too restrictive.) We shall distinguish accordingly between deterministic (I) accounts, i.e., all adequate natural order accounts, and de-

16. Nagel, *Structure of Science*, pp. 77-78. Cf. Arthur Pap, *An Introduction to the Philosophy of Science* (New York: The Free Press, 1962), pp. 313 ff.

terministic (II) accounts, i.e., adequate natural order accounts which meet the additional requirement just specified.[17]

8. MULTIPLE ACCOUNTS OF THE SAME OCCURRENCE

Does any account of a particular occurrence that satisfies the requirements formulated in chapter I terminate the natural order line of questioning and provide a complete and adequate answer? In particular, should additional requirements be specified so that natural order thinking about any given occurrence can terminate in only one account? A number of possible additions to our list of requirements come to mind.

1. It might be considered a requirement of an adequate natural order account that it specify the *immediate* as contrasted with the *remote* determining conditions, "immediacy" and "remoteness" having reference to either temporal or spatial characteristics. For example, this requirement could eliminate the possibility, in the case of a closed system, of giving an indefinite number of natural order accounts of the state of the system at a certain time, accounts otherwise made possible by a nomological universal formulating for that kind of system a regular relation between its state at any time and its state at a given time. With the added requirement, the one and only determining state would be the one temporally "immediate" to the state being accounted for, *provided that* "temporally immediate" was restricted to mean "immediately previous" *or* "immediately subsequent"—otherwise there could still be two determining states (i.e., the one immediately previous *and* the one immediately subsequent), and therefore two natural order accounts.

2. It might be considered a requirement of an adequate natural order account that it present as determining conditions traits belonging to the *most fundamental level of analysis*. If, for example, a "molar" description of the determining conditions of an occurrence can be translated into "molecular" terms, the account of this occurrence in molecular terms would be held to constitute the ade-

17. Bernard Berofsky has formulated another requirement which presumably also pertains to deterministic (II). We apply this requirement when, for example, we judge that the length of a pendulum determines the period of its swing but not vice versa, even though there is a deterministic (I) relation between period and length. Although familiar enough in practice the requirement is not simple to formulate, and since it is not a source of confusion in discussions of historical thinking we mention it only in passing. See Berofsky, "Determinism," pp. 240-52.

quate answer to the question "Why?" in terms of regular relations between states of affairs.

3. A requirement might be added that would disqualify correlative "effects" of a common "cause" as determining conditions. Consider the following account of an occurrence e: "A sufficient condition of the end of a period of fair weather in the Mississippi Valley was the experiencing of rheumatic pains by persons of a certain type living in that area." Such accounts assert as the sufficient condition of e an occurrence e^1 having as *its* sufficient condition a state of affairs (in the example, a drop in air pressure in the Mississippi Valley area) which was a sufficient condition of e. An additional requirement disqualifying occurrences of type e^1 as determining conditions would eliminate this kind of multiple account.

Even if it were possible to formulate these additional requirements unambiguously and uncontroversially, however, it would remain questionable whether they are essential. Our doubts as to the plausibility of adding requirements that would reduce to one the number of adequate natural order accounts of a particular occurrence are increased when we consider still other cases of multiple accounts which are consistent with the requirements set forth in chapter I and which would therefore have to be reckoned with. We shall mention just two. (a) An occurrence can have two sets of sufficient conditions in the sense that it is "overdetermined"; that is, given either set of conditions, e would have occurred when and where it did. For example, the personnel of a remote trading post are considering returning home because of native hostility and shortage of food. On the same day their reserve food supply is destroyed by fire and their leaders are killed in an ambush. Either one or the other event, under the circumstances, would have sufficed to cause the men to abandon the post. Since both events took place, either of two sets of sufficient conditions could be cited as accounting for their departure, i.e., their departure was "overdetermined." (b) Two sets of sufficient conditions can be comprised of traits (qualities and relations) and existential conditions in one case concurrent with e, in another antecedent to e and related to e by different nomological universals. For example, a natural order account of the length of a flagpole (occurrence e) might be given either in terms of the length of its shadow and the angle of the sun in conjunction with principles of optics, or in terms of "antecedent events and laws of succession and referring to the temporal genesis of the flagpole as an artifact."[18]

Such multiple accounts, one would suppose, are all appropriately classed as adequate accounts relative to the objectives of natural order thinking. In certain contexts, to be sure, our questions may happen to be specific, and we would not be satisfied with one or another of these alternative natural order accounts. It is not apparent, however, that there is any reason other than contextual for preferring one account to all others; no reason, therefore, for regarding one account as providing an intrinsically more adequate disclosure of the regularities among states of affairs.

It still might be argued that we have already departed from essential (as contrasted with contextual) requirements in distinguishing deterministic (II) from deterministic (I). This we did in deference to the way "determinism" is used in the context of discussions about history. Why not, then, add other contextual requirements to the concept of deterministic (II) relations? The reason is the lack of a consensus among historians regarding criteria of *the* determining or sufficient conditions. The class of deterministic (II) accounts does exclude some deterministic (I) accounts, thereby reducing the number of multiple accounts of some particular occurrences. But it cannot be inferred that the systematic exclusion of alternative natural order accounts is a peculiarity of historical intelligibility. Therefore, since there is no basis in the logic of natural order questioning itself for additional requirements that would eliminate multiple accounts of the same occurrence, one underlying assumption of disputes about *the* cause of an event has been eliminated.

9. OBJECTIONS TO THE PLAUSIBILITY OF THE IDEAL OF NATURAL ORDER INTELLIGIBILITY

There are three principal objections to the concept of natural order intelligibility as an ideal of the intelligibility of occurrences in terms of regular relations among states of affairs. These objections apply equally to deterministic (II) intelligibility, since the requirements of the latter include those of natural order, i.e., deterministic (I), intelligibility. (i) It is said that assertions of nomological regularity are trivial inasmuch as *any* combination

18. A. Grünbaum, "Explanation and Prediction," in *Philosophy of Science: The Delaware Seminar,* ed. Bernard Baumrin (New York: John Wiley and Sons, 1963), I (1961-1962), 90.

of discernible traits and existential properties in *any* spatio-temporal relationship to each other can be formulated as an instance of a nomological relation. (ii) It is said that no nomological universal can ever be conclusively confirmed or falsified, hence that there is no conclusive evidence of any natural order. (iii) It is said that it has become quite pointless to conceive of the intelligibility of occurrences in natural order terms (or "deterministic" terms, to use the phraseology often employed in stating this objection) because contemporary science has quite different objectives.

We shall consider these objections in the order given. Note that we are not discussing the plausibility or meaning of the thesis that *all* discriminable traits and existential conditions can, in principle, be made intelligible in terms of natural order, but rather the plausibility of natural order intelligibility as an ideal in accounting for *any* world happening.

(i) TRIVIALITY

According to this objection the distinction between nomological and non-nomological relations among states of affairs has no objective basis. The objection is supported by the argument that *any* combination and sequence of traits can be accounted for by means of a functional equation. Granted that the happenings are "discernible and describable, then it must be possible also to represent them by means of equations."[19] Bertrand Russell, who formulates the objection on the assumption that the determining conditions are measurable quantities, comments: "It is true that the formulae involved may be of strictly infinite complexity, and therefore not practically capable of being written down or apprehended. But except from the point of view of our knowledge, this might seem to be a detail: in itself, if the above considerations are sound, the material universe *must* be deterministic, *must* be subject to laws."[20]

It has been argued against this charge of triviality that it can be sustained only by allowing equations that violate the requirement that the nomological universal not contain absolute spatial or temporal specifications of the particular occurrences to which it applies. Since, however, there are devices by which explicit ref-

19. Henry Margenau, "Meaning and Scientific Status of Causality," *Philosophy of Science*, I, No. 2 (1934), 136.

20. Bertrand Russell, *Mysticism and Logic* (London: George Allen and Unwin, 1917), p. 204 (italics in the original).

erence to specific times can be avoided[21]—and presumably the same applies to specifications of place of occurrence—it is well to point out a more essential flaw in the triviality objection.

Contrary to what the objection assumes, not all equations suffice to provide deterministic accounts even when the specific time (and space) reference is eliminated. If not just any account in terms of an equation is a deterministic account then it is correct to say that not every order of traits and existential conditions is natural order (deterministic (I)). What is the requirement of a natural order account that some equation-represented happenings (for example, those in regard to which the fact of their occurrence at a specific time appears as a determinant) would not satisfy? It is the possibility of there taking place other instances of a certain kind of occurrence. Any equation which when interpreted so as to apply to happenings does not state a relation between *kinds* of traits, does not state a nomological or natural order relation. The kinds must be described so that it is possible for us, in principle, to encounter in experience and to discriminate between an indefinite number of instances of them. Or, in the language sometimes employed in discussing determinism: a "system" represented by an equation is not a natural order or deterministic system unless the system is defined so as to allow for an indefinite number of instances of any "state of the system."

The requirement of indefinite scope of predication thus emerges as the crucial one in defending our concept of natural order intelligibility against the charge of triviality. Even granting that any order is representable in an equation, it is not the case that any equation-represented order is natural order. The quest for natural order intelligibility is then a meaningful one, it being possible to differentiate between success and failure by referring to criteria implicit in the definition of a natural order (deterministic (I)) relation.[22]

(ii) VERIFIABILITY AND FALSIFIABILITY OF NATURAL ORDER ACCOUNTS

The issues raised by the objection that no natural order account can ever be conclusively confirmed or falsified are highly complex and we shall not attempt to treat them at length. It

21. See, e.g., Nagel, *Structure of Science*, p. 321 n. 39.
22. See Berofsky, "Determinism," pp. 309-23.

must suffice to clarify our concept of natural order intelligibility with regard to a few crucial considerations.

It is charged that the ideal of natural order intelligibility is arbitrary because confirmation of any instance of determination by sufficient conditions is impossible. Absolutely conclusive confirmation is indeed impossible because counter-instances of a strictly universal empirical generalization with indefinite scope of predication are always conceivable. But the conceivability of counter-instances and their detection is the very basis upon which rules of confirmation are constructed. These rules (such as Mill's "method of difference"), far from eliminating the possibility of our encountering counter-instances and recognizing them for what they are, call for instituting tests appropriate for disclosing counter-instances.

It is also objected that the ideal of natural order intelligibility is unrealizable in practice, even in the so-called exact sciences, either because the sufficient conditions can never be fully ascertained and formulated or because even careful experimentation and observation do not yield uniform results; on the contrary, it is said, the more careful and thorough our experiments and our observations, the greater range of variation we find. Thus empirical evidence never more than approximates the precisely formulated qualities and relations specified in a nomological universal.

The stubborn factor of experimental error is enough to discredit a reply to the effect that it is only a matter of time before investigators perfect their techniques and compile evidence that is uniformly in precise accord with the nomological universals it is used to confirm. This reply is further discredited by recognition that some well-established nomological universals include determining factors which we will not conceivably ever be able to measure exactly (e.g., instantaneous velocity).

A more cogent reply to this objection would stress the proven success of persistent inquiry that aims at natural order intelligibility in various domains, success in refining our ideas of natural order in these areas. In the light of this success it does not seem appropriate to interpret our inability to discern the sufficient conditions of occurrences and to avoid experimental or observational error as evidence against natural order. On the contrary, it is plausible to assume that we have evidence of natural order in some areas even though we are not able to realize completely the ideal of natural order intelligibility.

(iii) THE OBJECTIVES OF CONTEMPORARY SCIENCE

But it is argued that it is idle to debate whether we do or do not have convincing evidence of natural order in some areas and whether or not it is plausible to think of natural order intelligibility as the termination of a differentiated and refined line of questioning about what goes on in the world: the ideal of natural order intelligibility, we are told, is *passé*. Those today who seek regularities among states of affairs are said to be no longer looking for natural order. Their principal aim is to furnish us with the tools for making useful predictions, and they have discovered that this can frequently best be achieved by ignoring the ideal of natural order intelligibility. The following quotation exemplifies this viewpoint.

The aim of science is to describe the world in orderly language, in such a way that we can if possible foresee the results of those alternative courses of action between which we are always choosing. The kind of order which our description has is entirely one of convenience. Our purpose is always to predict. Of course, it is most convenient if we can find an order by cause and effect [i.e., deterministic]; it makes our choice simple; but it is not essential.

What we are looking for, in science as much as in the day-to-day of our lives, is a system of prediction: is, as it were, a predictor. The principles which guide us in our predictions are in the end nothing more than steps in the calculation. And life is not an examination; we do not get marks for the steps; what matters is getting the right answer. So it is perfectly possible to base a system on no principle except getting the right answer. . . . The business of prediction, and of science, is to get us to do roughly the right thing at roughly the right time.

Science is a way of ordering events: its search is for laws on which to base the single predictions. This is the stroke which rounds our picture: that science is systematic in method because it seeks a system of prediction.

Anticipating the future is the fundamental activity. . . .

Science is a great many things, and I have called them a great many names; but in the end they all return to this: science is the acceptance of what works and the rejection of what does not. . . .[23]

23. J. Bronowski, *The Common Sense of Science* (New York: Vintage Books, n.d.), pp. 81, 82, 114, 117, 146.

Maintaining that the thesis of universal determinism, which we shall discuss shortly, has hardened into a "scholastic formula," the same author has this to say:

For the idea which has given a new vigour to science in our generation is larger than the machinery of cause and effect. It stipulates no special mechanism between the present and the future. It is content to predict the future, without insisting that the computation must follow the steps of causal laws. I have called this the idea of chance, because its method is statistical, and because it recognizes that every prediction carries with it its own measurable uncertainty.

This is the method to which modern science is moving. It uses no principle but that of forecasting with as much assurance as possible, but with no more than is possible. That is, it idealises the future from the outset, not as completely determined, but as determined within a defined area of uncertainty.

This is the revolutionary thought in modern science. It replaces the concept of the *inevitable effect* by that of the *probable trend.* Its technique is to separate so far as possible the steady trend from local fluctuations. The less the trend has been overlaid by fluctuation in the past, the greater is the confidence with which we look along the trend into the future. We are not isolating a cause. We are tracing a pattern of nature in its whole setting. We are aware of the uncertainties which that large, flexible setting induces in our pattern. But the world cannot be isolated from itself: the uncertainty *is* the world.[24]

Controversy about the objectives of science is reflected in controversies over the nature of history. One aspect of this controversy may be mentioned here: the disputed implications of science in regard to free will, moral responsibility, and man-made history. It is scarcely surprising to find our spokesman for the prediction-oriented interpretation of science taking the following stand: "These are the ideas of chance in science today. They are new ideas: they give chance a kind of order. . . . But we have not yet begun to feel their importance outside science altogether. For example, they make it plain that problems like Free Will or Determinism are simply misunderstandings of history. History is neither determined nor random. At any moment, it moves forward into an area whose general shape is known, but whose boundaries are uncertain in a calculable way."[25]

24. *Ibid.,* pp. 145, 86, 87 (italics in original).
25. *Ibid.,* p. 88.

A related but less extreme interpretation of modern science is exemplified in views expressed by Carl Hempel. The major objective of scientific research, he has maintained, is to make theoretical generalizations based on experience, "which enable us to anticipate new occurrences and to control, at least to some extent, the changes in our environment."[26] What we have called giving accounts of particular occurrences has been treated by Hempel in analyses of the concepts of "explanation" and "prediction." He assimilates explanation to prediction by defining the former in terms of anticipation or expectation, by which he means not a psychological state of mind but "rational scientific anticipation which rests on the assumption of general laws."[27] Thus in his account of "rationally acceptable explanations," one generic feature is: every rationally acceptable explanation of an occurrence takes the form of "showing that, in view of certain particular circumstances and general laws, its occurrence was to be expected."[28] There are two sub-types of rationally acceptable explanations. In deductive-nomological explanations the expectation takes one form: the occurrence is to be expected in *all* cases. In probabilistic explanations, the expectation takes another form: the occurrence is to be expected with some degree of "inductive" probability, i.e., relative to the inductive evidence, the statement that it will occur in any given case is more or less likely.[29]

Deductive nomological explanations are, in our terminology, adequate natural order or deterministic (I) accounts; probabilistic explanations are not. But, according to Hempel, neither is intrinsically superior to the other. Presumably we might prefer a probabilistic explanation if it satisfied our practical requirements for anticipation and control in any given area.

Let me comment on these two conceptions of modern science. In Bronowski's more extreme interpretation, the issue is never squarely confronted: Is natural order questioning plausible? We are told that nomological universals can be *convenient;* but suppose that what we want is not efficacious prediction but intelligibility. Suppose that we simply persist in asking *why* precisely

26. Carl G. Hempel and Paul Oppenheim, "Studies in the Logic of Explanation," *Philosophy of Science,* XV (1948), 138.

27. Hempel, "The Function of General Laws in History," in *Aspects,* p. 235.

28. Carl G. Hempel, "Reasons and Covering Laws in Historical Explanation," in *Philosophy and History,* ed. Sidney Hook (New York: New York University Press, 1963), p. 146.

29. Hempel, "Explanation in Science and in History," pp. 13-14.

this occurrence there and then (past, present, or future), in terms of regular relations among states of affairs? Hempel's explicit recognition of the plausibility of deterministic (I) accounts has similar implications, which he does not develop. Knowledge of natural order enables us to know what to expect, but when it does our expectation can be devoid of any practical significance beyond the prospect of intellectual excitement and satisfaction. And is it not plausible to say that we would know more about what is to happen if, in regard to a particular occurrence, we were able to explain and predict in natural order terms rather than merely probabilistically? Granted that prediction in natural order terms fixes more precisely what is to happen than do probabilistic predictions, are we to say that a scientist is naive who persistently pursues the natural order line of questioning simply as a line of questioning, without regard to the possible utility of the more precise predictions that might become possible?

"Science" is not a univocal concept. Scientific inquiry and scientific knowledge can be either essentially predictive in orientation or essentially a quest for natural order intelligibility. Man's interest in the regular relations among states of affairs is twofold. Only one direction taken by this interest is a quest for natural order intelligibility. This calls for deterministic thinking. By contrast, sometimes our observation, experimentation, and generalization are not essentially directed at ascertaining sufficient conditions: all we want to do is to be able to predict successfully— successfully *relative to a practical exigency.* Practically it may be quite enough to know that the chances of a certain event coming to pass are nine out of ten. Thinking with this orientation we shall call *predictive science.*

Those who state the objective of empirical science as "explanation and prediction"[30] do not always make it clear whether or in what sense these are distinct or complementary aims. The goal of precise prediction *can* be a manifestation of deterministic thinking. On the other hand, explanation can be for practical purposes (such as enabling us to take preventive action) which affect what is considered to be an adequate explanation. Bronowski's extreme interpretation has the merit of showing that when practical considerations prevail the form, content, and interpretation of judgments about regular relations among happenings are subservient to their function as tools. The concept of an objective orderliness to

30. E.g., Nagel, *Structure of Science*, p. 79.

be disclosed is inappropriate; "orderliness" is a function of what works best in our handling of specific problems or types of problems under pressures of time and circumstances.

Generalizations closely resembling nomological universals may subsequently be found more useful than at present, but even were this to happen the two orientations of thinking would not merge into one. Predictions for practical purposes that utilized these generalizations would not have the same significance as natural order accounts, for they would still answer different questions and have different presuppositions. Meantime, if there is a trend among professional scientists away from deterministic thinking and toward the predictive orientation—a trend geared to compelling needs and shaped by an expanding vision of the potentialities of man's technical prowess—then reflection on history with its conventional focus on accounting for past events is uniquely fitted to sustain the ideal of natural order intelligibility with its presumption of determinism. For in dealing with what has already happened, deterministic thinking seems especially apropos. Knowing what *did* happen, the historian is not primarily interested in what could have been predicted. When events have transpired, when the battle's lost or won, when once pressing practical issues have become dead issues, we all respond readily to the fascination of trying to find out why, in fact, things turned out the way they did, a cognitive goal unmistakably grounded upon natural order rather than practically efficacious prediction.

Natural order intelligibility permits precise prediction, but it is not equivalent to being able to predict precisely. Even when the concept of predictability is broadly conceived to include "could have been predicted precisely" (as well as "can be predicted precisely"), natural order intelligibility is not equivalent to predictability. We can imagine circumstances in which precise prediction would be possible without knowledge of natural order, indeed without natural order. "Imagine if possible a perfectly arbitrary universe with a god agitating it according to his ever-changing desires," and suppose that this god "should give the scientist exact forewarnings of his actions."[31] Natural order intelligibility not only makes precise prediction possible but makes it possible in a distinctive way: the particular occurrence is predictable as objectively necessary relative to a nomological relation among particular occurrences.

31. Margenau, "Meaning and Scientific Status of Causality," p. 136, 140.

10. EXPLANATIONS AND NATURAL ORDER INTELLIGIBILITY

Many writers have based their analyses of scientific or historical thinking on the concept of *explanation*. There were substantial reasons for our shying away initially from a concept that has recently been shown to be so ambiguous. Consideration of the concept of explanation at this point, however, will clarify and support the claim that we have been developing throughout this chapter, namely, that there is an *ideal* of natural order intelligibility.

We are indebted to the anti-systematic, scrupulously descriptive bent of some contemporary philosophers for salutary emphasis on the multifariousness of explanations in everyday life, in science, and in ordinary historical writing. But we need to go on from there and take a closer look at those different meanings. Are they just different or are they interrelated in significant ways? Do apparently different explanations involve any common suppositions? Are all sorts of explanations equally ultimate? Do some depend less than others on the context of questioning? In following out such questions as these one becomes increasingly aware of the plausibility of maintaining that there are certain fundamental meanings of "explanation," so that not all of the ordinary meanings of "to explain" are on a par with one another.

In these excerpts from a recent article, John Passmore makes some pertinent observations:

In everyday life there is a wide variety of circumstances under which we may offer, or be offered, what we should describe as "an explanation" of an occurrence. Consider the following:

(1) "As I got into the street-car, I noticed a large brown cylinder which was emitting a continuous clicking noise. The driver explained that I was to put my fare into it."
In this instance, I am confronted by an object which I do not know how to use. The explanation tells me how to use it, "what it is for."

(2) "On the menu, there was something called 'scrod.' The waitress explained that this is young cod."
As in case (1), I am being taught how to use something—a word. But the explanation now takes the form of a definition.

(3) "I asked him why I had to submit a report on a student at mid-term. He explained that this is the common custom in American universities."
My puzzlement in this case revolved about what I took to be an unusual procedure; the explanation consists in telling me that it is not unusual, that there is nothing to be puzzled about.

(4) "One of my students did not hand in his mid-term paper. I asked him to explain."

Here what I seek as an explanation is an excuse, a justification.

(5) "I found one passage in his essay very obscure. I asked him about it, and he explained what he was getting at."

To explain is, in this case, to elucidate, to paraphrase, to make clear how something fits into a general context.

(6) "I asked him how he had got home, and he explained that he first caught a subway, then a street-car, then a taxi."

The explanation fills in detail. I already know that he got home; the explanation tells me by what stages he did so.

(7) "I thought Mary was winking at me, but they explained that she had a tic."

In this case, to explain is to re-classify, or re-interpret.

(8) "I had always been told that all Americans were hearty hail-fellow well-met sort of people, but he explained that this is only true of the Mid-Western."

"Explained to me" because I am puzzled about the discrepancy between what I had been told and what I have experienced; the explanation tells me that I have wrongly taken to be a universal characteristic of Americans what is, in fact, characteristic only of a special class of American.

(9) "I asked him why he wrote badly, and he explained that his school course laid very little stress on English composition."

The explanation, in this case, refers to precedent conditions—this is a typical causal explanation.

These types of cases, no doubt, flow into one another; on the other hand, there may be, almost certainly are, other distinguishable instances. Enough has been said, however, to indicate under what a variety of circumstances a piece of information can be offered as an explanation. The only common factor, so far as I can see, is that in each instance I am puzzled; the explanation sets out to resolve my puzzlement. It is not just that there is something I do not know; there is something I do not know when I ask: "At what time does the train leave for New York?", but that is not a request for an explanation. Being puzzled is a special sort of not knowing, not knowing "what to make of" a situation. The puzzling situation presents characteristics which are, from our point of view, unexpected; it interrupts the smoothness of our dealings with the world. The explanation, if we accept it, gets us moving again.

An explanation need not even be a reply to a question; we may offer an explanation to somebody who is standing before a turnstile and obviously does not know what to do next, or to a child whose voice sounds puzzled as he reads aloud. In such an instance, although we are not puzzled ourselves, we recognize what there is about the situation which, in some sense, "calls for" an explanation. This is a matter of experience; we have to know that the turnstile is an unusual one, or that the child has never met the kind of behavior about which he is now reading. For, of course, no situation is intrinsically puzzling. It is puzzling only to somebody who has not yet developed particular habits, particular forms of expectation. The turnstile is not puzzling to a daily commuter, although it may be quite baffling to a visitor from abroad. The Boston-bred will, no doubt, have learned the meaning of "scrod," or acquired the habit of putting his fare into a cylinder, not by asking for explanations but simply by imitation; he will not be puzzled by the withdrawn behavior of New Englanders because he will not expect anything else of his neighbors. . . .

Everything depends, then, on what I know and what I want to know. . . .

It follows from all this that there can be no purely formal definition of an explanation. The schema:

"All X are Y, P is an X, ∴ P is a Y"

can sometimes be used to explain why P is a Y, but it can also be used to test the hypothesis that all X are Y, to prove that P is Y, to calculate that it is Y, to predict that it will be Y. How the schema is used will depend on what we know and what we want to know; and these are not formal considerations. . . .

. . . The historian's way of using the word "explanation" is, indeed, almost as liberal as that of the man in the street—certainly, it lies closer to his usage than to the physicist's.[32]

Having read this, one is resolved to avoid the mistake of presuming that "explanation" or "historical explanation," as ordinarily used, have just one meaning. The only puzzling thing is why such apparently sober and untendentious observations as Passmore's have not put an end to the insistence by some historians and philosophers that the logic of historical explanations is not so different from that of explanations in physics or in the physical sciences in general.

A more radical attempt to set wayward historians and philosophers straight has been made by other philosophical analysts intrigued by how explaining actually gets done. The ideal of scientific history has heretofore been based, as they see it, upon a misapprehension of the nature of scientific explanation. Even the physicist's explanations are really not as rigorous, tidy, clear-cut, and complete as the logician's scientific model led us to believe. The most telling argument against the ideal of scientific explanation in history, then, does not consist in showing that historians, like the man in the street, simply explain things differently from the scientist, but in exposing the ideal of scientific explanation:

32. John Passmore, "Explanation in Everyday Life, in Science, and in History," *History and Theory*, II, No. 2 (1962), 106-10.

allegedly it does not even correspond to the way explaining actually gets done in the most highly developed physical sciences. Once we see this, the new argument goes, we shall be rid of the specious sharp dichotomy between scientific and unscientific explanations. No explanations are really scientific. No one, then, should feel uneasy when told that history is not scientific.

But this radical effort to end controversy has, like Passmore's milder form of descriptive analysis, not had its intended effect. We are moved to ask: Is there some good reason, after all, behind the reluctance of historians and philosophers to repudiate the idea of an exacting explanation model? The preceding pages indicate that there is a good reason: one form of explanation, an accounting for occurrences in terms of determining conditions, answers to a fundamental line of questioning having requirements of completeness or adequacy that can appropriately be called essential. We could have made "explanation" the central concept, established criteria of completeness and accuracy, and distinguished between contextual aspects of explanation, on the one hand, and essential or non-contextual aspects of explanation, on the other. But our task is facilitated when, instead of explanation, we speak of a *way of thinking* ideally terminating in adequate *accounts* by virtue of which occurrences are intelligible to us. Among other advantages, this makes it easier to show both the significance of interrelationships between types of explanations and the significance of so-called contextual requirements.

It is especially noteworthy that contextual requirements can be related to fundamental requirements in different ways. Contextual requirements can call for the completion of a natural order account. In such cases, depending upon what is missing (and what we or someone else therefore seek to find out), the appropriate account, contextually speaking, may be an account that shows what conditions determined the occurrence according to already established laws; or it may be that what is called for is a statement of the nomological universal relating two or more events (as cause and effect) which we have some reason to believe are nomologically related.[33] But in other cases fulfilling contextual requirements may leave essential requirements unfulfilled. Thus we are sometimes entirely satisfied with a statistical account or an account merely establishing one necessary condition of an occurrence. In still other cases the contextual requirements may dictate which of multiple

33. Cf. Nagel, *Structure of Science,* p. 32n.

possible adequate accounts (relative to essential requirements) is the appropriate one: *which* set of sufficient conditions of an "overdetermined" occurrence; whether *immediate* conditions *or remote* conditions, and if remote, which ones; or at *which* level of analysis the sufficient conditions are to be sought.

What is acceptable as an explanation? Passmore's view is that "everything depends" on what I know and what I want to know.[34] William Dray, among others, has called attention to this "pragmatic dimension" of explanation.[35] But we must not overlook ways in which human beings find the world *questionable,* whether or not they consciously differentiate and follow up these lines of questioning. We must not overlook the fact that these lines of questioning have requirements of completeness or adequacy, whether or not we care to or are able to persist in questioning until the requirements are met. Thus, it makes sense to ask about any occurrence: Upon what determining conditions did this depend? And what counts as an explanation when this is asked depends ultimately on what the determining conditions were, *not* upon what happens to be important to the inquirer or upon any other feature of the particular explanation-context.

Passmore's examples impress upon us that what is immediately appropriate as an explanation depends on what we already know and want to know. But much remains to be said. We need to remember that varying contextual requirements presuppose a background or framework of assumptions about the way in which it is plausible to pose and answer questions about occurrences. Thus in the case of number 9 on Passmore's list the assumptions are not spelled out, but we can tell that the occurrence is presumed to have depended upon other occurrences which made it possible or necessary. Example 7 presupposes a differentiation between alternative natural order accounts. Examples 2, 3, 5, 6, and 8 have a common feature which Passmore does not mention: In every case what is asked for could be said to be a description of the world—either of a particular occurrence (in example 5: the intention of a person at a particular time and place to communicate something), or of a similarity manifested in occurrences (examples 3 and 8), or of a sequence of events (example 6), or (as in example 2) of the "neutral meaning" intended by the use of a

34. Passmore, "Explanation in Everyday Life, in Science, and in History," p. 108.

35. Dray, *Laws and Explanation,* pp. 20, 98.

word on a certain occasion or range of occasions. Example 4 is interesting precisely because of its vagueness: Is what is called for a natural order account of determining conditions or is it a rational explanation from the standpoint of the agent?[36]

One difference between descriptions and natural order accounts is worth emphasizing—a difference that does not depend on context. We can ask the natural order question about any described state of affairs, but we cannot ask for any other *kind* of explanation of natural order. There is an ultimacy about the natural order way of accounting for occurrences which is not characteristic of descriptions.

In the light of these remarks, is the idea of a generic concept of explanation, an idea favored by proponents of the "unity of science," defensible or not? We conclude that it is—once the requisite distinctions and qualifications have been made, the variety of meanings of "to explain" in ordinary usage notwithstanding.

11. NATURAL ORDER AND UNIVERSAL DETERMINISM

Up to this point we have not been concerned with universal determinism—i.e., the view that *all* particulars can be accounted for, in principle, in terms of natural order (i.e., of deterministic (I) relations). One thing is clear: neither natural order accounts of particular occurrences nor assertions of nomological universals depend for their meaning or their confirmed status upon an a priori thesis of universal determinism. Yet this idea is an important constituent of the scheme of natural order intelligibility. Our comments will be directed principally to its foundation and status. We shall begin with a vastly simplified, schematic reconstruction, tracing the main steps in the process of reflection leading to the formulation of a thesis of universal determinism.

Apparent regularity is at first not clearly distinguished from real regularity. Disclosure that some regularities are merely apparent suggests tests for "real" regularity. Finding regularities among worldly happenings which stand up under these tests, we proceed to postulate (1) that there really are such regularities and (2) that this way of making sense out of the world is applicable to an indefinite range of things in the world. Combining these postulates and reformulating them in terms of the sophisticated concept of natural order, we have postulate (3): *In respect to an indefinite number of kinds of occurrences, apparent nomological regularity,*

36. See below, chap. IV, sec. 3, and chap. VIII.

when subjected to methodical scrutiny, turns out to be real nomo-logical regularity (i.e., it passes tests for discriminating "apparent" from "real" regularity). Every instance of confirmed nomological regularity supports the plausibility of postulate (3) which then functions as a rule of inquiry, directing our attention to evidence of possible regularity and making us suspicious of apparent exceptions to well-confirmed nomological universals.

Postulate (3) is not, however, the thesis of universal determinism; it leaves indefinite the scope of determinism. But reflection advances another step. Noting that by close scrutiny we can discover regularities in areas of the world where our prevailing impression had been one of irregularity, it occurs to us that nomological regularity might be characteristic of *all* occurrences; in other words, we hit upon the idea of pervasive natural order, of *universal determinism.* Indeed, the evidence supporting this idea is so considerable that we judge it plausible. We postulate universal determinism, presuming that, pending evidence to the contrary, *any* given occurrence is an instance of natural order. This presumption also functions as a methodological rule: we think it plausible to look for natural order in all areas. Evidence contrary to this presumption is not ruled out, but it must be more substantial than merely apparent disorder. Even though *definitive* standard tests for *in*deterministic occurrences cannot be devised, this does not obliterate the difference between a superficial appearance of disorder and experimentally verified disorder. As one philosopher has expressed it, the idea of universal determinism "is not analytic, nor is it an inductive generalization that could be refuted by contrary instances. It is best described as a *guiding principle*" of deterministic thinking, a principle that owes its plausibility and

its successes to a contingent feature of the universe. It "guides" the scientist in his search for a difference in antecedent conditions to account for the fact that apparently similar antecedents were followed by dissimilar effects. Whether in this conception it can be claimed to be a true, or at least a well-confirmed proposition, or should be accorded the status of a "rule of procedure" that cannot properly be called true or probably true, is really a matter of taste since the distinction between a proposition and a rule of procedure becomes somewhat fuzzy as we ascend on the ladder of inductive generalization.[37]

37. Arthur Pap, *An Introduction to the Philosophy of Science* (New York: The Free Press, 1962), p. 311 (italics in original). He calls it "the principle of causality."

But the only available example of experimentally verified *dis*order is in the field of quantum mechanics. Currently accepted quantum mechanics theory does not permit adequate natural order accounts of certain occurrences: "the detailed individual behavior of electrons and other subatomic elements."[38] The only account physicists can give of the detailed behavior of individual electrons is a statistical account. Even here we do not find unanimity of informed scientific opinion. And even if there were unanimity among quantum physicists as to the indeterministic character of sub-atomic phenomena, this would not appreciably weaken the presumption of determinism for other phenomena. Acknowledged indeterminism in sub-atomic phenomena would certainly not imply indeterminism either in macroscopic physical phenomena or in such domains as human behavior, much of which does not lend itself readily to description in "physical" terms.[39]

The crucial considerations, then, are these: It is possible to define "deterministic relation" sufficiently unambiguously to permit the formulation and application of rules of inquiry directed at disclosing such relations as well as disclosing *whether or not* certain kinds of occurrences take place deterministically. The burden of experimental evidence warrants our presuming not only that some occurrences take place deterministically but that all do, with the possible exception, in the present stage of inquiry, of sub-atomic phenomena. The thesis of universal determinism is a presumption supported by past experience. Thus there are two senses in which—relative to the ideal of natural order intelligibility—we say that an occurrence is unintelligible: (a) when we believe that it did not or will not take place deterministically (as in the area of sub-atomic phenomena), and (b) when we presume that it did take place deterministically but are unable to provide a natural order account. It is not strictly accurate today to speak of a plausible presumption of universal determinism, but aside from sub-atomic phenomena, the scope of natural order (deterministic (I)) intelligibility as an ideal does remain unrestricted. In practice, investigators are not always *interested* in pressing forward an inquiry into sufficient conditions and thus putting the presumption of deterministic (I) relations to the test, but the idea of natural order emerges as an appropriate possible objective in pursuing the intelligibility of *all* (except sub-atomic) occurrences.

38. Nagel, *Structure of Science,* p. 309.
39. *Ibid.,* pp. 312 ff.

Our discussion of the plausibility of a presumption of determinism has been in terms of deterministic (I) relations, i.e., the sense in which a deterministic relation is equivalent to natural order. To the extent that deterministic (II) relations, which comprise a special class of deterministic (I) relations, are the center of controversy in debates over historical determinism, we should raise the question here as to the plausibility of a presumption of determinism in the more restricted sense of deterministic (II) relations. Remembering that the natural order intelligibility of the same occurrence can in principle be achieved through more than one form of natural order account, the question at issue can be phrased as follows: Is it plausible to presume that (except for sub-atomic phenomena) all occurrences manifest deterministic (II) relations and that they can accordingly, in principle, be made intelligible in terms of deterministic (II) accounts? Inspection of the different types of relations involved discloses that it is plausible, because it is a characteristic of those deterministic (I) relations that are not deterministic (II) relations that whenever the former are manifested the latter are also. More precisely, whenever it is possible to deduce what happened at a certain time from knowledge of *subsequent* states of affairs (and a nomological universal)— as in the case of closed systems—it is presumably possible to give a deterministic (II) account of the same occurrence. The presumption of determinism in terms of deterministic (II) relations is, then, no stronger a presumption than the presumption of determinism in terms of deterministic (I) relations. If the latter is plausible so is the former, and we have shown that this is the case.

It may be helpful at this point to comment briefly on the way we form concepts of occurrences.

What is the intelligible structure of the world—the real world? The historian, like the scientist and like most of us most of the time, takes the world for granted as an indefinite field of variegated empirical content, spatially and temporally ordered. This variegated content is just there; we find ourselves experiencing it as sheer qualitative likeness and diversity, spatially and temporally ordered, before we think more about it. The qualitative and the spatio-temporal distinctions employed by us may be crude and unself-consciously taken for granted or they may be consciously and critically refined, but we cannot think them away completely. The enterprise of refinement, thinking about the world, reflects our interests: practical, aesthetic, theoretical, etc. Does it also reflect the nature of things-in-themselves? We readily suppose that it does, but a more critical judgment is that it is idle to speculate about things-in-themselves. The fact is that in the course of our dealings with the world we have framed one idea of the world as manifesting pervasive natural order, so that in principle, *by making suitable discriminations,* we should always be able to discern sufficient conditions. This is one idea that guides us in the formation of concepts of occurrences, controlling what we consider as "an occurrence."

There appears to be no way in which conceptualization in accordance with this idea could issue—as the classical atomistic philosophers, for example, might have maintained—in a disclosure, an inventory as it were, of the "really real" things and relations which constitute the spatio-temporal universe. On the other hand, our conceptualization is not arbitrary. Relative to the critically grounded presumption of determinism, what we consider as an occurrence or a thing will not depend on what we immediately and undiscriminatingly find there, or on what *happens* to follow what or to be co-present with what in *our* experience; it will be influenced by whether or not qualities, relations, and existential conditions discriminated and conceptually conjoined in a certain way, exhibit relations of sufficient conditions. I say "influenced" because there seems to be no way of deciding just how decisively and completely our pursuit of such relations controls our discriminations and conceptualizations. It would appear that we begin our natural order thinking using a host of discriminations found ready at hand, discriminations which reflect vital needs or linguistic or social conventions—in other words, non-theoretical influences. There is also, apparently, a certain flexibility in the way the ideal of natural order intelligibility can be realized, opening the way to the continuing "legitimate" influence of practical interests upon our way of discriminating and conceiving occurrences, our way of carving up the world into things, point-events, particles, fields, or whatever. But this continuing involvement of practical (or other) interests should not obscure the fact that there is a fundamental theoretical consideration involved, a test that all conceptual distinctions must pass: Does this way of carving up the stuff of experience enable us to discern deterministic relations?

Plain men and historians do not usually talk of "occurrences" in the technical sense in which I have been using the word. We speak of deeds of valor, of elections, of plots and revolutions, of victories and defeats, of ambitions, acts of revenge, love affairs, and so on. These conceptualizations are so familiar to us that it is easy to suppose that the occurrences are there to begin with and that all we do is label them. We suppose that either an occurrence as "given" manifests nomological regularity, or that our presumption of determinism has run afoul of an exception. Actually, however, what we begin by thinking of as an occurrence usually already bears the stamp of some human interest, some chance concrescence or concatenation. In concentrating on the quest for sufficient conditions, we rework our concepts; what we end up thinking of as "an occurrence" or "an event" reflects this dominant interest. Relative to this interest, when no natural order is manifest in respect to what we have been conceiving of as "an occurrence," it is always appropriate to abandon that concept and start over.

Disputes about the ultimate structure of reality are therefore to little purpose. We do not even know the meaning of "real structure." We certainly cannot aspire to discover structure by putting aside the categories and distinctions of our ways of thinking about experienced content: pre-reflective experience is unintelligible. What we usually call an occurrence, therefore, or discriminate as an event or a condition or a thing, is conceived selectively out of the world relative to *some* way of regarding what is experienced. *One* fundamental way of regarding the world is to view it as exhibiting natural order. From this standpoint, we discriminate and conceptualize spatio-temporal contents or combinations of contents which facilitate discovery of determining conditions.

The questions we have treated in chapters I and II are involved in most historical investigations and reconstructions, but our approach to them, dictated by considerations of precision and comprehensiveness, may have struck the historian as excessively abstract. Doubtless the area in which historians most frequently come in contact with the issues discussed is causal explanation, about which we have so far had little to say. Before turning to the specific consideration of history in the following chapters, I shall therefore restate all the principal conclusions regarding natural order intelligibility so as to show their application to that familiar historiographical terrain.

A causal explanation, in one form at least, is an assertion that an occurrence was bound to happen at a certain time and place given the occurrence of certain attendant circumstances or conditions. Causal explanations, when fully worked out, terminate the line of questioning directed to answering: "Why did precisely this happen just there and just then?" Obviously many incomplete assertions can be made about the "causes" of events; for example, an assertion to the effect that an occurrence was likely under the circumstances or that it would not have happened had it not been for such and such. Whenever incomplete assertions such as these cannot be completed by us, the happening in question is still open to further causal inquiry. The requirements of completeness in causal inquiry are not to be confused with contextual requirements such as the satisfaction of our curiosity, giving just the answer that someone has asked for, or making the best of the limited information at one's disposal. (Chap. II, especially secs. 2 through 5 and sec. 10.)

When we can give a complete causal explanation of a particular occurrence, the occurrence is deterministically intelligible. It is plausible to presume that all human happenings—embracing the conventional subject matter of history—are deterministically intelligible. Stated in the simplest terms, we have argued the plausibility of historical determinism. (Chap. II, secs. 7, 9 and 11.)

The particular human occurrences that the historian seeks to make intelligible by causal explanations are non-duplicable, i.e., there could not be two just alike. (Chap. I, sec. 2.) Yet we maintain that every causal explanation presupposes a general relation between the particular as an instance of a kind and its causes as instances of kinds. (Chap. I, sec. 3.) We have further maintained that the generalizations about particulars of certain kinds presupposed in causal explanations have certain peculiarities setting them apart from other generalizations: they assert a necessary connection that is not logical (analytic) in character (chap. I, sec. 6); unlike some generalizations about matters of fact they are indefinite in scope of predication (chap. I, sec. 4); and they require indirect evidence (chap. I, sec. 5). All of these latter characteristics, however abstruse they may appear, come to light when we ask about the nature of a causal connection or about the form of a plausible answer to the question "Why did precisely this happen just there and just then?"

Furthermore, when we ask searchingly about what sorts of traits or combination of traits can qualify as causes (which is one way of asking when a causal inquiry is complete), we discover the requirement of "unrestricted universality": a causal account is incomplete if we cannot remove from the description of causes references to particular times, places, persons, and things. (Chap. I, sec. 6 and chap. II, sec. 6.)

What we have proposed to the historian, then, is the following: What is called causal explanation in history can be clarified by seeing it as one form of a fundamental way of thinking about the world (i.e., natural order thinking); this is a plausible line of questioning which he can pursue in regard to any human happening; and this line of questioning involves criteria of completeness or adequacy such that complete causal explanation is tantamount to deterministic intelligibility.

Chapter III.

The Historian's Commitment
to Determinism
Some Objections Answered

1. INTRODUCTION

The preceding discussion culminates in these three remaining chapters of Part One. Assuming that we have developed a sound conception of deterministic thinking, we have now to show that this conception is relevant to history. If we succeed, we shall have at the very least put a damper on controversy between partisans of the pro-scientific and anti-scientific conceptions of history. We shall have shown that in one by no means trivial sense of science, the same scheme of intelligibility applies to history and science alike.

According to this meaning of science, to say that history is a science is to say that natural order intelligibility is an appropriate objective for human thinking about particular human occurrences (or, in deference to conventional usage: *past* human occurrences). Natural order accounts are equivalent to deterministic (I) accounts. We have noted that the ideal of natural order intelligibility allows for the possibility of more than one natural order account of the same occurrence. Among the possible types of deterministic (I) accounts is that type which we have distinguished as deterministic (II) and, as we have noted, it is in terms of the latter that the appropriateness of deterministic historical thinking has usually been attacked or defended. Accordingly, throughout these three chapters we shall be dealing for the most part with deterministic thinking in the form of thinking directed at ascertaining deterministic (II) relations.

We shall not maintain that every historian at least occasionally thinks deterministically or that some historians always do. Our claim is that *many* historians often do so. Many historians often think deterministically, but we are not to expect to find them making open and unambiguous declarations to this effect. Our thesis has to be tested by going behind occasional, casual remarks, trying to gauge their import. We must make explicit the usually unstated assumptions of these remarks. We must reconstruct the thinking of the many historians who divulge nothing at all about their own historical thinking.

This chapter is devoted chiefly to a consideration of various objections raised against the idea of deterministic historical thinking. The objections dealt with in sections 3 through 5 are based on alleged characteristics of historical *subject matter;* those in sections 6 through 10 pertain mainly to characteristics of *historical accounts* and the reasoning behind them.

With each of these objections our task is to show that they vanish once we bring to bear a suitable conception of the nature and status of determinism. Only when such a conception is lacking do these objections appear convincing, giving credence to sweeping assertions to the effect that "history proper" is one thing, "science" quite another.

2. ARBITRARY RESTRICTION OF SUBJECT MATTER

Conventional ideas as to the subject matter of history are various and indefinite. Suppose, however, that we accepted the widespread notion that history is about human societies in the past. Suppose even that it were shown that most written histories are in fact accounts of human societies in the past. What must be emphasized is that such a circumscription of the subject matter of history *in itself* signifies nothing at all as to the distinctiveness of historical thinking. It might reflect nothing more than a contingent selectivity or conventional carving up of the happenings of the world and assignment of labels to respective sectors. It is perfectly possible that all of these sectors can be thought of deterministically.

It is easy to exaggerate the significance of conventional labels and to fall victim to the illusion that there are discontinuities

where, in fact, there are only artificial divisions, divisions so artificial that a back-up system of cross-reference is needed to do justice
to the interconnections. The latter are nonetheless stubbornly regarded as less essential than the divisions which are cross-refer-
enced. So it is, in the case of history, that the very idea of a common scheme of intelligibility—such as natural order—can appear
inappropriate because history is thought to have its special domain: the past of human societies. Natural order thinking as such,
however, involves no presuppositions as to where the quest for
orderliness will lead. What occurrences will turn out to be sufficient conditions of what other occurrences is always a problem for
investigation. More strikingly, the scheme of natural order intelligibility involves no essential discontinuity between past, present,
and future occurrences.

The point is this. If we start with an uncritical notion of the
real unity of "the past of human societies" and identify this with
the subject matter of history, we shall be wary of accepting the
idea that the historian's way of thinking can be that of deterministic science. Correspondingly, if it should appear upon examination that one form of historical thinking is deterministic,
then the way is open to full appreciation of the links between human and non-human phenomena, between the social and the
personal, and between past, present, and future. We shall not be
disturbed by the fact that autobiography and biography are so
much like "history" yet do not have human societies as their central
focus. We shall not think it paradoxical to speak of the present as
history[1] or of the future as history.[2] We shall not think it imperative
that discussion of the natural conditions of human events be confined to introductory chapters dealing with "background." And
so on. The conventional conception of history creates an initial
bias against the claim that natural order intelligibility is relevant
to historical thinking, although once this claim is presented in a
way the historian finds applicable and persuasive, it has a liberat-
ing effect on historical studies.

3. THE FALLACY OF MISTAKEN REFERENCE

Here is an excellent illustration of the difficulties encountered
in straightening out our notions of history. We have already pointed

1. E.g., Paul Sweezy, *The Present as History* (New York: Monthly Review
Press, 1953).
2. E.g., Robert L. Heilbroner, *The Future as History* (New York: Harper
and Brothers, 1959).

out that as one way of historical thinking, deterministic thinking does not preclude other ways of thinking. But sometimes the initial mistake is made of *attributing a characteristic to the subject matter that should be attributed to the way of thinking.* The mistake shows up clearly enough when one develops its consequences with thoroughness. It shows up as soon as we find ourselves holding that the same occurrences have and do not have sufficient conditions or that the same occurrences essentially have and do not have practical significance. In short, it shows up in contradictions that underscore the importance of not committing what we might call the fallacy of mistaken reference. Sooner or later, if we are thorough, we come to see that occurrences *intrinsically* neither have nor lack sufficient conditions and practical significance. In other words, whether or not they have them depends on how we think of them.

Suppose it is objected that historical occurrences cannot be thought of deterministically because the occurrences are *intrinsically* endowed with some kind of meaning or significance that is incompatible with universal determinism. The burden of proof lies with the objector who presumes to know that things-in-themselves have such-and-such a character. No philosopher whose position forces him to shoulder this burden has met the challenge successfully. Therefore we may be allowed to say to him: You might be correct if you were to assert that historians sometimes think of occurrences in terms, say, of practical significance, a way of thinking fundamentally distinct from deterministic science. We cannot, however, accept your inference that because it is possible to think of occurrences in practical terms it is intrinsically impossible to think of them deterministically.

Isaiah Berlin's anti-scientific conception of history is instructive in this regard.[3] It might appear irrelevant inasmuch as he makes no explicit metaphysical claim to the effect that some occurrences are *really* undetermined; what he says is that we cannot refrain from thinking and talking about some occurrences as undetermined, so deeply engrained are these modes of thinking and talking. Berlin then infers that this rules out universal determinism, for clearly the same occurrence cannot be conceived of as determined *and* undetermined. We notice, however, that there is a concealed

3. See especially his discussion in *Historical Inevitability* (London: Oxford University Press, 1954) which we examine at greater length below in chap. VIII, sec. 5.

metaphysical premise, namely, that a way of thinking about an occurrence defines the nature of the occurrence. This turns out to be only a more devious instance of the philosophical error we have just been considering.

Berlin overlooks one crucial fact: not all historians and scientists think the way he says they do; they *do* sometimes commit themselves to *universal* determinism, and they do this not naively or impulsively but out of professional conviction that it represents a distinct and ultimate form of intelligibility. One could argue that Einstein and de Broglie were just old-fashioned in their presupposition of determinism. But is this plausible? My point is that, all things considered, it is less plausible than the alternative view we have been developing here: to think of *all* occurrences deterministically does not make any of them *be* the way they are thought of. The most we can say is that our experimentation with questioning and answering shows that this is a way of making sense out of the world. Nothing prevents our discovering that we can think of the *same* occurrences in *other* ways. If we find that there are certain other "engrained"—and critically plausible— ways of thinking of the same occurrences, well and good; we can proceed to explore their mutually incompatible or incommensurable aspects. But nothing that we find in this exploration can warrant our reverting to a denial of the soundness of any way of thinking that imposes itself upon us in critical reflection. This would be our reply to Berlin's claim that historical thinking *cannot* be deterministic because it is a thinking of events as partially undetermined. We say that one way of historical thinking postulates universal determinism and that this does not, in principle, preclude another way of historical thinking which involves a restriction on deterministic thinking.

4. COMPLEXITY AND UNIQUENESS

Sometimes the case against the assimilability of history to science is based on the complexity of human phenomena, at least the complexity of those human phenomena with which historians characteristically deal. This argument, if it had any force at all, might seem to be particularly telling against our conception of deterministic intelligibility. Complexity is said to make it impossible, or next to impossible, to formulate any strictly deterministic laws. With complex phenomena, so it is said, the best any inquirer can hope to come up with are probabilistic laws. But the complexity argument is vague and only superficially persuasive. As Nagel says in reference to social phenomena, "the complexity of a subject matter is at best not a precise notion," and even though, in some vague sense of the term, "social phenomena may indeed be complex, it is by no means certain that they are in general more complex than physical and biological phenomena for which strictly universal laws have been established."[4]

Einmaligkeit, the uniqueness of historical events, is also the basis of an argument against scientific history, an argument no more telling than the "complexity" argument but one that is more common, seemingly more cogent, and definitely more revealing about the nature of history.

The essence of the uniqueness argument is as follows: assuming that it is characteristic of natural order intelligibility to involve nomological universals (an assumption that we have explicitly endorsed), it will not be possible to render unique events deterministically intelligible, for experience cannot possibly provide a basis for comparison, for analysis, and, ultimately, for generalizations about unique events. Historical events, being characteristically unique, are for that reason deterministically unintelligible.

Are historical events unique? As we defined "occurrence," one property of a particular occurrence is being non-duplicable. If "unique" means non-duplicable and if we assume that historical events are particular occurrences, then historical events are indeed unique. But we have seen that uniqueness, in this sense of non-duplicability, is not incompatible with deterministic intelligibility. If one is to argue their incompatibility one must maintain that historical events are not—or at least are not thought of by the historian as being—instances of a kind.

It is very easy to make out a persuasive, although specious, case for this view. We find it so easy to believe that there never was or will be another event just like Caesar's crossing of the Rubicon, just like Michelangelo's painting the ceiling of the Sistine Chapel, just like the first successful flight at Kitty Hawk. We find it very easy to believe that the uniqueness of these events involves more than non-duplicability at the *same* time and *same* place. It involves, we suppose, non-duplicability at any time or place. The doctrine of "eternal recurrence," to be sure, would upset this supposition,

4. Ernest Nagel, *The Structure of Science* (New York: Harcourt, Brace and World, 1961), p. 505.

but how far-fetched that doctrine is! How much more persuasive is the view, espoused by Bergson and Collingwood, among others, that human history *must* be composed of utterly unique events because it is a cumulative process, the past surviving in the present. Awareness of what went before qualitatively differentiates otherwise similar events.[5] So we find ourselves believing that two instances of the same historical event never did occur and never will, at another time or place; that no generalizations about such events are or will be possible; in short, that the natural order intelligibility of these events is sheer delusion.

In undermining the superficial persuasiveness of this argument against the applicability to history of the ideal of deterministic intelligibility I shall make three points. These do not conclusively refute the argument. Their effectiveness lies in this: once they have been made, the issue will have been reformulated in terms that make constructive discussion possible.

First: We must not allow our feelings regarding the plausibility of the uniqueness argument to precipitate us into affirming that it is obvious that historical events are not instances of a kind in any relevant sense. In other words, we must be on guard against a dogmatism that cuts analysis short or precludes all discussion. There is no such thing as a priori synthetic knowledge; the uniqueness argument is no exception to this philosophical truth. Analysis and discussion could only be ruled out a priori by *defining* "historical event" in such a way that not being an instance of a kind was part of the definition. Merely verbal tactics of this sort would settle nothing.

Second: There is general agreement that historians do often intend to account for happenings in terms of necessary conditions, and we do sometimes accept their findings as a fulfilment of this intention. In other words, we have to confront the acknowledged fact that historians do achieve (or approximate) explanations of this sort. To be sure, it is often not apparent exactly in what sense an historian is asserting that an occurrence was dependent on a circumstance, but there is general agreement that this is sometimes what the historian is asserting in "explaining why."

We cannot do better than to cite the view of one contemporary philosopher, William Dray, who has been concerned to differentiate historical from nomological explanation. It is significant that he

5. See, e.g., R. G. Collingwood, *The Idea of History* (London: Oxford University Press, 1946), pp. 224 ff.

does not question that historians (sometimes) look for the causes of occurrences and that sometimes, in representing something as the cause of a particular occurrence, the historian's intention is to assert that some circumstance ("the cause") "was really necessary, i.e. that without it what is to be explained would not have happened."[6] Let us start with this statement as a partial construal of the historian's intention. The question is: How can the historian ascertain that a circumstance was necessary, i.e., how can he ascertain this causal connection?

There are two alternative answers: (a) this ascertainment is not possible without explicit or implicit consideration of other occurrences, which afford *generalizations* about how *kinds* of circumstances are *regularly* related to the occurrence of other *kinds* of happenings and, ultimately, a generalization about the *kind* of occurrence to be expected from a combination of certain *kinds* of circumstances, and (b) "particular, historical causal connections, may sometimes be [and typically are] established without either experimental or theoretical justification" by "an exercise of the historian's judgment in the particular case. . . ."[7] Answer (a) is our answer; answer (b) is Dray's.

Answer (b) is relevant because it affirms that at least some historical events, events to be explained, are not instances of a kind, or at least that viewing them as instances of a kind is not an essential feature of the logic of causal explanation in terms of determining circumstances. If answer (b) is correct then at least some historical causal explanations differ fundamentally from our conception of deterministic explanation. Usually answer (b) is combined with the view that all or most (Dray's view) historical causal explanations are of this non-deterministic sort, and with an affirmation of the uniqueness of historical events. If they are not asserted to be *really* unique in some metaphysical sense they are held to be unique *as conceived* by the historian. As Dray expresses it: in "typical explanations in history" the historian is concerned with an event "as *different* from other members of its class."[8] This kind of difference, according to our view (i.e., answer (a)), would make deterministic explanation impossible. In our view, an historical event that was unique *in this sense* would in principle be deterministically *inexplicable*.

6. William Dray, *Laws and Explanation in History* (London: Oxford University Press, 1957), p. 98.
7. *Ibid.*, pp. 55, 106.
8. *Ibid.*, pp. 46, 47.

Now if it is correct that historians do explain why certain events in fact took place, and if it is correct that this is sometimes tantamount to asserting that one or more circumstances were necessary conditions of those events, we are moved to ask: How can an historian explain an event that is conceived of by him as *different* from other members of *its class*? Methodologically speaking, the way the historian arrives at his explanation may be any of an infinite number of ways, but how can his judgment, "*x* was a necessary condition of *e*," be a warranted judgment *unless* it be construed as a judgment to the effect that "*e*'s presupposing necessary condition *x* was an instance of the regularity of phenomena"; *unless*—by whatever means he arrived at his conclusion—he can, upon request, furnish support for his judgment in the form of empirically confirmed generalizations as to the regular dependence of the occurrence of certain *kinds* of relevant empirical phenomena on the occurrence of other *kinds* of empirical phenomena? We have held that the only critically plausible way of explaining why a particular occurrence in fact occurred involves conceiving that occurrence as an instance of a kind. Has Dray, has any historian or philosopher, ever come forth with an analysis showing how it is possible for the historian to make "independent" judgments of causal connection in particular cases involving events conceived of as *sui generis*? Neither he nor anyone else has succeeded in doing this. Failing such an analysis this objection to our position cannot be taken seriously.[9]

Third: The residual plausibility of the "uniqueness" argument, once we have noted that its proponents have never made good their claims, stems from our difficulty in seeing how the conception of deterministic intelligibility can actually be relevant to accounting for events that seem to us not to be instances of a kind. This continues to be the Achilles' heel of the "unity of science" position. We have made a precious forward step, however, simply in discovering what the central problem for analysis is: reconciling our feeling as to the incomparability, i.e., the one-of-a-kind "uniqueness" of historical events, with the thesis that historians do think about these events deterministically, looking for sufficient (or at least necessary) conditions. How, we must ask, is this sort of thinking possible in regard to that sort of event? Sections 4 and 5 of chapter V deal with *this* question.

9. Cf. Carl G. Hempel, *Aspects of Scientific Explanation* (New York: The Free Press, 1965), p. 241 n. 7.

As we proceed with our discussion we shall find that historians and philosophers have entertained various ideas as to the peculiar way in which historians think about their subject matter, ideas that might lend respectability to the uniqueness argument. But these allegedly distinctive ways of thinking either do not provide accounts as to why anything in fact happened or they turn out to involve nomological generalizations characteristic of deterministic thinking.

5. CONTINGENCY

In speaking about history as full of contingencies some philosophers and historians have thought that they were speaking about a trait that rendered historical explanation different in kind. Suppose we ask in what sense (or senses) history is full of contingencies and how this is reflected in historical explanations.

"Contingent" is often contrasted with "necessary," but this alone is scarcely illuminating. An occurrence might be said to be contingent (i.e., not necessary) in any of the following respects: (1) not presupposing sufficient conditions; (2) not necessary relative to selected facts and laws; (3) unusual; (4) unexpected; or (5) having a plurality of causes.

The first sense of contingency is by no means clear,[10] but we can safely assume that it has no relevance to this discussion of differences between historical and scientific explanation. For if an occurrence does not have sufficient conditions, then the fact of its occurrence cannot, strictly speaking, be accounted for at all in terms of its relation to other states of affairs.[11]

The second sense is probably the most deceptive; let us momentarily reserve comment about it. As to the third, to say that an event was contingent in the sense of "unusual" means that it was not deducible from at least some and possibly all the knowledge that we have of things or circumstances of the kind involved in the occurrence, namely, knowledge about what usually in fact happens to things of this kind or what usually happens under circumstances of this kind. If "all," then we may be curious to find out more, but it may be that we know perfectly well what brought about (in the sense of nomologically necessitated) this departure from the normal course of events.

10. Cf. Nagel, *Structure of Science*, pp. 332 ff.
11. For an example of an historian's confusion about this see the quote from H. A. L. Fisher and the accompanying comment in Sidney Hook, *The Hero in History* (New York: The Humanities Press, 1943), pp. 141-46.

Contingent in the fourth sense can mean not deducible from (a) any knowledge that *we* had and any facts that *we* were aware of prior to its occurrence, or it can have the same meaning (b) *relative to what persons involved in the occurrence* knew or did not know.

In the fifth sense of the term, *what* is "contingent" about a particular occurrence is *which* set of conditions determined it— "contingent" here means "not deducible simply from any knowledge that we have about this *kind* of occurrence."[12]

The meaning of "contingent" in the second sense is close to but different from sense (3). Suppose we are recounting and explaining a certain sequence of occurrences (e.g., a "chain of events" in the career of some "entity" such as a person, group, country, institution, etc.). Some of the occurrences in the sequence may be said to be contingent, not because they are *unusual* or *unexpected* (in sense (a) or (b)), but because in accounting for them we mention as determining conditions persons (e.g., an assassin) or things (e.g., a volcano) that have not been *so far* discussed. They have not been relevant; up to a certain point, these persons or things in no way affected the occurrences we have been explaining. Perhaps they did not even exist throughout much of the period covered by our story. At a certain point, however, they become "relevant": they are then mentioned as determining conditions. Such determining conditions are often called "contingent" when their presence in the historical account as determining conditions is in no way itself a consequence of the "chain of events" that we selected to tell about and regard as the main thread of our story. Nothing we have said in telling—and fully explaining—a story accounts for (explains the "why in fact" of) the presence of these facts as determining conditions of the events in that story now to be explained. Such determining conditions are contingent *relative to that portion of world happenings that we have told about and explained up to that point.*

We can agree that history, as ordinarily presented, is "full of contingencies" in all of these senses except (1). We can agree that the historian is more likely to comment on the contingent character of the events he is recounting—contingent in one sense or another—than is the scientist, when the scientist turns his hand

12. To avoid complicating this discussion any further, we ignore the distinction between necessity as a relation between statements in a reasoning process and necessity as a relation between occurrences.

to explaining particular occurrences. But when we ask ourselves whether contingency is peculiarly characteristic of historical subject matter or, which is really the heart of the matter, whether explanations involving contingency in senses (2) through (5) are fundamentally different in their presuppositions from scientific explanations, it is obvious that they are not.[13]

6. RESTRICTED UNIVERSALITY

It is argued that the historian's way of thinking, unlike the scientist's, cannot be deterministic because the historian cannot possibly explain occurrences in terms of regularities of unrestricted universality. Unrestricted universality is the requirement that in adequately formulated nomological relations the descriptions of the kind of occurrence and kinds of determining conditions include no restrictions as to specific time or place, nor even any specific segment of time or region of space, and no restriction as to particular objects.[14]

Collingwood, for example, remarks: "In order that behaviour-patterns may be constant, there must be in existence a social order which recurrently produces situations of a certain kind. But social orders are historical facts, and subject to inevitable changes, fast or slow. A positive science of mind will, no doubt, be able to establish uniformities and recurrences, but it can have no guarantee that the laws it establishes will hold good beyond the historical period from which its facts are drawn."[15] It will be noted that this argument is different from the uniqueness argument already considered, at least in the latter's most extreme form, although, like that, it might also be said to derive from a characterization of the subject matter of history.

The restricted universality argument is readily answered. There is no "guarantee" that there is natural order in any domain. Natural order is *presumably* found in most domains at most levels of description, and it is conceived to be unchanging.[16] Changes in "social order" are plausibly presumed to have their own sufficient

13. On the meanings of contingency see also Sidney Hook, "Some Problems of Terminology in Historical Writing," in *Theory and Practice in Historical Study: A Report of the Committee on Historiography* (Social Science Research Council Bulletin 54 [New York, 1946]), pp. 115 ff.; Nagel, *Structure of Science*, pp. 324 ff.
14. See above, chap. I, sec. 6.
15. Collingwood, *Idea of History*, pp. 223-24.
16. See above, chap. II, secs. 6 and 11.

conditions, but again there is no "guarantee" that these changes are manifestations of natural order any more than there is a "guarantee" that any of our formulations of nomological relations are faultless. The argument overlooks the fact that natural scientists often work with generalizations of restricted universality (although indefinite in scope of predication)—referring to regularities of phenomena "in our solar system," "under terrestrial conditions," "among individuals of the same species," etc. They may do this for reasons of convenience, being ready, if called upon, to account for the restricted universality in "purely qualitative" terms. Even when they cannot account for it we can often recognize that their thinking is tied in with the natural order line of questioning (granting that at other times their orientation is that of *predictive science*), and so we judge that the ideal of natural order intelligibility—with its requirement of unrestricted universality—applies to their domain of inquiry. Why should we judge history differently?

It has been argued that the historian has "a much larger stake in limited generalizations" (i.e., restricted universality) than the natural scientist because the historian's interest is focused on "the understanding of particular events" rather than on "the formulation of universal generalizations."[17] This view, as we shall show, is not tenable.

"Limited generalizations" are said to be "genuine law-like statements" in that they are not merely descriptive summaries of particular events and do have counterfactual force; they are, however, distinctively "rooted in *transitory regularities*, deriving from the existence of temporally restricted technological or institutional patterns."[18] Generalizations are said to be limited "either tacitly or expressly": "tacitly" when they can be correctly interpreted to mean that some of the circumstances mentioned as determining conditions, although known to have occurred at some era in history, "cannot reasonably be expected to recur"; "expressly" when proper names (including names of specific periods of time) are used in the formulation of the generalization.

It is noteworthy, however, that whether or not generalizations are "tacitly" limited (i.e., judged to be *de facto* inapplicable to all historical periods but one) is in itself quite irrelevant to his-

17. Carey B. Joynt and Nicholas Rescher, "The Problem of Uniqueness in History," *History and Theory*, I, No. 2 (1961), 158.
18. *Ibid.*, p. 156 (italics in original).

torians' interest in understanding particular events. An event is not more intelligible because its occurrence exemplifies a nomological relation judged unlikely ever to be instantiated except between the two dates delimiting a certain historical period. As for generalizations that are "expressly" limited, these we have characterized as restricted in universality. Why has the historian any special "stake" in them, a "stake" deriving from a concern to understand particular events? Are particular events only intelligible or, perhaps, more intelligible than they otherwise would be, when subsumed under "expressly" limited generalizations as contrasted with generalizations of unrestricted universality? They are so only if we deem the line of questioning directed toward reformulating them in *un*restricted form inappropriate in principle to historical subject matter (i.e., particular *human* events). Joynt and Rescher do not defend this thesis, which we also have rejected. To account for the historian's stake in "expressly" limited generalizations, then, we must look not to the focus on *particular* events but to historical practice and to conventions about historical understanding. Historical understanding *is* considered by many historians and readers to be consummated at a certain point *even though* plausible questions remain unanswered as to precisely why this or that particular event happened precisely when and where it did, questions looking toward unrestricted universality, i.e., toward the elimination of (among others) proper names of specific periods of time. In other words, "expressly" limited generalizations are important to the historian only because in practice historical questioning and answering so often stop short of the ideal of natural order intelligibility.

It is not difficult to see how we would answer the restricted universality argument when it refers specifically to dispositional accounts. According to this version, the dispositions that historians cite as determining conditions are frequently restricted to particular persons or objects; therein their universality is restricted. Natural science accounts of occurrences cite dispositions sometimes too, but these dispositions characteristically are either formulated in "purely qualitative" terms (and therefore are not restricted) or can be derived from nomological universals formulated in "purely qualitative" terms. It is concluded that this constitutes a fundamental difference between historical and scientific explanations. Dray, for example, contrasts the following two dispositional accounts: "The glass broke when the stone hit it because it is brittle," and "Disraeli attacked Peel because he [Disraeli] was ambitious."[19] He comments: "Just as, in the case of the breaking glass, we may assume that the dispositional property holds by virtue of certain physical laws concerning the behavior of glass and bricks, so the dispositional properties attributed to human agents may appear to be applicable because of there being regularities in human behavior which are formulable in terms of laws (however 'loose')." But, he maintains, we are mistaken if we suppose "that a dispositional explanation of a particular human action depends in any way on the truth of such laws," for:

. . . 'ambition' is not a *general* characteristic of men (or even, perhaps, of politicians) in the way 'being brittle' is of glass. To say 'Disraeli attacked Peel because he was ambitious' draws attention to the general pattern of action into which his particular action fits, but it implies nothing about the kind of men from whom this kind of action can be expected. It merely implies that action of this general pattern can be expected from Disraeli; it subsumes his action under a regularity said to hold for a particular person, rather than a regularity said to hold for all persons of a certain type.

Now historians surely do frequently cite dispositions of restricted universality. (We shall not ask whether, perhaps, natural scientists commonly do so as well.) And historians often would not at present be able to overcome the restricted universality implied in their accounts even if they succeeded in replacing dispositional terms with nomological generalizations. This latter point has been made recently, for example, with regard to rationality as a dispositional trait often attributed to individuals in accounting for their actions. It has been maintained that we can sometimes convert such dispositional accounts into law-like accounts *of restricted universality.*

We know of no reasonably well-confirmed law that connects wants, beliefs, and actions for all persons in every choice situation, for the case of deliberative action. But, in the case of some individual we know well, we can sometimes know some statement like this to be true of *him*: 'At any time *t*, *he* will perform that action among those he believes possible which he *thinks* will maximize expectable utility for him,' where 'utility' is defined in some way in terms of the agent's intensity of want for any event in question. To make this sort of statement about a person, or about a person at a particular time, would be to classify him as a rational agent, in

19. Dray, *Laws and Explanation,* pp. 145-46.

one possible sense of "rational." Evidently, not everyone is rational in this sense, and in fact probably no one is rational at all times. Hence we cannot assert something corresponding to the above statement, as a general law true for everyone. What we can know is a "law-like" fact about some particular individual over some period of time. . . .[20]

We do not hold that the meaning or the truth of a dispositional account of which the component dispositional statement is restricted in universality depends on the latter's being derivable from unrestricted nomological universals. We do say, first, that the intent of even a dispositional account of which the component dispositional statement is restricted in universality, is to make some particular occurrence intelligible in terms of regular relations between states of affairs. This is natural order thinking. And we further say that the natural order line of questioning has its ideal of intelligibility. The applicability of this ideal to historical subject matter is not jeopardized by the fact that historians do not strive to apply it nor by the fact that natural order thinking at present, generally speaking, certainly cannot provide deterministic accounts (requiring unrestricted universality) of particular occurrences of the human past. The point is that there is no ground for singling out the conventional subject matter of history as a domain in which unrestricted universality is inappropriate as a requirement of natural order intelligibility. Those who base the distinctiveness of historical thinking on the argument here under scrutiny do not have a cogent case.

7. Narratives as Explanatory

A number of philosophers and historians have maintained that historical accounts typically tell a story, and that to tell a story is to make happenings intelligible in a distinctive way. Does the typical historical narrative afford a kind of intelligibility fundamentally different from deterministic intelligibility? That is our problem.

When an historian explains "why" by telling a story, what does he do? He depicts a number of happenings as having occurred in temporal sequence. These various happenings constitute not merely a temporal succession; they are presented as belonging to the career of something: an idea, a person, a group, a movement,

20. Richard Brandt and Jaegwon Kim, "Wants as Explanations of Actions," *The Journal of Philosophy,* LX (1963), 432.

an institution, and so on, or as belonging to a "chain of events" that "leads" from one state of affairs to another, states of affairs that happen to interest us.

Sometimes a story is told merely as a way of accounting for the event that concludes the story, for example, a narrative oriented toward answering the question: How did the discovery of America come about? But narratives are also written in which just as much interest attaches to the coming about of the intermediate events. The terminal event of a narrative can be quite incidentally terminal, as in the case of an account that ends with the present only because nothing more *has* happened in the career being narrated. The "course" of the events narrated can be well defined: a "rise" or "fall," the genesis and resolution of a crisis, etc.; but some stories are relatively formless, exhibiting no familiar over-all pattern or qualities.

Given these diversities in the character of historical narratives, what can we say about their underlying scheme of intelligibility? It would be an exaggeration to claim that the intelligibility of narrated events reduces to deterministic intelligibility.[21] As we shall have occasion to observe subsequently, most historical writing displays various modes of intelligibility; the typical historical narrative is no exception. But we look in vain for a fundamental scheme of intelligibility peculiar to the narrative form itself, a way of accounting for happenings in terms of interrelationships among occurrences. In so far as a narrative accounts for what took place in terms of interrelationships among occurrences, it does so in terms of determining conditions. The line of questioning is that of natural order thinking; the ideal of this line of questioning is deterministic intelligibility. The sequence of narrated events is then intelligible as a "causal" sequence, and the relevant basic criterion for deciding what events are to be included in the narrative is causal relevance. The only peculiar feature of deterministic intelligibility in its narrative form is that it involves an interrelated succession of deterministic relations: A is the cause of subsequent state of affairs B, which is the cause of subsequent state of affairs C, and so on. The crucial point, however, is that:

. . . the successive stages singled out for consideration surely must be qualified for their function by more than the fact that

21. It is no less exaggerated—and gratuitous—to identify historical narrative with "understanding." See, e.g., Cushing Strout, "Causation and the American Civil War," *History and Theory*, I, No. 2 (1961), 184-85.

they form a temporal sequence and that they all precede the final stage, which is to be explained: the mere enumeration in a yearbook of "the year's important events" in the order of their occurrence clearly is not a genetic explanation of the final event or of anything else. In a genetic explanation each stage must be shown to "lead to" the next, and thus to be linked to its successor by virtue of some general principles which make the occurrence of the latter at least reasonably probable, given the former.[22]

It would be superfluous to inquire here why the historian chooses to trace just the "causal chain" that he does choose, i.e., to tell just the story that he does tell. It is pertinent, however, to emphasize that none of the necessary conditions in a set of sufficient conditions is more necessary than any of the others. The story told by the historian is not intrinsically more explanatory than any of the many other stories that might have been told by tracing other relevant causal chains.

Why do historical narratives, then, appear so unlike scientific explanations of particular occurrences, even when we focus on their common objective of accounting for occurrences in terms of interrelationships among occurrences? The chief reason is that they are characteristically so casually structured: logical interrelationships are obscured and relevant facts are interspersed with additional information and interpretive commentary. We are usually so unaware of the implicit generalizations that we are surprised when we realize that they must be there. Our attention is often focused upon *what* the antecedent events were, especially when their causal relevance is considered "obvious." And, as in the case of some of the complex explanations we shall consider, even if the historian has to make out a case for the relevance of an event in his narrative, he will often do this not by citing a well-established law but by refining upon working generalizations or combining generalizations. This latter process[23] is not usually carried out completely and explicitly. Much more commonly the historian will talk informally about the details of the events in question, trusting that his readers will follow his elliptical argument without difficulty and will concur with him as to the reasonableness of the implicit general knowledge.

Historical narratives have sometimes been declared *sui generis*

22. Hempel, *Aspects*, pp. 448-49. See also Maurice Mandelbaum, "Historical Explanation: The Problem of 'Covering Laws,'" *History and Theory*, I, No. 3 (1961), 239; Nagel, *Structure of Science*, pp. 564 ff.

23. See below, chap. V.

by contrasting them with scientific explanations that utilize "developmental" or "historical" laws.[24] Since historical narratives account for unique sequences, they cannot invoke historical laws. So the argument goes. It is true that some efforts at making history more "scientific" have taken the form of searching for developmental laws extending to all of the traditional subject matter of historians. Opponents of "scientific" history have sought to capitalize on the failure or very limited success of these ventures, citing it as evidence of the non-scientific character of history. But this argument is only relevant when scientific explanation is arbitrarily identified with a special type of explanation. It would be relevant if restated: "since historical narratives account for unique sequences, they cannot presuppose *any* nomological universals"; relevant but not convincing, for it is based on a misconception already exposed in the preceding section.

8. ONE EVENT—MANY EXPLANATIONS

One of the most commonly drawn distinctions between what historians actually do and what might be expected if history were scientific pertains not to a characteristic of individual works of history, but to the fact that there are so many historical explanations of the same event. Thinking from the scientific standpoint, it is assumed, cannot yield more than one valid complete explanation of the same event. Historians, by contrast, *seem* to operate with more liberal criteria and often look favorably upon a number of explanations of the same event.

The apparent plurality of historical treatments of the same event often turns out not to presuppose the admissibility of more than one complete account of the same event. Closer scrutiny reveals one or another of the following: (1) The several historical works are not all approved of *as* explanations, at least not as natural order explanations. Each one represents a different genre of historical thinking. One is perhaps prized for its descriptive detail; another for making the past come alive so that we understand better what it felt like to be living then; another for the present-mindedness of the historian who has used the past to illuminate some aspect of our current situation; another for its insight into the time-transcending meaning of human doing and suffering; and still another is highly regarded as a natural order account which

24. Gustav Bergmann, *Philosophy of Science* (Madison, Wis.: University of Wisconsin Press, 1957), pp. 124 ff.; Nagel, *Structure of Science,* p. 76.

does indeed explain why things happened as they did. (2) Several works which are prized as explanations of why one and the same thing in fact happened may complement each other in the sense that they focus on different necessary conditions. (3) They may not be explanations of exactly the same thing, even though the same words are used to designate the subject matter (e.g., one history of the United States of America may be a social history, another economic, another intellectual, etc.); and several economic histories of the United States may supplement each other by accounting for different occurrences. (4) In cases where it has not been possible to agree upon a warranted explanation, historians may approve of several works because all present plausible hypotheses. (5) Finally, various historical treatments of the same subject can be valued as expressions of divergent viewpoints reflecting the historians' economic class, religious affiliation, political bias, and so on. No doubt this list could be extended.

If, in addition to the many ways in which historical works on the same subject can really be complementary, there persists an indulgence regarding those competing deterministic explanations which in their nature cannot be regarded as "equally true," why is this? Taking a charitable view of the matter, one might account for it by noting that historians are accustomed to a relaxed critical attitude which accords well with the formidable obstacles that beset the explaining historian. A less charitable observer might call attention to the defensiveness of historians when their easygoing attitude is called into question, and ascribe this to a hardly defensible but cherished carelessness with which historians customarily formulate their explanations—a carelessness which makes it difficult to know what explanation a historian has actually proposed, let alone whether it is worth anything. Historians, it may be said, sometimes prefer to congratulate one another in a display of fraternal solidarity instead of trying to establish the intrinsic merits of their competing claims.

It remains to question one premise of this entire argument, namely, the assumption that there is only one valid complete scientific explanation of any one event. Reflection upon scientific thinking does not substantiate this premise. The possibilities for multiple deterministic accounts of the same occurrence are not confined to conventional historical subject matter.[25] There is

25. See above, chap. II, sec. 8.

apparently, then, no basis to be found through a comparative study of the logic of scientific and historical thinking for the conclusion that the latter is not deterministic because it admits of multiple accounts—multiple accounts *within* the framework of natural order intelligibility.

9. THE USE OF CAUSAL TERMINOLOGY

It is claimed that historians talk about *causes*, whereas scientists today do not; therefore, history and science are fundamentally unlike. But the alleged peculiarity of the historian's talk about causes often turns out to reflect nothing more than the *type* of natural order account favored by historians or the *degree* of completeness of their natural order accounts.

We have already noted that various characteristics commonly supposed to differentiate causal accounts from non-causal accounts do not differentiate causal accounts from natural order questioning.[26] Consider, for example, the view that a cause is only one of a set of conditions and that the historian characteristically looks only for one or some of the set of sufficient conditions, not for the entire set.[27] The historian looking for a necessary condition is a scientist working at a specific task. More accurately, he *can* be and often is.

As Nagel, Gardiner, and Dray, among others, have pointed out, the historian may be thinking with practical considerations in mind.[28] In that case the concept of cause has pragmatic connotations built into it. But we only invite confusion if we give *this* concept of cause our exclusive endorsement. If you ask an historian whether the pragmatically selected cause suffices to account for the state of affairs he is explaining, he will immediately see that it does not—that a complete account would mention other determining conditions. Though historians seldom if ever state the sufficient conditions of an occurrence, they nonetheless recognize the appropriateness of a scheme of intelligibility which essentially ignores practical considerations; they do not feel that all questions of natural order should automatically be referred to a non-historian specialist in sufficient conditions. They sense the possibility of shifting their standpoint as historians back and forth between a

26. See above, chap. II, sec. 4.
27. See, e.g., Nagel, *Structure of Science*, pp. 559 ff.
28. *Ibid.*, pp. 582 ff.; Patrick Gardiner, *The Nature of Historical Explanation* (London: Oxford University Press, 1952), pp. 99 ff.; Dray, *Laws and Explanation*, pp. 97 ff.

pragmatically conditioned standpoint and what by contrast we could call the disinterested natural order standpoint.

To review all the allegedly non-deterministic aspects of causal accounts would be unnecessarily repetitious. One, however, deserves mention. It is sometimes maintained that non-pragmatic causal accounts do not yield deterministic intelligibility because they do not presuppose nomological universals. There are obvious reasons why historians and others find this argument persuasive, and we shall deal with these in due course.[29]

10. Some Peculiarities of Historical Generalizations

A simple reply can be made to a number of arguments citing alleged peculiarities of history, all pertaining to the character of historical generalizations: Our concept of deterministic thinking encompasses these peculiarities (just as, e.g., it encompasses restrictive universality), therefore they cannot differentiate historical thinking from deterministic thinking.

It is maintained that the generalizations implicit in historians' explanations (a) are at best statistical, or (b) are often merely law-like dispositional statements, or (c) are not systematized by means of comprehensive theories. Now the important thing about arguments such as these on behalf of the peculiarity of history is that they do grant that the historian's accounts presuppose independently warranted generalizations; it is that very feature, appropriately analyzed, that is the clue to their "natural order" character (especially inasmuch as the thinking of historians only rarely has the alternative orientation of predictive science). The peculiarities, even if correctly attributed to historical generalizations, do not suffice to render historical thinking different in kind from natural order thinking. This is a conclusion we have already developed at some length. We need only recall that the relevance of the scheme of deterministic intelligibility is not disproved by historians' recourse to statistical generalizations (as the best available generalizations or as the *appropriate* answer to a non-pragmatic question calling for a statistical explanation or prediction); or by their recourse to dispositional explanations (with the qualifications already discussed); or by the fact that the generalizations they employ in explaining are not systematically ordered by means of comprehensive theories. We should keep in mind with regard to the unsystematic character of historical generalizations that

29. See chap. V below, especially sec. 2.

indirect confirmation is a requirement of adequate nomological universals. Historians are just as shy of mere "universals of fact" as other inquirers, and it is safe to assume that, without being fully aware of why they do it, they look for interconnected generalizations that can serve as indirect evidence. Finally, it may well be that, in practice, refining upon generalizations usually goes hand in hand with theory formation, but elaborate, hierarchical ordering of laws is not an essential requirement of natural order intelligibility.

Chapter IV.

The Deterministic Intelligibility of Rational Action

1. INTRODUCTION

R. G. Collingwood can serve as initial spokesman for the thesis that history is not assimilable to science on the ground that natural order intelligibility is unsuited to consciously rational, purposive behavior.

The processes of nature can therefore be properly described as sequences of mere events, but those of history cannot. They are not processes of mere events but processes of actions, which have an inner side, consisting of processes of thought; and what the historian is looking for is these processes of thought. All history is the history of thought.

But what kind of thinking can be its object? . . . In order . . . that any particular act of thought should become subject-matter for history, it must be an act not only of thought but of reflective thought. . . . Reflective acts may be roughly described as the acts which we do on purpose, and these are the only acts which can become the subject-matter of history.

From this point of view, it can be seen why certain forms of activity are, and others are not, matter of historical knowledge. It would be generally admitted that politics is a thing that can be historically studied. The reason is that politics affords a plain instance of purposive action.[1]

Collingwood goes on to consider other human activities that involve purposive thinking and that therefore provide proper

1. R. G. Collingwood, *The Idea of History* (London: Oxford University Press, 1946), pp. 215, 307-9.

subject matter for historians: warfare, economic activity, moral action, art, science, religion, and philosophy.

Whether or not it is sound to conceive of rational activity as the *only* proper historical subject matter is a question we shall bypass here. It is certainly *sometimes* the subject matter of history. The question is whether natural order intelligibility is appropriate to rational activity. In Collingwood's own opinion, because the subject matter of history is rational activity, natural order intelligibility is inappropriate.

In considering what lies behind this alleged inappropriateness we shall not confine ourselves to Collingwood's particular viewpoint. Instead we shall organize the discussion so as to bring out the major issues in recent controversy and thus confront the main objections to our own position.

The kind of intelligibility achieved by historical thinking, according to Collingwood's notion of it, is sometimes called "teleological explanation." This expression is used in more than one sense. In particular it is sometimes used broadly to mean any explanation of characteristics of phenomena by reference to certain ends or purposes which those characteristics are said to serve. In this sense of "teleological explanation," there is no delimitation to human phenomena and no requirement that the human being or beings in question be pursuing ends with deliberation, i.e., consciously thinking how to accomplish ends-in-view and acting on the basis of this "calculation."[2] Collingwood's idea of historical explanation pertains only to deliberate purposive activity, therefore it is "teleological explanation" only in this narrower sense of that term. The *deliberate,* purposive activity of *human beings* is also our topic here.

It is sometimes supposed that what sets teleological explanations fundamentally apart is that they cite future occurrences as determining conditions. The fulfilled purpose, i.e., something that has not yet occurred at the time of the purposeful action (the occurrence to be accounted for), is supposedly among the determining conditions of that action consciously done to bring about that result. Is this a good reason for contending that historical accounts (as teleological) are *sui generis*? On those terms, teleological accounts would not be just different, they would be unacceptable

2. Cf. Ernest Nagel, *The Structure of Science* (New York; Harcourt, Brace and World, 1961), pp. 23-25.

according to canons of inductive confirmation. Explanations cast in that form are either unverifiable (because lacking unambiguous empirical reference) or empirically unwarranted. The prevalent view among philosophers of science is that, given an appropriate analysis, there is no ground for asserting that in rational behavior "the future acts causally on the present," that "goals or ends of activity are dynamic agents in their own realizations."[3]

[One argument against the fundamental similarity of all scientific explanation] . . . insists that the explanation of any phenomenon involving purposive behavior calls for reference to motivations and thus for teleological rather than causal analysis. . . . Unquestionably, many of the—frequently incomplete—explanations which are offered for human actions involve reference to goals and motives; but does this make them essentially different from the causal explanations of physics and chemistry? One difference which suggests itself lies in the circumstance that in motivated behavior, the future appears to affect the present in a manner which is not found in the causal explanations of the physical sciences. But clearly, when the action of a person is motivated, say, by the desire to reach a certain objective, then it is not the as yet unrealized future event of attaining that goal which can be said to determine his present behavior, for indeed the goal may never be actually reached; rather—to put it in crude terms—it is (a) his desire, present before the action, to attain that particular objective, and (b) his belief, likewise present before the action, that such and such a course of action is most likely to have the desired effect. The determining motives and beliefs, therefore, have to be classified among the antecedent conditions of a motivational explanation, and there is no formal difference on this account between motivational and causal explanation.[4]

Taking cognizance of these considerations, we could very properly have introduced a suitable—though odd-sounding—restriction into our definition of deterministic (II) relations; i.e., the restriction that an occurrence subsequent to e cannot be an antecedent (or concurrent) determining condition of e. This restriction would not, of course, preclude *references* to subsequent occurrences in the formulation of necessary conditions.[5]

3. *Ibid.*, pp. 24, 402.
4. Carl G. Hempel, *Aspects of Scientific Explanation* (New York: The Free Press, 1965), p. 254.
5. See, e.g., Hempel's remarks in "Explanation and Prediction by Covering Laws," in *Philosophy of Science: The Delaware Seminar*, ed. Bernard Baumrin (New York: John Wiley and Sons, 1963) I (1961-1962), 109.

2. PECULIARITIES OF INTENTIONS, PLANS, ETC. AS DETERMINISTIC CONDITIONS

The preceding quotation presupposes that scientific explanation of purposeful behavior (whether strictly deterministic or not) will mention motives, intentions, and/or plans among other determining conditions. Considerable attention has been given lately to this type of determining condition, and conflicting views have been expressed as to its proper analysis. This disagreement is reflected in disagreement as to the relevance of the scheme of natural order to historical intelligibility. The analysis of motives, intentions, etc. is a topic that has to be dealt with if we are to make good our claim that rational activity is deterministically intelligible. From this perspective, the chief issue is the following: *unless* we can show how motives, intentions, etc. can enter into natural order accounts as determining conditions, doubt will remain as to whether accounts of rational activity can be in accord with our conception of deterministic thinking; we shall wonder whether, perhaps, in so far as historians do endeavor to make rational activity intelligible, they necessarily do this in some way peculiar to their profession.

In *The Nature of Historical Explanation,* Patrick Gardiner poses this question: "What does it mean to give an explanation of somebody's action in terms of what he wants, intends, or plans?" Suppose the historian says "*x* did *y* because his intention was *w*." Is he asserting a causal relation between two events? Gardiner concludes that he is not. The reason given is that there are not two events involved. Having an intention is not an event at all; it is a disposition. To say that "*x* had intention *w*" is to make a statement that is "analyzable into both categorical and hypothetical elements."[6] Such "elements" might be: "*x* at some time thought about *w*" (categorical); "*x* could have put his intention into words had there been occasion for it" (hypothetical); "*x* would have experienced feelings of pleasure if state of affairs *s* (which would have facilitated intention *w*) had come about" (hypothetical).

So the historian is not asserting a causal relation between two events when he asserts "*x* did *y* because his intention was *w*." Instead, says Gardiner, the function of the "because" is "to set a statement referring to a specific action within the context of a general statement," which "can be 'unpacked' into an indefinite

6. Patrick Gardiner, *The Nature of Historical Explanation* (London: Oxford University Press, 1952), pp. 120, 124.

range of statements concerning his [the agent's] reactions to various kinds of circumstances. It represents, if you like, an *instance* of how he can in general be expected to behave under certain conditions."[7] It sets the action within a pattern of normal behavior.

Gardiner thus argues for the distinctiveness of some historical explanations on the grounds that they are dispositional and, as such, non-causal. These allegedly distinctive dispositional explanations are not confined to explanations of deliberate activity—our present topic—but do include the latter. Certainly "planning"— if not also "wanting" and "intending"—implies deliberation. In Gardiner's view it is as dispositional rather than as referring to deliberation that some historical explanations of deliberate activity are distinctive. But they would, nonetheless, be distinctive in a way that concerns us. As it turns out, "cause" for Gardiner means "determining condition." A non-causal explanation would, then, lie outside the natural order (i.e., deterministic) line of questioning. We must first ask: In so far as any historical explanations are dispositional are they non-deterministic?

Gardiner's dispositional interpretation of "mental conduct concepts" owes much to Ryle's *The Concept of Mind,* and we have already seen that dispositional accounts of occurrences, as conceived by Ryle, although they do not fully meet the requirements of natural order intelligibility, do fall within the framework of natural order intelligibility.[8] That dispositional explanations are not deterministic accounts is pointed out by Gardiner himself: they only inform us that the action in question was an instance of how *in general* the agent can be expected to behave or "is likely to behave."[9] We are not told what the sufficient conditions of the action were, for we are not told the precise conditions under which "the pattern of normal behavior" is realized. Gardiner's analysis does not bring out the fact that the historian can plausibly aim to supplement, fill in, or refine upon indeterminate "many-tracked" (or "single-tracked") dispositional generalizations, telling us, in effect, of at least one set—the relevant set—of further conditions which *together with those mentioned in the dispositional hypothetical* constitute a set of sufficient conditions.

It is pertinent to distinguish between cases in which dispositional statements function as generalizations—as statements of a regular

7. *Ibid.,* p. 125 (italics in original).
8. Chap. II, sec. 5 above.
9. Gardiner, *Explanation,* p. 125.

relation of which a particular occurrence is an instance—and cases in which dispositional statements function as descriptions of the determining conditions (or kind of conditions) of a certain occurrence (or kind of occurrence). Gardiner correctly observes that the mental action concept "having a motive" (or "plan," or "intention") does not refer to *an* event, at least not in the usual sense of event. But this alone does not render accounts of occurrences utilizing dispositional terms different in kind from deterministic accounts. For if the statement employing dispositional terms is functioning as a generalization we have only to point out that no natural order generalization refers to *an* event; and if, on the other hand, the dispositional terms are utilized in describing determining conditions we have only to point out that it is arbitrary to insist that a determining condition can only be *an* event. If it is plausible to assume, as we have done, that any combination of qualities, relations, and existential conditions can be determining conditions, then the only remaining doubt as to the assimilability of the historian's dispositional explanations to natural order thinking centers upon whether or not the relevant dispositional terms are analyzable into these. Gardiner himself does not undertake any extensive analysis, but his remarks about the "unpacking" of dispositional statements indicate that he considers such analyses feasible in principle.

It is sometimes maintained, however, that "mental conduct concepts" resist analysis, and the inference is drawn that dispositional explanations employing these concepts differ significantly from deterministic accounts. Studies now exist, however, which show that they can be analyzed. A model for such a study appropriate to the scheme of natural order intelligibility is the analysis in "Wants as Explanations of Actions," by Richard Brandt and Jaegwon Kim. Their conclusions are very much to the point:

So it is proper to say that we do have explanations of actions on the basis of wants; but these everyday common-sense explanations, whether of deliberative or nondeliberative actions, on the basis of wants, presuppose and derive their explanatory force from an everyday common-sense scheme of psychological knowledge of people in general or of the preference scale (etc.) of a given agent in particular, which can be unpacked in more or less precise statements, some of which we have tried to sketch. Thus, when we say "He stole the money because he badly wanted a new car for his honeymoon," we are using information about the agent's preference scale (etc.) and general propositions about what people ordinarily do in certain circumstances, inferring deductively or inductively the explanandum statement, very much as we do when we offer the explanation, "The radiator leaks because the temperature fell to 10° last night and there was no anti-freeze in the radiator." Explanations of this kind may not have much theoretical power or interest; but to grant this is only to concede that they *are* common-sense explanations. Trivial and obvious as they seem, these explanations are not fundamentally different in logical and methodological requirements from their counterparts in natural science. Truly deductive explanations of actions may be difficult and even impossible to attain, but we must remember that even in physical science deductively complete explanations are often found only among theoretical explanations of laws and theories and seldom among explanations of specific events and states. . . .

Are the explanations of action on the basis of wants as we have outlined them "causal explanations"? There is the extreme view, endorsed by many philosophers, which categorically denies that they are causal explanations—and indeed that any alleged explanation of action on the basis of wants could succeed in being a genuine causal explanation. However, what these philosophers mean by 'causal explanation' is often unclear, and, when it is clear, it is not at all certain that all the familiar explanations found in the natural sciences are "causal" in any single required sense. . . .

What we think clear and important in this dispute is the question of whether or not sensible explanations of human actions exhibit the appropriate inferential and nomological pattern of explanations found in physical and biological sciences—in other words, whether explanations of action form a unique type of explanation with special logical and methodological requirements distinct from those of explanations in natural science. Obviously, if our analysis of wanting and of explanations of action in terms of wants is plausible, at least in basic outline, it is one good reason for thinking that explanations of action do not differ from explanations in natural science, in inferential nomological pattern.[10]

We shall not then readily be impressed by any argument to the effect that dispositional accounts of purposeful action—or of any other occurrences, for that matter—constitute as such a fundamentally distinct way of making occurrences intelligible, and that in so far as historians provide such accounts historical intelligibility is unlike deterministic intelligibility.[11]

10. Richard Brandt and Jaegwon Kim, "Wants as Explanations of Actions," *The Journal of Philosophy*, LX (1963), 433-35.

11. See also above chap. III, sec. 6, for comment on another argument involving dispositional statements, namely, the argument that the historian's teleological explanations are distinctive because the dispositions that he cites in them are characteristically of restricted universality, i.e., they pertain to particular places, periods, persons or objects.

3. REASONS

Gardiner's discussion of mental conduct concepts places no particular stress on the *rational* aspect of purposeful activity. In so far as "being reasonable" figures as a dispositional term in accounts of human activity it would appear that we have only to defend the thesis that "being reasonable"—as well as the whole family of rational disposition terms that this calls to mind—is no different from any other "mental conduct concept": all are in principle analyzable in terms of qualities, relations, and existential conditions. Discussions of the status and function of references to reasons and rationality in accounts of purposeful activity are immensely complicated, however, by a number of persistent ambiguities and confusions. These stem chiefly from failure to take cognizance of the different types of reasons, reasoning, or rationality (using these terms just as broadly as they are used ordinarily), and of the various orientations from which reasons can be "cited" by historians and comprehended by readers of history. Accordingly, we shall first differentiate two principal types of "reasons" or, as we shall call them, meaning relations; we shall then discuss different orientations from which reasons of the different kinds can be referred to and comprehended, i.e., different ways of regarding meaning relations. Applying these distinctions, we will be able to show what is involved in a deterministic account of rational action.[12]

We shall maintain that occurrences characterized as rational are, in principle, within the scope of deterministic thinking. Historians' accounts of *rational* actions are often dispositional. Sometimes only a dispositional account is called for. Sometimes a dispositional account is the best we can provide. But the presumption of the applicability in principle of the deterministic ideal of intelligibility to rational actions is, in any case, altogether appropriate. Thus we maintain that historical explanation cannot be essentially differentiated from natural order thinking by contending that rational action can only be made intelligible by dispositional or causal accounts having a scheme of intelligibility other than natural order.

12. Attention is called to the extensive treatment of rational action in Part Two below, especially chaps. VIII and IX. There, however, we are dealing with thinking about rational actions from the standpoint of living in the world. This standpoint is mentioned briefly here as one of the orientations from which reasons can be referred to and comprehended. See (C.2) in the outline below.

(i) TYPES OF MEANING RELATIONS   MANIFESTATION

I. *Formal-Logical* $\begin{cases} \text{experienced} \\ \text{or} \\ \text{objectified} \end{cases}$

II. *Human Meaning Relations* $\begin{cases} \text{experienced} \\ \text{or} \\ \text{objectified} \end{cases}$
(Correlates of Human Attitudes or
Standpoints)

(ii) WAYS OF REGARDING MEANING RELATIONS

WHICH RELATIONS
SO REGARDED

A. *Descriptive Understanding*   I or II
(Pure description or ancillary in
function, serving (B) or (C))

B. *Thought About (made intelligible)*   I or II
*From The Standpoint of Natural
Order*

C. *Identifying Understanding*   II only

C.1 Human meaning relations understood identifyingly as manifestations of the *natural order
standpoint.*
("cognitive attitude")

C.2 Human meaning relations understood identifyingly as manifestations of the *standpoint of living
in the world.*
("emotional attitude")
valuational
("volitional attitude")
action-oriented

(i) TYPES OF MEANING RELATIONS

I. *Formal-Logical Meaning Relations.* Ordinary discourse
tacitly recognizes relations which are not analyzable in spatio-
temporal terms; relations in connection with which we often speak
of things or symbols as having certain "meanings."[13] It is character-

13. The term "meaning" is not used here in a technical sense which deserves to be explicitly stated. A historian concerned with any of these types
of subject matter is often said, in ordinary discourse, to be dealing with

istic of this class of relations that they do not essentially involve any distinctively human meaning, i.e., meaning relations correlated with human attitudes or standpoints. Some examples of Type (I) meaning relations are: (1) the formal relation between a universal of any sort (concept, rule, practical principle, etc.) and an instance of the universal; (2) the relation between a symbol and its definition; (3) the relation between a symbol and things which it denotes; (4) the formal relation between a signal and the "meaning" of the signal; and (5) the relation between component "parts" of a structured "whole."

In their most familiar guise we encounter these relations *in systems*, e.g., in logical, mathematical, or linguistic systems (such as our native language). These may be more or less abstract, more or less versatile, with respect to the kind of content to which they can be applied. "If *a* is smaller than *b*, and if *b* is smaller than *c*, then *a* is smaller than *c*" illustrates one sort of versatility. "The symbol '*Au*' stands for the chemical element gold" illustrates another sort of versatility. The important thing is that they can be thought of, and often are, as self-contained meaning systems constructed out of the formal-logical meaning relations we mentioned just above. Because we can and do think of them in this way as self-contained meaning systems, because what interests us often happens to be the meaning relations as such within any given system, it is appropriate to call these systems "neutral meaning" systems, in the sense that the relations they comprise have, as such, no essentially human reference, no human meaning.

II. *Human Meaning Relations (Correlates of Human Attitudes or Standpoints).* When we scrutinize the conceptualizations that pervade our experience we find some types of relations which can be qualified as distinctively human. Even "neutral" systems, of course, have human reference. Human beings know the meanings of formal-logical symbols; human beings know the rules and perform operations with symbols according to rules. The systems are contrived by human beings—at least discovered

---

meaning—meaning that is objectively there in the subject matter and not, e.g., what the subject matter subjectively means to him. As it turns out, the relevant ordinary meanings of "meaning" are so diverse that it would be a thankless task to try to say what they have in common, by virtue of which they are all meanings of "meaning." We might remark, however, that none of the meaning relations of types I and II is a mode of the nomological relation.

by them—and used for human ends. And, in the case of natural languages, certainly the dictionary definitions of many words involve human reference of one sort or another. Nonetheless it seems plausible to say that there is nothing distinctively human about the relation between a rule and a case that illustrates a rule or comes under it, and nothing distinctively human, therefore, about what we come to understand when we have rules or word-meanings identified for us as such. It is quite incidental that a particular neutral meaning system or a particular use of such a system can be humanly revealing, as—to take an extreme example—Spengler found that mathematical systems furnished general insights into the "spiritual" form of their respective cultures.

It may not always be easy to distinguish formal-logical meaning relations from those correlated with human attitudes or standpoints, yet the distinction is useful. In reading the following quotation from Sorokin, for example, one readily sees the need for further analysis of his concept of the "logico-meaningful" along the lines of our distinction between neutral meaning and human meaning. Speaking about one way in which "cultural elements" are integrated, a way he calls "logico-meaningful," he writes:

In what does it consist? What are its qualities? Suppose we have before us the scattered pages of a great poem, or of Kant's *Critique of Pure Reason,* or fragments of the statue of Venus de Milo, or the scattered pages of the score of Beethoven's Third Symphony. If we know the proper patterns of meaning and value, we can put these pages or parts together into a significant unity in which each page or fragment takes its proper place, acquires a meaning, and in which all together give the supremely integrated effect that was intended. . . . The functional or causal or probabilistic connection of separate units is almost always inferential and external; it rarely gives us an internal comprehension of the connection. . . . Different is the feeling we have in regard to logically integrated unities. The properly trained mind apprehends, feels, perceives, senses, and understands the supreme unity of Euclid's or Lobachevski's geometry of perfect mathematical deduction; of Platonic metaphysics; of Phidias's Athena; of a suite or concerto by Bach; of a Shakespeare drama; of the architecture of the Parthenon or the Cathedral of Chartres.[14]

Our immediate interest is in discriminating modes of human meaning as distinctive *subject matter* for historical inquiry. We shall find, however, that differentiated lines of questioning and schemes

14. Pitirim Sorokin, *Social and Cultural Dynamics* (rev. and abr. ed.; Boston: Porter Sargent, 1957), pp. 7-8, 11.

of intelligibility are associated with modes of human meaning. Accordingly, differences in modes of meaning are reflected in the variety of ways in which historical subject matter—including reasons—can be regarded and presented by the historian and comprehended by readers.

It must suffice to sketch the modes of distinctively human meaning in broad strokes, and as suggestively as possible, in a manner congenial to the objectives of this study. I shall have recourse to Wilhelm Dilthey's distinctions and descriptions.[15] He differentiates three basic human "attitudes," i.e., ways in which we approach, treat, or conduct ourselves toward experienced content. These ways are: (1) the "objective" or "cognitive attitude," which is directed toward knowledge of objective reality; (2) the "volitional attitude," directed toward formulating and accomplishing goals; and (3) the "attitude of the emotional life." Corresponding to each of these ways of approaching the world there are meaning relations. The relations among things, and our relations to things corresponding to these different approaches, are modes of meaning. Things are meaningful as "known," as "valued," or as "willed." These three attitudes and their corresponding meaning relations are the roots of all distinctively human meaning.

Having stressed their interpenetration in "each lived experience," Dilthey proceeds to discuss the development of meaning relations corresponding to the respective attitudes. The attitude

in which we apprehend the lived and the given, produces our picture of the world, our concepts of reality, the particular sciences among which the knowledge of this reality is distributed—accordingly, the purposive system of the knowledge of reality. At every stage of this process inclination and feeling are at work. They are

15. Dilthey, in published and unpublished works, returned again and again to the task of describing what he called the "mental structure" (*psychische Struktur*) of human experience. His most fully developed account—too lengthy for our purposes—is to be found in the posthumously published "Zweite Studie," *Gesammelte Schriften* (Leipzig and Berlin: B. G. Teubner, 1942), VII, 24-69. Whereas Dilthey distinguishes three "attitudes" and their corresponding modes of meaning relations, we draw a fundamental distinction between two "standpoints"; the subdivision we shall make within the standpoint of living in the world (see Part Two, chap. VII, sec. 1) corresponds roughly to two of his "attitudes." The correspondence (which is shown in the accompanying outline) between his distinctions and ours is thus very close. It should be pointed out that although the account we give here of the modes of meaning is sketchy, we have already presented in chapters I and II a detailed analysis of the scheme of intelligibility correlated with one of the attitude-standpoints as a differentiated and refined way of thinking.

the center of our mental structure; from this point all the depths of our being are stirred. We seek an affective state which in some way or other stills our desires. Life is continually approaching this goal. Now life seems to have grasped it; now again the goal recedes. Only the progress of experience teaches each individual what are the enduring values for him. Here the chief work of life is to come through illusions to the knowledge of what is genuinely worth while for us. The system of processes in which we test the values of life and of things, this I call experience of life. It presupposes knowledge of what is, hence our understanding of the objective world. And, as a means to this experience of life, our acts of will, whose immediate purpose concerns changes outside or in ourselves, can serve at the same time for evaluating the elements of our lives as well as external things, in case our interest points to these. Through knowledge of man, through history and poetry, the means to experience of life and the horizon of that experience are enlarged. And in this field also our life can win its security only through elevation to universally valid knowledge. (Can this knowledge, indeed, ever answer the question of absolute value?) The consciousness of life's values is the basis of a third and last system, in which we voluntarily strive to organize and guide movements, men, society, and ourselves. It includes purposes, goods, duties, rules of life, the whole vast business of our practical activity in administration of justice, economy, social regulation, and control over nature. Within this attitude also consciousness advances to higher and higher forms. We seek as the last and highest an activity based on universally valid knowledge, and again the question arises, how far this goal is attainable.[16]

I would stress—as Dilthey himself did—that although the three attitudes are interwoven in concrete experience, they undergo differentiation and elaboration. Each of them harbors the potentiality of dominating our relation to the world. In everyday life now one dominates, now another. When the cognitive attitude prevails, the world becomes identified with sheer facts in their objective relationships. The volitional attitude becoming dominant, our entire experience finds its focus in appropriate action; knowledge of the world is then essentially transformed into an instrument which we use in finding out and doing the appropriate thing. Or, finally, the attitude of emotional life evolves to the point where it can take in the whole world; so "taken in," the world becomes for us the spectacle of human doing and suffering. Individuals, however, and even whole societies at certain times, may view the

16. Wilhelm Dilthey, *The Essence of Philosophy*, trans. S. A. and W. T. Emery (Chapel Hill, N. C.: The University of North Carolina Press, 1954), pp. 35, 39, 63, 64.

world predominantly in terms of one attitude, a phenomenon to which Dilthey devoted considerable attention in his analysis of world-views.

Manifestations of distinctively human meaning include both highly personal and shared meanings of all sorts. We note particularly the formation of relatively stable quasi-autonomous "cultural systems." The cognitive attitude gives rise to science as a collective, institutionalized endeavor continuously sustained throughout the flux of generations. The volitional attitude is reflected in "economic life, law, and technology." The emotional attitude produces art and play, which have their respective institutional manifestations.[17]

Each mode of human meaning relations, as the quotation from Dilthey indicates, can be more or less articulated and systematic. Marks of what we shall call the rational development of an attitude are: a disposition to treat meaning relations as questionable rather than taking them for granted; elaboration, refinement, and co-ordination of relevant concepts and generalizations; and conscious, explicit methodological inquiry and judgment.

(ii) WAYS OF REGARDING MEANING RELATIONS

A. *Descriptive Understanding.* It is possible for an historian simply to state the meaning relations involved in particular occurrences. He may give either a general description of meaning relations common to an unspecified number of occurrences, or a description of the meaning relations involved in a single occurrence. To grasp and be able to state meaning relations in general form or as involved in particular occurrences is to understand what happened. By means of such descriptions historians often afford us this understanding, i.e., *descriptive understanding.*

The meaning relations thus described and understood can be either formal-logical or distinctively human. The occurrences in which the meaning relations are manifested can have the form either of "subjective" experience or publicly observable "objectifications" (marks, shapes, sounds, pictures, gestures, behavior, etc.).[18]

17. *Ibid.,* pp. 37-39.
18. We note in passing an important characteristic of "meaningful" objects. In analyzing "what" they mean we have not only to employ the distinction between formal-logical and human meaning relations; we have also often to distinguish between an "essential" meaning and the "particular" supplementary meaning they have for a person (or persons) in a situation. The latter aspect is not the same as a personal opinion (correct or incorrect)

In the case of neutral meaning systems, "giving the meaning" may be tantamount to giving the conventional meaning of symbols (what they represent, signify, stand for, designate, etc.), or it may take the form of stating the rules for manipulating the symbols (formation rules, rules of syntax, etc.). As historical subject matter requiring explanation, the historian's task may be that of reconstructing and displaying the "dictionary" and the "rules"; he explains a meaning system which was in use at a certain time and place. Michael Ventris' decipherment of the Linear B script on the prehistoric tablets discovered in Greece and Crete exemplifies this sort of "historical explanation." If the meaning system is a natural language we are likely to call the historian a philologist or linguist. If his task were reconstructing the logic of the ancient Stoics, we might call him a logician or historian of philosophy. The explanation problem is different when what is called for is the explanation of a specific passage in a book or document by reference to the dictionary and rules of a mathematical system or language. The question "How can we account for this word or letter or punctuation mark on this page?" can be answered in terms of the rules and/or dictionary of the system represented.[19] When so answered, we shall call the account descriptive. To be able to give such a descriptive account one must know the meaning relations involved. It is this knowledge and the knowledge afforded the reader of the descriptive account that we call descriptive understanding: *descriptive* in that it tells what happened; *understanding* in that it pertains to meaning relations. In order to distinguish as clearly as possible this way of presenting and comprehending meaning relations we have intentionally ignored the fact that in practice other ways (especially (B) and (C.2)) of regarding the occurrences manifesting meaning relations are usually conjoined with descriptive understanding.

Our particular interest is in historical accounts that cite *reasons.*

---

as to what the symbol, sentence, gesture, etc. essentially means—an opinion which is correct or incorrect relative to the essential-meaning defining criteria, whatever they may be. We can distinguish between the essential meaning of some poems and what the poems, of which I know *the* meaning, mean to me, i.e., the supplementary "particular" meaning. The "essential" meaning and its relation to the "particular" meaning differ in character depending upon the character of the manifestation, i.e., upon whether the latter is literal, pictorial, ritualistic, poetic, etc.; hence sound generalizations applying to them all are rare.

19. Cf. Erwin Panofsky's remarks on iconography, *Meaning in the Visual Arts* (Garden City, N.Y.: Doubleday and Company, 1955), pp. 27, 31-32.

Our problem is to find out whether such accounts must be non-deterministic. In the area of neutral meaning systems relevant instances are provided by mathematical and logical systems, for we commonly do speak of the rule-governed operations of such systems as reasoning processes; "mathematical reasoning" is used in this sense, as is "syllogistic reasoning." Now the situation might arise in historical investigation that the fact to be accounted for was a step in a reasoning process of the sort referred to. Explaining the fact might take the form of "citing reasons" in the sense of showing that the step taken was in accordance with a set of rules. Whether our historian had to point out for us a rule of which we were ignorant or had to show us that a well-known rule did indeed apply here, in either case his explanation of the fact would involve this distinctive way of "citing reasons": descriptive understanding.

Descriptive understanding (in the form of generalized accounts or accounts of specific occurrences) of distinctively human meaning relations (as objectified or as lived experience) may also involve "citing reasons" if the human attitudes of persons involved in the occurrences were rationally developed so that reasoning occurred and cognitive claims were made. Corresponding to the respective attitudes, these "reasons" and "claims" may be concerned with matters of fact and natural order (the cognitive attitude), with rules and norms of action (the volitional attitude), or with values (the emotional attitude). Formal-logical relations figure prominently in rationally developed human meaning relations.[20]

In practice, therefore, the historian frequently has occasion to exercise descriptive understanding of both types of meaning relations in connection with a description of the same particular occurrence. For example, if the occurrence were a process of deliberation on the part of a commanding officer as to how best to dispose his troops in meeting an enemy attack, descriptive understanding of that occurrence would likely include an account of how a certain step in that process was a logical inference from premises (a formal-logical relation). The premises of this inference (perhaps called "reasons") could include statements of fact, nomo-

20. This applies to a vast number of "intellectual" and "cultural" historical studies in which there is little or no explicit mention of "reasons"; e.g., large sections of Adolf Harnack's *Outlines of the History of Dogma* (Beacon Paperback edition; Boston: Beacon Press, 1957) or Otto Gierke's *Natural Law and the Theory of Society: 1500 to 1800* (Beacon Paperback edition; Boston: Beacon Press, 1957).

logical universals, principles of evaluation, or principles of action.[21] In describing or understanding the content and function of those premises *as*, respectively, statements of fact, nomological universals, principles of evaluation, or principles of action, one would have to be aware or become aware of specific meaning relations which are correlates of human attitudes.

Preparatory to commenting on confusions regarding the logic of "rational explanations" in history, let us complete our coverage of pertinent distinctions by noting briefly how meaning relations, as comprised in a description of what happened, can be regarded and, in certain cases provide intelligibility (cf. (B) and (C) in the outline). This will oblige us to touch briefly on matters more fully treated in Part Two.

B. *Thinking from the Standpoint of Natural Order.* Meaning relations of both types—formal-logical and distinctively human—can, we maintain, figure in descriptions of occurrences that are thought about and made intelligible from the standpoint of natural order. Among other occurrences, *rational actions* can be descriptively understood and thought about from the natural order standpoint. In other words, they can in principle be accounted for deterministically, and deterministic accounts of rational actions can cite reasons as causes.[22]

C. *Identifying Understanding. Identifying understanding* is descriptive understanding *together with an awareness* that the *kinds* of distinctively human meaning relations that characterize the subjective or objectified manifestations we are understanding, are *the same kinds* of meaning relations that characterize *our* subjective experience and that are involved in meanings objectively manifested in *our* artifacts, institutions, and behavior. These kinds of meaning are correlates of human standpoints—common ways of confronting the world, of asking questions about what goes on, and of striving for intelligibility.

These confrontations can be but need not be rationally developed; they can be but need not be critically differentiated and refined. Our own conception of the ways men confront the world is based on an analysis of human thinking about the world. What

21. The latter two are discussed below in chap. VII, sec. 2 and chap. VIII, sec. 2.

22. This conclusion, central to the entire chapter, is elaborated upon and defended below in sub-section (iv).

in this study we call standpoints of thinking *are* the character-istically human confrontations or "attitudes" rationally developed, critically differentiated, and refined. Analysis of human attitudes as developed, differentiated, and refined standpoints of thinking, discloses that there are two of these: natural order (correspond-ing to Dilthey's "cognitive attitude"), and the standpoint of living in the world (combining Dilthey's "volitional" and "emotional" at-titudes). There are, accordingly, two kinds of human meaning rela-tions which we can understand identifyingly.[23]

When the historian takes note of judgments which other human beings have made about the world, he cites reasons in distinctive ways. Natural order thinking (i.e., "reasons"), which the historian has descriptively understood, can be and sometimes is regarded and presented identifyingly. An instance of this—not as tangential as it might seem—is provided by the case of an historian who is engaged in trying to ascertain the determining conditions of an occurrence *e*, and who finds in the work of an author contemporary with that occurrence an opinion about its determining conditions. The historian finds his predecessor's opinion suggestive although not entirely sound. In his own work, the historian *describes* what the earlier author thought about *e*: this is *descriptive understanding*. He then presents this opinion for our scrutiny as an hypothesis concerning the determining conditions of *e*, sharing with us, his readers, his appraisal of the opinion; this identification of the other's problem as his own—and our own—involves what we call *identifying understanding*. The historian, himself thinking about *e* from the natural order standpoint, regards the other's thinking about *e* as being from the same standpoint. This identifying under-standing is presupposed by the historian's criticism of the other's contribution to the deterministic intelligibility of occurrence *e*.

The same relationships between the historian's thinking and the citing of past reasons are found in the historiography of science whenever the historian of science is describing, identifying with, and, perhaps, criticizing the natural order thinking of past con-tributors to natural order intelligibility.

Most analyses of rational explanation in history say nothing about citing reasons in the way just considered. They focus in-stead on explanations of *actions* which cite the *agent's* reasons (corresponding in the outline to the sub-division "action-oriented" under (C.2)). Utilizing our distinctions we may note that an

23. Each kind is understood by identifying with its corresponding stand-point. Cf. (C.1) and (C.2) in the outline.

agent's reasoning about what he is going to do is carried out from the standpoint of living in the world. It would seem plausible to suppose that in respect to past rational actions, the historian can (a) describe, (b) make intelligible from the standpoint of natural order, *or* (c) understand identifyingly from the standpoint of living in the world.[24]

(iii) CITING REASONS

In view of persistent confusions evident in discussions of rational action and determinism, the following points deserve emphasis: 1.) There are different types of "reasons." Of those reasons correlated with human standpoints, one sub-type qualifies as a reason for doing an action from the standpoint of the agent. Obviously, then, not all the reasons that *can* be cited by historians are even likely candidates for determining conditions of rational actions. This does not jeopardize the plausibility of the thesis that reasons of *some* sort *can* be causes. 2.) There are different ways in which historians can cite reasons. In some of these, the historian is certainly not giving a deterministic account of a rational action. This does not automatically strip them of cognitive significance. 3.) On the other hand, even assuming that there is a way of citing reasons (namely, from the standpoint of the agent) that is not merely descriptive understanding, that does make a past rational action intelligible, and yet that does not consist in citing reasons as determining conditions, this fact does not affect the possibility of there being deterministic accounts of rational actions in which reasons *do* appear as determining conditions; nor can it be assumed that intelligible accounts of actions of this other form (i.e., from the standpoint of the agent) are intrinsically superior to deterministic accounts, should the latter be possible. 4.) "Understanding" may be merely descriptive in import, merely comprehending *what* happened, but even as such it may be exactly what is called for in a certain context of puzzlement. In other words, descriptive understanding alone can constitute an explanation of sorts. 5.) Descriptive understanding can also serve (in an ancillary capacity) in making practical reasoning intelligible when the latter is understood identifyingly as reasoning from the standpoint of the agent. The identifying understanding here in-

24. We shall maintain in Part Two that through identifying understanding of another's rational action, the historian makes that person's action intelligible in a distinctive way. See below, chap. VI, sec. 3.

volved is not intended to serve natural order thinking about the practical reasoning as a determining condition of rational action. Consequently, it cannot be criticized for failing to contribute to the natural order intelligibility of rational actions. 6.) On the other hand, descriptive understanding can serve natural order thinking (in an ancillary capacity): knowing what happened we can ask questions about determining conditions. When what happened was a rational action (the description of which involves meaning relations), the reasons or reasoning of the agent might be expected to figure in the description of the determining conditions of the action—at least in one possible natural order account of the rational action. This positive contribution of understanding to natural order thinking is quite independent of the hermeneutic-methodological function of understanding (not discussed here) whose limitations certain philosophers of science have correctly insisted upon.[25] 7.) Understanding meaning relations as such (including reasons of whatever type) is never tantamount to accounting for an occurrence deterministically.

In the discussion that follows we shall elaborate on some of these points.

A *description* of something as, for example, being in accordance with a rule, does not account for the occurrence of the thing in question. When the historian has evidence that in a certain instance it was being used intentionally or habitually in accordance with a rule, he can perhaps go on to cite determining conditions for its occurrence. But the difference between the description and the deterministic account is easily lost sight of. Simply by describing a word, letter, mark, or whatever as used-according-to-rule the historian usually has *already* conveyed to us his implicit judgment that this description is relevant to why the thing in question occurred then and there; he has already let it be known that, in his judgment, it did not just *happen to be* in accordance with a rule but *was used as being* in accordance with a rule. Through our awareness of the natural order significance of the description of the thing to be explained, we mistake what is actually relevant description of the latter for an assertion of its determining conditions. Strictly speaking, in citing the formal-logical reasons, the historian is *not* accounting for why the fact occurred; he is merely pointing out that a relation between rule and case obtains. The rule in this explanation is *not* a rule about

25. See, e.g., Hempel, *Aspects*, p. 239.

the conditions under which occurrences take place. This kind of "rational explanation" is different in kind from asserting the sufficient conditions of an occurrence; it is not a form of natural order account. When this kind of rational explanation is all that has been provided, we know more about *what* happened but nothing about *why* it happened. The occurrence has not been thought about or made intelligible from any standpoint of thinking at all.

Some additional examples will help to show how descriptive understanding of formal-logical and human meaning relations can enter into causal accounts of occurrences, i.e., accounts falling within the deterministic line of questioning and answering.

We have already noted that the historian often has to describe meaning relations of both types. Such is the case when, in citing the "reasons" for an occurrence, he describes it not only as according-to-rule, as established procedure, or as having definite symbolic significance (formal-logical meaning), but also as being an instance of the fulfilment of some function in the operation of a cultural system (human meaning). Why, for example, was John F. Kennedy, at that time Senator from Massachusetts, visiting the villages of Wisconsin's Tenth Congressional District in March of 1960? In explaining this occurrence, Theodore H. White describes the prescribed legal procedure for presidential primaries in the United States of America and, in particular, the law of the state of Wisconsin bearing on this matter.[26] Kennedy's visit to Wisconsin on that occasion is understood as an instance of procedure according to rules (formal-logical meaning). White also describes certain features of the American political system, and obviously assumes considerable further knowledge along these lines on the part of his readers. Among other things we are told of the theoretical purpose of presidential primaries and of the rationale of the particular form of primary required by Wisconsin law. It is assumed that we already know what purposes are served by the election of a president in the American political system, knowledge which, in turn, presupposes a general understanding of the rationale of that cultural system itself (distinctively human meaning). All of this descriptive understanding is relevant to explaining the occurrence in question; relevant because White maintains that one determining condition of the Wisconsin trip was Senator

26. Theodore H. White, *The Making of the President 1960: A Narrative History of American Politics in Action* (New York: Atheneum, 1961), chap. IV.

Kennedy's grand strategy for winning the presidential election of 1960 to enable him, as chief executive, to influence the destiny of his country. The "reasons why" Kennedy was in Wisconsin thus involve an understanding of a cultural system—one form of distinctively human meaning.

The same would be true of the reasons cited in stating the determining conditions of the fact that the Cathedral of Chartres has the form of a cross with the central axis aligned east to west or of why, on November 25, 1963, the flags on the public buildings of New York City were flying at half-mast. Or suppose an historian is to explain why the majority of the United States Supreme Court ruled in 1954 that racial segregation in public schools was unconstitutional. He can be expected to discuss rule-governed legal grounds for the decision (neutral meaning). Presumably he will also have to consider the view that one function of the Supreme Court is to "advance the principle of organic law in a Federal union," and that by means of its decisions the Constitution of the United States of America is developed in response to new concerns, aspirations, needs, and insights.[27] Thus, whatever his conclusions as to the determining factors of the occurrence, his explanation will be constructed on the basis of descriptive understanding of an instance of legal reasoning in the narrow sense (formal-logical meaning), and of the operation of a particular legal system—a cultural system involving distinctively human meaning.

When the historian is interested—either primarily or incidentally—in accounting for the character of a particular cultural system, rather than in accounting for a particular occurrence or state of affairs that is a manifestation of the cultural system, we would not usually speak of his description as "citing reasons." But in any case, whether he is ultimately engaged in giving a deterministic account of a particular occurrence or in providing us with a general understanding of the cultural system as such, as long as he is *describing* a meaning relation he is not accounting for why in fact anything happened, occurred, changed, or is as it is. And because he is not doing this at all, it cannot be that he is doing it in some way fundamentally different from deterministic thinking.

We reach the same conclusion when we consider what the historian is about when he is engaged in understanding particular experienced meanings in cases where practical reasons or reason-

27. Paul Freund, review of Anthony Lewis' *Gideon's Trumpet*, in *New York Times*, June 21, 1964, Sec. 7, p. 1.

ing are involved. For example, an historian wants to know what the members of the United States Senate had in mind when they approved the 1963 Test Ban Treaty. He might formulate his findings as follows: they looked on the Treaty as offering the prospect of a gradual lessening of international tensions and a start toward the progressive elimination of the danger of nuclear war without concurrently jeopardizing national security. It might be inferred from this that the voting majority thought of international peace and national security as the relevant ends with highest priority and, furthermore, that when making practical decisions these men regarded it as reasonable to choose a feasible alternative conducive to the attainment of ends with highest priority. But assuming that the historian is *only* trying to convey their point of view, all of this would be intended as descriptive understanding, nothing more.

Or suppose the historian seeks to answer the question: "Why did King Edward VIII of England abdicate the throne? If he aims simply at understanding, he will have to present the King's state of mind and feeling, showing him confronted with a moral dilemma, obliged to choose between loyalty to tradition and to country and love for a woman. The historian would presumably cite the reasons that the King had in mind in deciding to abdicate. Neither in this case nor in the preceding example would citing the reasons be accounting for why anything in fact happened; they would not be cited as causes. The historian would only be describing *what* happened; what happened in these cases involved meaning relations, more specifically, reasons. Certainly this sort of description is often the one that is sought for and given where human phenomena are concerned, but it is not an accounting for occurrences in terms of natural order. It is communicating what someone else experienced—getting us to see *what* someone was thinking. Of course, what the other person was thinking may have been: 'I'll do x because of w" and it may be that the historian finds it natural to communicate this as "He decided that he would do x because of w" or "w was the reason why he decided to do x." But we should not be deceived here by the "because" or "the reason why." The historian can simply be saying that these were the meaning relations such and such a person had in mind on such and such an occasion.

In the latter examples above, the reasons that it would be contextually appropriate for the historian to cite are directly related to action, to what Dilthey calls the "volitional attitude" and we call the standpoint of the agent. In other cases the reasoning that a person engaged in might be related to the "cognitive attitude," i.e., the standpoint of natural order thinking (e.g., for what reasons did Copernicus think that the geocentric theory was defective?), or with the so-called "attitude of the emotional life," i.e., the standpoint of evaluation (e.g., on what grounds did St. Augustine conclude that it was good for Christian virgins to have been raped by Gothic invaders?). It may be a characteristic tendency of descriptive understanding to emphasize selectively one or the other of the different modes of human meaning relations, leaving out some strands of concretely experienced meaning even though, as Dilthey credibly maintained, all three attitudes are merged in subjective experience. But whether the historian aims at complete description or has a selective focus, the fact remains that description, even when it is descriptive understanding, does not by itself account for why anything happened when, where, and as it did happen.

It must be obvious from our account of the deterministic relation how misguided it is to suppose that one could ever directly apprehend these relations, even within his own "inner" states. Whatever it is that philosophers, such as Dilthey,[28] have had in mind when they have said that human beings have a direct inner experience of causality, this could not be an awareness of a deterministic relation. It follows that we cannot apprehend causal connections (which are equivalent to or which presuppose deterministic relations) vicariously by an identifying understanding of the subjectively experienced meaning relations of other persons, i.e., *their* alleged inner experience of causal connections. What we understand identifyingly are meaning relations, not deterministic relations.

(iv) DETERMINISTIC INTELLIGIBILITY

We have not yet established that rational actions are in principle deterministically intelligible. Our thesis is that all that distinguishes a "rational" deterministic explanation from any other deterministic explanation are some of the sorts of things and relations that are included in the description of the determining conditions: objectives, beliefs, practical principles, certain personal traits, and features of situations. Meaning relations are implicit in the very concept of objective, belief, practical principle, rea-

28. See, e.g., *Essence of Philosophy*, pp. 34 ff.

sonable, and so on. Describing these meaning relations (descriptive understanding) is, in such explanations, part of the job of describing *what* the determining conditions were; it does not disclose them *as* determining conditions. Only when we ask about these meaning relations as descriptive of determining conditions of an occurrence do we engage in natural order questioning, in the pursuit of a nomological relation or something approximating thereto: "That sort of person in that sort of situation with those objectives and beliefs will invariably decide to act that way."

For purposes of analysis we shall differentiate between citing rationality as a cause and citing reasons as causes. A rational deterministic account of an action is one that mentions either the agent's rationality or his reasons (or both) in the description of the determining conditions.

"Rationality" or "being reasonable" can be and assuredly mostly is a dispositional concept; whether when unpacked it is unpacked as a "many-tracked" or a "single-tracked" disposition, it cannot be analyzed as a nomological universal. A nomological universal, strictly speaking, specifies sufficient conditions; a dispositional concept does not do so, even tacitly.[29] Dispositional accounts of occurrences, however, fall within the scope of natural order questioning even though they are not adequate natural order accounts. Consider, then, the claim that an historian's rational explanation is different in kind from natural order accounts because it includes reference to "being reasonable." *This* claim can be countered by pointing out that "being reasonable," like other dispositional concepts, can be unpacked in terms of qualities, relations, and existential conditions and, although the analysis does not allow a specification of the sufficient conditions of the action in question, it is nonetheless plausible to presume that a specification is in principle possible. Perhaps historians' rational explanations typically do cite the agent's "being reasonable"—or some other rational disposition term—in accounting for actions, but this does not warrant the claim that historians' rational explanations are distinct in kind from natural order accounts; it only signifies that their explanations are typically inadequate accounts within the natural order line of questioning.

One obvious reason for overlooking the natural order character of many explanations that mention or imply the "reasonableness" of the agent and that are presumably oriented towards natural

29. See above, chap. II, sec. 5.

order intelligibility, is that the historian does not formulate even
the implicit loose generalization: he does not bother to point out
that the reference to reasonableness renders the agent's action
intelligible by disclosing the action to have been an instance of a
relation between certain traits characterizing a person (together
with other states of affairs) and a person's acting in such and
such a way in such and such a situation. And it goes without saying that the historian does not usually go a step further and point
out that in respect to the line of questioning in which he is engaged, the loose generalization implied in his rational explanation
of the person's action imperfectly approximates a pertinent deterministic relation which would "complete" the intelligibility of the
action but which the historian for some reason has not disclosed
in his account.[30]

Can reasons—as distinguished from rationality—be causes? Yes,
in the sense that the sorts of things that are ordinarily cited *as*
reasons for actions (whether or not they are also cited *as* causes)
can, in principle, figure in descriptions of states of affairs which
together with other states of affairs are nomologically related (as
necessary conditions) to occurrences ordinarily referred to as actions. What sorts of things are cited as reasons for actions? Traits
like the following: Wanting something, thinking that one has an
obligation, thinking that something would be beneficial, feeling a
sudden urge to do something, believing (or knowing, perceiving,
noticing, remembering) something.[31]

Consider, for example, the statement: "John F. Kennedy went
to Wisconsin in March of 1960 because he wanted to become the
nominee of the Democratic party for President of the United States
of America and because he believed that it would be advantageous
to compete in the Wisconsin primary election." Without assuming
that this is a causal account we could ask what reasons for Kennedy's action are mentioned in the statement. Presumably there

30. On "rationality" as a "broadly dispositional" explanatory concept, see
Hempel, *Aspects*, pp. 472 ff.
31. Cf. Donald Davidson, "Actions, Reasons, and Causes," *The Journal
of Philosophy*, LX (1963), pp. 685-86. He finds that among the reasons
commonly cited are "desires, wantings, urges, promptings, and a great variety
of moral views, aesthetic principles, economic prejudices, social conventions,
and public and private goals and values in so far as these can be interpreted
as attitudes of an agent directed toward actions of a certain kind." Most of
Davidson's analysis accords with our own, although in Part Two we take a
position at odds with his supposition (p. 693n.) that his account *suffices* to
define the relation of reasons to the actions they explain.

are two: "wanting to become Democratic nominee for President" (r_1), and "believing that competing in the Wisconsin primary would be advantageous" (r_2). These reasons are part of a description of a state of affairs at a certain time: "At such and such a time a certain person was conscious of r_1 and r_2." There is no a priori reason why the state of affairs so described could not be among the sufficient conditions of what occurred: Kennedy's act of going to Wisconsin in March of 1960. Reasons can, in principle, be causes.

It is said that historians commonly reconstruct the workings of the agent's mind—that they reconstruct "the agent's *calculations* of means to be adopted toward his chosen end in the light of the circumstances in which he found himself."[32] But we would insist that the distinction between meaning relation and determining conditions be kept ever in mind, otherwise confusion will result when we ask about the nature of these reconstructions. If the historian's intent is to account for the decision, to make it intelligible as something that *happened,* then he must do more than show the "reasonableness" of the concatenation of ideas entertained by the agent. If he only does the latter, we may choose to classify his explanation as "rational," but it is *not* an alternative way of accounting for why something in fact occurred. For obviously, according to our analysis, a rational action will not have been accounted for *simply* by narrating *descriptively,* however vividly, a thought process, i.e., simply by setting forth or communicating, by whatever literary devices, the meaning relations involved.

This concludes the main argument on behalf of the thesis that rational action is no exception to the presumption that all happenings are deterministically intelligible. We shall briefly mention one other source of confusion. It has often been maintained that a person's calculating what he should do involves private psychic states and "meaningful" categories. The assumption is then made that explaining rational activity—explaining why certain acts were done and not others—must be done in terms of psychic states and "meaningful" categories. It is but a step further to the inference that such explanations must be entirely different from "causal" explanations. The assumption, however, is without foundation.[33] That there are psychic states and meaning systems in no way affects

32. William Dray, *Laws and Explanation in History* (London: Oxford University Press, 1957), pp. 122, 150.
33. Cf. Nagel, *Structure of Science,* pp. 473 ff., 544 ff., 554 n.5.

the legitimacy of descriptions of rational activity in behavioristic terms or the acceptability of causal accounts that cite other than psychic determinants. In so far as the issues involved are not merely verbal (i.e., deciding upon the definitions and uses of the terms "rational activity," "calculation," etc.), they are issues within scientific inquiry itself. It is for the scientist to discover, if he can, any determining conditions of rational activity described in whatever way they can be described.

4. Critiques

The force of our conclusions on these issues will become clearer if we examine critically some specific contrary opinions about historical thinking. Let us begin with a closer examination of Collingwood's position. How does he formulate the inappropriateness of natural order-type accounts of rational activity?

The historian, investigating any event in the past, makes a distinction between what may be called the outside and the inside of an event. By the outside of the event I mean everything belonging to it which can be described in terms of bodies and their movement: the passage of Caesar, accompanied by certain men, across a river called the Rubicon at one date, or the spilling of his blood on the floor of the senate-house at another. By the inside of the event I mean that in it which can only be described in terms of thought: Caesar's defiance of Republican law, or the clash of constitutional policy between himself and his assassins. The historian is never concerned with either of these to the exclusion of the other. He is investigating not mere events (where by a mere event I mean one which has only an outside and no inside) but actions, and an action is the unity of the outside and inside of an event. He is interested in the crossing of the Rubicon only in its relation to Republican law, and in the spilling of Caesar's blood only in its relation to a constitutional conflict. His work may begin by discovering the outside of an event, but it can never end there; he must always remember that the event was an action, and that his main task is to think himself into this action, to discern the thought of its agent.

In the case of nature, this distinction between the outside and the inside of an event does not arise. The events of nature are mere events, not the acts of agents whose thought the scientist endeavours to trace. It is true that the scientist, like the historian, has to go beyond the mere discovery of events; but the direction in which he moves is very different. Instead of conceiving the event as an action and attempting to rediscover the thought of its agent, penetrating from the outside of the event to its inside, the scientist goes beyond the event, observes its relation to others, and thus brings it under a general formula or law of nature. . . .

In this penetrating to the inside of events and detecting the thought which they express, the historian is doing something which the scientist need not and cannot do. . . . For history, the object to be discovered is not the mere event, but the thought expressed in it. To discover that thought is already to understand it. After the historian has ascertained the facts, there is no further process of inquiring into their causes. When he knows what happened, he already knows why it happened.

This does not mean that words like 'cause' are necessarily out of place in reference to history; it only means that they are used there in a special sense. When a scientist asks 'Why did that piece of litmus paper turn pink?' he means 'On what kinds of occasions do pieces of litmus paper turn pink?' When an historian asks 'Why did Brutus stab Caesar?' he means 'What did Brutus think, which made him decide to stab Caesar?' The cause of the event, for him, means the thought in the mind of the person by whose agency the event came about: and this is not something other than the event, it is the inside of the event itself.[34]

Is Collingwood maintaining that a deterministic account of rational activity is inappropriate because impossible? Not exactly, for he says that it is "beyond question" *possible* to discover "similarities or uniformities" among the facts of historical activity (i.e., rational activity). Why then is it inappropriate to make these discoveries and to utilize them in deterministic accounts? Because, apparently, such accounts are superfluous, and therefore valueless:

. . . any estimate of the value of such a science, based on the analogy of natural science, is wholly misleading. The value of generalization in natural science depends on the fact that the data of physical science are given by perception, and perceiving is not understanding. The raw material of natural science is therefore 'mere particulars,' observed but not understood, and taken in their perceived particularity, unintelligible. It is therefore a genuine advance in knowledge to discover something intelligible in the relations between general types of them. What they are in themselves, as scientists are never tired of reminding us, remains unknown: but we can at least know something about the patterns of facts into which they enter.

A science which generalizes from historical facts is in a very different position. Here the facts, in order to serve as data, must first be historically known; and historical knowledge is not perception, it is the discerning of the thought which is the inner side of the event. The historian, when he is ready to hand over such a

34. *Idea of History*, pp. 213, 214, 255.

fact to the mental scientist as a datum for generalization, has already understood it in this way from within. If he has not done so, the fact is being used as a datum for generalization before it has been properly 'ascertained.' But if he has done so, nothing of value is left for generalization to do. If, by historical thinking, we already understand how and why Napoleon established his ascendancy in revolutionary France, nothing is added to our understanding of that process by the statement (however true) that similar things have happened elsewhere. It is only when the particular fact cannot be understood by itself that such statements are of value.[35]

How can Collingwood say that once we understand the purposive thinking of historical agents then "nothing of value is left for generalizations to do"? To the extent that this opinion is more than the expression of a subjective preference, we can account for it as follows. Collingwood was aware of the distinctiveness of the "volitional attitude"—the standpoint of the agent. His "idea of history" is: understanding the subjective experience of others with this selective focus. He was correct in maintaining the distinctiveness of this attitude. In particular, he correctly asserted that causal generalizations (nomological universals or approximations thereof) are not implicit in identifying understanding as such. But he failed to grasp clearly the difference between understanding the practical reasons or reasoning of others and thinking from the standpoint of natural order, a failure connected with his faulty conception of understanding. He mistakenly supposed that when the historian understands, happenings (actions, in this case) thereby become intelligible *in the same way* that deterministic accounts make them intelligible. In other words, Collingwood supposed that the historian, understanding identifyingly, already knows the determining conditions of certain happenings. He supposed that understanding is an alternative account of the same kind. In this he was mistaken. Had he seen his mistake he could have gone on to consider more circumspectly the possibility, in principle, of deterministic accounts of rational activity, explanations for which nomological universals, far from being superfluous, are indispensable.

Related to that mistake was Collingwood's failure to distinguish clearly between descriptive and identifying understanding. To appreciate this distinction is to see that descriptive understanding places rational activity at the disposal of the historian-scientist: *what* happened was purposive thinking, the solving of a *particular*

35. *Ibid.*, pp. 222-23.

problem (an emphasis repeatedly made by Collingwood); the historian-scientist's problem then is to find out the determining conditions of the fact that the agent reached the decision that he did reach, solved his problem as he did solve it, and acted on the basis of his decision as he did act.

William Dray's views on rational explanation owe much to Collingwood. Dray, it should be noted, states that something cannot be correctly termed a "cause" unless it was a necessary condition of its effect.[36] There are, however, different kinds of causal necessity. One such kind, apparently, holds between two events (as we may call them for convenience): Given any two events, x and y, if x be the cause and y its effect, then y is an event that has already occurred and that would not have occurred without x (or: without x, y "would have been different in important respects"). A second kind of causal necessity—Dray calls it "rational necessity"—holds between reasons and an action: Given any reasons r and any action a of a person P, if r be the cause and a the effect (an action that has already occurred), then r comprises reasons thought of by P as "good" or "sufficient" reasons for regarding a as the appropriate action.[37]

A rational explanation of an action, according to Dray, consists in presenting the reasons of the agent, reasons thought of by him as sufficient reasons for regarding what he did as the appropriate action. The reasons are presented so as to bring out their character *as* sufficient reasons from the agent's point of view. There are, he maintains, two ways in which historians give rational explanations: (1) from the standpoint of the agent, and (2) from the standpoint of a spectator. Agents do not look upon their own reasons as causes; spectators often do look upon an agent's reasons as causes. Sometimes in giving rational explanations from the standpoint of a spectator, the historian cites the agent's sufficient reasons as causes. The kind of causal necessity here involved for the spectator, namely, *rational* necessity, is, however, also involved from the standpoint of the agent in the very concept of "good" or "sufficient" reasons. To give a rational explanation from either standpoint, therefore, is to bring out the relation of rational necessity.[38]

36. Dray, *Laws and Explanation*, pp. 98, 102, 154.
37. *Ibid.*, pp. 102, 126, 154.
38. Dray's "standpoints" do not correspond to our distinctions and the differences are important. For elucidation see below, the concluding pages of chap. VIII, sec. 6. Where I have said "sufficient reasons for regarding doing what he did as the appropriate action," Dray is apt to say "sufficient reasons

Referring back to Dray's differentiation between kinds of causal necessity, we note that neither way of giving a rational explanation accounts for an action on the basis of a necessary connection between two events. The necessity in a "rational explanation" is always *rational* necessity. Is it *possible*, in principle, for actions to be explained in terms of the first kind of causal necessity distinguished above? Dray, like Collingwood, answers affirmatively, and even concedes that sometimes—"perhaps only rarely"[39]—historians actually do this. The typical historical explanation of a rational action, however, he says is a "rational explanation"; furthermore, it is an explanation from what he calls the standpoint of the agent.

There is nonetheless a curious ambiguity in Dray's analysis, indicating that he has not been altogether successful in excluding causal necessity of the first kind from his own account of typical "rational explanations" in history.

Dray says that an account of an action as rationally necessary suffices to explain the action. Strictly speaking, what is it that we know by virtue of having been provided with such an account? Only that the act which the agent performed was an act which the agent thought he had "good" reason to do. We know something in particular about how the agent regarded the act. Now if what the historian and his readers wanted to know was whether the agent thought he had good reasons for regarding what he did as appropriate, then, indeed, the descriptive account of the meaning relations which Dray calls a "rational explanation" explains what they were curious to know. But Dray reveals his own awareness that this is not all that historians and their readers "typically" want to know. Often they want to know whether the way the agent regarded the doing of *a* was a factor determining the occurrence of *a*—whether, that is, there was a relation of causal necessity *of the first kind* between the agent's regarding the doing of *a* in the way that he regarded it and his performance of *a*. Historians often seek to find out about reasons because they are curious as to the necessary conditions of actions in the first sense as well as in relations of rational necessity. In fact, ascertaining the latter is often deemed significant only when done in connection with an interest

for doing *a*." Using the latter form of expression, however, makes it exceedingly difficult to bring out the ambiguity in his concept of "rational explanation," for the ambiguity is sustained by the form of expression.

39. Dray, *Laws and Explanation*, p. 117.

in or claim concerning a relation between reasons and action that corresponds to the first kind of causal necessity. Which relation historians and readers happen to be *immediately* puzzled about in some particular instance will often depend upon contextual considerations, e.g., upon which of the two types of relation they know less about at the moment. Often the historian strongly suspects that there was a causal relation in the first sense between the agent's regarding the doing of *a* as appropriate and the fact that the agent did *a*. Having this suspicion, he deems it worthwhile to reconstruct the agent's reasons for regarding *a* as the appropriate course of action. Often it is the reader's antecedent belief in or assumption of such a relation that gives point to the historian's account of the agent's "sufficient reasons." In such cases, the puzzle that knowledge of the agent's "sufficient reasons" resolves is: What reasons, *presumed to have been a necessary condition* (in the first sense) *of the performance of the action,* did the agent have for regarding it as the thing to do? Because the presumption is taken for granted, historians do not trouble to spell it out. The focal point is the agent's "sufficient reasons"; but this contextual focus and its significance to historian and reader derive from the unstated presumption.

Dray has been concerned to establish that typical historical explanations do not, as such, imply nomological relations. With regard to "rational explanations," *conceived of solely as establishing a relation of rational necessity* (i.e., descriptive understanding plus a claim that the description of the action judged reasonable by the agent is the same as the description of the action known to have been done), he correctly asserts that: (1) they *do not,* as such, imply a nomological universal; (2) they *are not* invalidated by "negative instances"; (3) they do not have as their point "to show that this is the kind of thing we can expect to be done by such a person in such circumstances"; and (4) they *do not* derive their confirmation from "experience of similar cases."[40] But, aware that historians' explanations of rational actions are often intended to be more than accounts of rational necessity (i.e., descriptive understanding), Dray allows himself to make claims for "rational explanations" which cannot be made for mere accounts of rational necessity. He claims that "In representing the action as the thing to have done . . . we to some extent license the conclusion that it

40. *Ibid.,* pp. 132-33.

was the thing to have expected."[41] But a mere account of rational necessity *would not license this conclusion at all*. Moreover, Dray says that a "rational explanation" has the form "'*A* did *x* because of *y*', where *y* is *A*'s reason for doing *x*."[42] But there is a significant difference between this and an assertion of the form "*A* thought that he had sufficient reason *y* for doing *x*." It is the latter and the latter alone that appears to tally with Dray's concept of accounts of rational necessity, the latter being conceived of as establishing solely a *rational* relation between an action done and the agent's reasons.

If we are correct in supposing that historians who cite an agent's reasons for his actions often are presuming that the reasons were a causally necessary condition of the action in the first sense of causal necessity, then causal claims *in the first sense of causal necessity*, citing reasons as causes, *are* often made by historians. Making such claims is not—as Dray suggests—an alternative and relatively unusual way of writing history; it is *one aspect* of a very common way of explaining actions. And, if this is the case, the question of whether historical explanations imply nomological relations must, as far as *these* reason-citing accounts are concerned, be asked with this in mind. In other words, it will not do to say that nomological relations are not implied by "rational explanations" because they are not implied by accounts of rational necessity; we must go on to ask whether nomological relations are implied by the other common component of "rational explanations": the claim or presumption of a *non*-rational necessary connection between the agent's having had sufficient reason for performing an action and his performing it. We have already argued that such causal claims *do* presuppose a nomological relation.[43] We have argued in this chapter that such causal claims are plausible in principle when made about reasons as causes. In chapter V we extend the argument to claims made in reference to the highly specific particular occurrences that historians often try to account for.

To summarize, Dray maintains explicitly that reasons typically are *not* cited by historians as causes—in the natural order sense of cause—of rational actions; some of his statements, however, imply that historians typically *do* cite them as causes in the natural

41. *Ibid.* See Hempel's critique of Dray in *Aspects*, pp. 469 ff.
42. Dray, *Laws and Explanation*, p. 133.
43. See above, chap. II, sec. 4.

order sense. His confusion in this regard stems from a failure to differentiate clearly and consistently between descriptive understanding, identifying understanding, and natural order thinking. These criticisms notwithstanding, Dray has made a signal contribution in calling attention to the "standpoint of agency."[44] And when the historian identifies understandingly with the rational agent, what happened *is* made intelligible in a way that does not involve citing reasons as causes in the natural order sense.

5. CONCLUDING REMARKS

In ordinary usage, one "meaning" ascribed to facts is precisely their causal relations to other facts or their being consequences of other facts. This usage is particularly common in our talk about historical events—in speaking of the meaning (or significance) of a certain action or alteration in the state of affairs. This meaning of "meaning" has misled scientifically minded thinkers into believing that the *only* meaning of facts is their cause-consequence relations. Equally obscurantist, however, is the claim of the anti-scientist thinkers when they point out that natural scientists, who are interested in regularities and determining conditions, rarely talk about the "meaning" of the phenomena they study (at least not in their technical formulations), and infer from this that the references to meaning characteristic of our talk about historical events can *only* refer to something not deterministically intelligible.

Our discussion has not exhausted the misconceptions that underlie controversy about "reasons as causes." Another source of confusion might be mentioned here, a common one if A. C. MacIntyre is correct about ordinary usage when he says: "the contention that . . . behavior is determined by causal factors is normally taken to mean 'determined by causal factors as contrasted with rational appreciation, etc.,'" that is to say, as contrasted with calculating the propriety or expediency of doing something.[45] Why is this ordinary usage a source of confusion? Because the distinction between causal determination and rational appreciation has to be refined, *correctly* refined, if it is to withstand criticism. Ordinary usage does not, presumably, take cognizance of the requisite re-

44. See especially *Laws and Explanation,* p. 140, and his remarks in *Philosophy and History,* ed. Sidney Hook (New York: New York University Press, 1963), pp. 132-33.
45. A. C. MacIntyre, "Determinism," *Mind,* LXVI (1957), 40.

finements. Using the crude distinction we are easily drawn into making controversial claims. There are two ways in which the distinction can be refined. First, the tenable refinement: determination by causal factors is to be contrasted with "rational appreciation" in the sense that relations of meaning as the content of "rational appreciation" are not, as such, occurrence-determining relations. Second, an untenable refinement: determination by causal factors is to be contrasted with "rational appreciation" in the sense that it can never be the case that the *occurrence* of a process of rational appreciation is a causal factor of behavior. What ordinary usage misses is the distinction between reasoning as involving meaning relations and reasoning as something that happens.

That I have not overstated the possibilities of confusion from this alleged ordinary usage is evidenced by the fact that, misguided by it himself, MacIntyre apparently argues from this "normal" usage to the existence of an absolute area of human freedom which science *cannot* conquer. Correctly apprehended, the distinction between causal determination and rational appreciation yields a much less dramatic inference: determinism (i.e., the deterministic relation between occurrences) does not have any application to meaning relations as such, for these are not occurrences.

The extended discussion of historical "meaning" in this chapter has been necessary in order to answer objections to the view that any human happening, rational actions not excepted, can be thought of deterministically. We have incidentally stressed the variety of other ways of dealing with meaningful human phenomena which are open to the historian, ways which in no respect compromise natural order intelligibility.

Chapter V.

Ordinary History Scrutinized

A Critique of Appearances

1. INTRODUCTION

Those who have argued the fundamental likeness of history and science have usually tried to formulate models or paradigms supposedly relevant to both history and science. Impressive in their simplicity, these models and paradigms undoubtedly have not faithfully represented some characteristics of historical thinking. Historians and philosophers who bothered to look at actual works produced by historians have been impressed by discrepancies between models and paradigms, on the one hand, and what, on the other hand, historians—*or* scientists, for that matter—actually profer as explanations. They have concluded that the models and paradigms are inapplicable to history and perhaps to science as well.

We shall begin by noting some pertinent features of the simplified models and paradigms, then take up a number of criticisms of the thesis that history is a science, criticisms that contrast the models and paradigms of science with characteristics of actual historical writing.

The simplified models and paradigms lead one to believe that a "complete" scientific explanation (1) requires an explicit and precisely formulated generalization, whether probabilistic or strictly universal; that (2) it takes the form of a direct subsumption of the occurrence to be explained under the relevant generalization, a generalization that is ready-at-hand with the status of a confirmed "law," and (3) that the relevant generalization is a single law, of which there have been many confirming instances.

With regard to (1) it has been argued that generalizations—at least precise, explicit generalizations—are not found in ordinary historical writing, and that this is no shortcoming (sec. 2). With regard to (2) it has been argued that "plurality of causes" and the lack of ready-at-hand generalizations together with the "uniqueness" and "richness" of typical historical subject matter are responsible for fundamental differences in the way historians ordinarily make occurrences intelligible (secs. 3 and 4). Finally, with regard to (3) it has been argued, on similar grounds, that a single law explanation model does not apply to history (sec. 5).

2. WHAT GENERALIZATIONS?

Examination of historical writing discloses many cases in which historians are presumably explaining why something in fact happened but do this without explicitly stating relevant generalizations about determining conditions; moreover, when we ask ourselves what generalizations their accounts tacitly imply, we find these difficult to formulate. Critics of the assimilation of history to science infer from this that historical explanations characteristically do not imply precisely formulated generalizations.

Let me refer here to the views of three such critics: William Dray, Patrick Gardiner, and Michael Scriven. All three have stressed the importance of analyzing the actual way in which practicing historians ordinarily do think and write.

(i) DRAY

In Dray's view, an assertion that a particular event happened because of a combination of circumstances need not and usually does not tacitly imply a precisely formulated empirical law. At most it could be said to imply a *principle of inference*. In making the judgment "e because of $c_1 , \ldots , c_n$" the historian commits himself to the truth of the covering general statement "If $C_1 , \ldots , C_n$ then E." But this covering general statement is a principle of inference, not an empirical law.[1]

According to our analysis, the historian's judgment *does* imply a nomological universal of the form "If $C_1 , \ldots , C_n$ then E." "Imply"

1. William Dray, *Laws and Explanation in History* (London: Oxford University Press, 1957), p. 39.

in what sense? In the sense that the existence of a generalization of this form is an integral part of the meaning of an assertion of sufficient conditions. Our analysis does not exclude the possibility that in certain contexts the same statement, "If C_1 , . . . , C_n then E," *could* function as a principle of inference. Then, as Dray says, "it tells us nothing about what is, has been, or will be the case; it tells us only what we should be able to say *if* so-and-so were the case." *So construed* it "belongs to the language of reasoning—of norms and standards, not of facts and descriptions."[2] But, of course, the question cannot be evaded: Upon what foundation does such a principle of inference rest—a principle which is obviously *not merely a stipulated* or *conventional* rule? Why is it "reasonable" for the historian to infer "If c_1 , . . . , c_n then e"?

Our analysis includes epistemic considerations involved in an assertion of sufficient conditions. Any such assertion implies a *confirmed empirical rule of occurrence,* a nomological universal. There is a direct interdependence between "implying a nomological universal" and "being supported by evidence." In terms of our analysis of deterministic accounts, there is no mystery about the kind of evidence relative to which it would be reasonable to infer "If c_1 , . . . , c_n then e." Dray's analysis, on the contrary, gives us no enlightenment on this point. He emphasizes that, unlike an empirical law, a principle of inference "does not show the *source* of its authority on its face." What, then, is the covert source of its authority? Typically, we are told, it is "an exercise of the historian's judgment in the particular case." And, at least sometimes, Dray maintains, such judgments have no "experimental or theoretical justification," the particular case being "independently judged."[3]

Dray's two claims are thus closely connected: one, that the generalizations implicit in ordinary historical explanations are merely principles of inference; the other that historians' judgments of necessary or sufficient conditions are of particular cases "independently judged." His denial that a nomological universal (or what he terms an empirical law) is implicit in historical accounts of why a particular occurrence in fact happened, points back to his thesis about historical judgment. The latter we have already criticized, and having found it inadequate we can discount his

2. *Ibid.,* pp. 40-41.
3. *Ibid.,* pp. 41, 55, 106, 107 (italics in original).

objections to the implicit law claim. They do not seriously challenge the basic similarity of historical and deterministic accounts.[4]

(ii) GARDINER

In his account of generalizations Gardiner attempts to refine upon ideas previously set forth by Hempel concerning the function of general laws in history.[5] Hempel had proposed two ways of accounting for the fact that historians seldom assert precise generalizations: 1) the generalizations presupposed in their explanations are sometimes too familiar, too obvious, to merit explicit mention, and 2) the historian sometimes simply does not have at his disposal a precise generalization covering just the sort of occurrence he is seeking to explain, and so cannot give a complete explanation. In the latter case Hempel speaks of the historian as providing an "explanation sketch" which, in principle, can be completed, filled in, through future inquiry. Either, then, an historical explanation is logically similar to a scientific explanation, or it is an incomplete scientific explanation; in any case there is no difference in kind. But Hempel also emphasized that historians are characteristically lax about formulating their explanation sketches; they seldom make it clear along what lines future inquiry would have to be developed in order to "fill in" the sketches. Unquestionably the impression we are left with is that historians can be expected to provide better explanations after receiving philosophical instruction in the nature of scientific explanation.

Gardiner makes an important qualification to this: In one sense of completeness, what constitutes a complete explanation depends on what we are after. It will not do to insist summarily that the historian ought always to aim at giving a precise, explicit, complete formulation of the sufficient conditions of particular occurrences. There would be no advantage in saying that an inquirer who is satisfied with less is not really an historian, properly speaking. This qualification is not, however, a qualification of our view that

4. See above chap. III, sec. 4. It is possible that the preceding account does less than justice to Dray's views. Occasional phrasing in less polemical passages suggests that Dray is taking a different tack. The thought in these passages, if developed, would issue in refinements of the "covering law" model similar to those proposed in the concluding sections of this chapter.

5. Patrick Gardiner, *The Nature of Historical Explanation* (London: Oxford University Press, 1952). Carl G. Hempel, "The Function of General Laws in History," *The Journal of Philosophy*, XXXIX (1942), 35-48; reprinted with minor revisions in Carl G. Hempel, *Aspects of Scientific Explanation* (New York: The Free Press, 1965), pp. 231-43.

there is a scheme of natural order or deterministic intelligibility with its own criteria of completeness. Relative to *these* criteria, Hempel's point of view is still substantially tenable.

In other respects Gardiner's refinements do *seem* to conflict with our version (and Hempel's) of the role of generalizations in historical explanations. Gardiner seems to be saying that the generalizations which historians do express, or which they would express if they were more articulate, are *characteristically*—not just contextually or conventionally—loose and "porous."[6] It becomes apparent from his discussion that generalizations of this type may not be the nomological universals implicit in the explanation as finally presented by the historian. They may be working generalizations, "guiding threads" or clues, which aid the reader, as they aided the historian, in discerning what the determining conditions were. "One is inclined to say that generalizations of the kind in question provide indications, and rough ones at that, of the sorts of factors which, under certain circumstances, we expect to find correlated with other sorts of factors; but that they leave open to historical investigation and analysis the task of eliciting the specific nature of those factors on a particular occasion, and the precise manner in which the factors are causally connected with one another." But if these loose and "porous" working generalizations were the only sort of generalizations involved in historical explanations, our analysis would indeed be faulty. We have been assuming that a generalization is an integral part of a *completed* explanation. Does Gardiner disagree? Must *this* generalization be loose and "porous" in the case of historical explanations?

He does affirm in one passage that in so far as generalizations "are enunciated by historians" they are of the loose kind, and that their function is *merely* to "assist the historian."[7] Nonetheless it appears (1) that Gardiner does recognize that there is also a generalization implicit in the resultant "explanatory" account, and (2) that he finds no reason why, in principle, these generalizations cannot be precise generalizations explicitly formulated. In fact, Gardiner appears to agree with our notion of a presupposed scheme of natural order intelligibility with respect to which any historical explanation might be appraised as incomplete when it does not state explicitly and precisely the sufficient conditions of a particular

6. Gardiner, *Historical Explanation*, p. 93.
7. *Ibid.*, p. 93; cf. p. 59: "Historical generalizations have not the status of scientific laws."

occurrence; a scheme of intelligibility in which regularity is implied in the very notion of "sufficient condition," so that every causal account implies that there is a nomological universal "covering" the particular occurrence in question.[8]

As champion of practicing historians Gardiner wants to make it quite clear that completeness as they conceive it is not necessarily equivalent to deterministic intelligibility. But he is not as explicit as he might be about what their objectives are. Piecing together his remarks one gets the following picture of the logic of historical explanation (in so far as the question is why a particular event happened): The historian is interested in explaining the occurrence of events that cannot be directly subsumed under any available "law." But he cannot establish the determining conditions of the occurrence other than by reference to "how things and people in general behave." When the historian finally states or implies that the particular occurrence happened "because" of such and such conditions, whatever force the "because" has comes from generalizations (nomological universals) postulated on the basis of observations and analyses of all sorts of other occurrences. The supporting generalizations and their foundation are usually set forth only in the sketchiest way by the historian who has himself used them in reaching his conclusions. Yet the historian who does not hand out worthless explanations will say enough to direct us to the confirming evidence, confident that "we know roughly the kind of factors" which are involved and can fill in the unstated qualifications or refinements. Thus any loose and "porous" generalizations that the historian articulates as part of his explanatory account are accompanied by explicit refinements or pointers, and the better the explanation, the more precise the ascription of causes implying a complex of nomological universals which can be made explicit by the reader or by the historian himself, should he be called upon to do so.[9]

We conclude that there are no fundamental differences between Gardiner's analysis of historical explanations and our analysis of natural order accounts in respect to the function of generalizations.[10]

8. See *ibid.*, pp. 54-55, 61-62, 82.
9. *Ibid.*, pp. 96-99.
10. It should be noted, however, that Gardiner occasionally seems inconsistent. The force of the "because" in explanations, he ascribes to "regularity." It is (sometimes) the historian's purpose to explain why events happened. Precise nomological generalizations are a prerequisite of precise explanations. Yet Gardiner denies that the historian is concerned with finding

(iii) SCRIVEN

Aside from their intrinsic interest, Gardiner's views provide an interesting contrast both with Dray's and with the views we are about to consider. Whereas Dray denies that any empirical generalization is implicit, Gardiner maintains that the force of the "because" in historical "explanations" presupposes such a generalization. Whereas Gardiner believes that in principle an implicit refined generalization can be formulated, Michael Scriven maintains that historians are among those the logic of whose judgments typically cannot possibly be formulated. Scriven does not conclude that this makes history unscientific. He would say that many historical explanations and scientific explanations simply do not accord with our analysis.

On one point Scriven is in complete and unequivocal agreement with us: the historian does often try to find out why a particular occurrence was bound to happen, not merely that it was probable under the circumstances. The generalizations that the historian will cite when called on to justify his account will not, then, be statistical statements, for "an event can rattle around inside a network of statistical laws."[11] But we should not therefore suppose, says Scriven, that the historian will cite precisely formulated nomological universals. Instead he will characteristically have recourse to *truisms*. Why did the Spanish conquistador Cortes send a third expedition into Lower California after two earlier expeditions had been failures? In his book, *The Rise of the Spanish Empire*, the English historian Merriman explains Cortes' action as being due to two factors: the prospect of immense booty, and Cortes' confidence that by leading the expedition himself the previous causes of failure could be overcome.[12] Now if the historian saw fit to justify this explanation or if we were to challenge him to justify its adequacy, he might mention certain generaliza-

---

precise regularities. A loose and "porous" generalization may be valuable as a guide to understanding, but if at some stage it is not made more specific our understanding (i.e., natural order intelligibility) remains sketchy. Thus Gardiner seems to vacillate between on the one hand regarding precise generalizations as a prerequisite to the fulfilment of the historian's purpose—adequate natural order accounts—and on the other hand maintaining that precise generalizations are out of keeping with this purpose. See Gardiner, *Historical Explanation*, pp. 54-55, 60-61.

11. Michael Scriven, "Truisms as the Grounds for Historical Explanations," *Theories of History*, ed. P. Gardiner (Glencoe, Ill.: The Free Press, 1959), p. 467.

12. *Ibid.*, p. 448.

tions about how persons behave who are self-confident and greedy—as Cortes was known to be—and he might add a vague proposition "to the effect that if a man has these characteristics and does undertake a hazardous voyage and there are no other apparent causes, then it is *very* probable these were the causes" of his action. This vague proposition and the other generalizations about human behavior are truisms. They characteristically state that something is true for all instances except under certain conditions. As used by the historian, a truism stating "what had to happen in *this* case unless certain exceptional circumstances obtained" is combined with a judgment to the effect that "in this case there were no exceptional circumstances." It is a linguistic characteristic of these truisms that although they contain no explicit list of the exceptional conditions, they do contain words which remind us of our knowledge of these, words such as "ordinarily," "typically," "usually," "properly," "naturally," and "under standard conditions."[13]

Scriven's analysis is illuminating; much more so than a single example can convey. He has differentiated significantly between types of loose and "porous" generalizations. Sometimes we do not have much of an idea of, much feeling for, the specific conditions under which a loose generalization would apply. A *ceteris paribus* clause signifies our ignorance. In these cases inquiry can be directed at filling in—making the generalization more precise. But in other cases, in the case of truisms, the looseness and porosity do not have the same character. We often know well the sort of conditions that could interfere with the determining relationship or the sort of conditions under which the relationship would "hold good," even though we would find it next to impossible to specify these and do not bother to do so. Often when an historian gives what by our analysis would be considered an incomplete account, one not stating the entire set of sufficient conditions, what he singles out as the causes reflects not contextual or pragmatic considerations, but which conditions *normally* result in that kind of occurrence. What he omits to specify as causes are conditions that would have prevented the occurrence had they been different but which *normally* are just what they were in this case.

Scriven argues that his discovery of truisms thoroughly discredits the assumption that adequate causal accounts specify the sufficient conditions and tacitly imply a correspondingly specific empirical generalization. Truisms are alleged to be the only gen-

13. *Ibid.*, pp. 458, 466, 465 (italics in original).

eralizations implicit in most historical causal explanations, and truisms are imprecise: they do not completely specify sufficient conditions. Closer inspection of this analysis, however, considerably weakens these claims.

There are two possible situations in which an historical explanation might be "justified" by citing a truism. First, the historian not only knows that "under normal circumstances" e occurs whenever x takes place, but his "trained" judgment—emphasized by Scriven[14] —has enabled him to ascertain that all of the relevant circumstances were indeed normal. Analysis of the historian's explanation in this case would require taking cognizance that, as modified by exercise of his trained judgment, the truism is transformed into a generalization specifying the set of *sufficient conditions*. It is the latter generalization, not the truism, which "justifies" his account. In the second situation the historian knows that "under normal circumstances" e occurs whenever x takes place, but his knowledge of the "normal circumstances" is vague and sketchy. When he cites the truism to justify his assertion that "e occurred because of x," its force is weakened by his ignorance. To be sure, he is not *aware* that there were any unusual circumstances, but he has no very clear notion of what to look for. He does not know why e was bound to happen.

In terms of our analysis there is nothing distinctive about the case of the first historian: the occurrence is deterministically intelligible, for him at least. By contrast, in terms of both analyses (Scriven's and our own) the second historian has not succeeded in making the occurrence intelligible: we are not told why it was bound to happen, nor does the historian himself know. Whether we interpret the function of truisms in terms of the first or the second situation makes no difference: in neither case does Scriven's analysis require that we qualify or modify our own on fundamental points.[15]

Scriven also emphasizes that the historian's judgment is characteristically not articulated, not formulated; indeed, he says that the judgment is "unformulizable."[16] Our analysis of historical intelligibility as deterministic would be faulty if the implicit nomological universals together with their confirmed status could not,

14. E.g., *ibid.*, p. 466.
15. Cf. Dray's critique of Scriven, "The Historical Explanation of Actions Reconsidered," in *Philosophy and History*, ed. Sidney Hook (New York: New York University Press, 1963), pp. 121-22.
16. "Truisms," p. 462; cf. pp. 458, 465, 471, 473.

in principle, be made explicit. But one looks in vain for any specification of the allegedly insuperable obstacles to explicit formulation. The only impediment mentioned, namely, the complexity of certain phenomena, is not insuperable in principle. It is one thing to be fascinated by the proven accuracy of unformulated judgment —"the trained eye of the lumberman or the tracker, the professional hands of the cheese-maker," or by the fact that remarkable skill in judgment (e.g., medical diagnosis) can be attained through practice as against instruction in rational principles; it is quite another thing to describe and to analyze the structure of schemes of intelligibility.[17]

3. Causal Analysis: Ordinary History Not an Ordinary Applied Science

Spokesmen for the "unity of science" have sometimes given the impression that explanatory history resembles applied science.[18] They concede, to be sure, that as a mere collector and verifier of data the historian feeds information to the generalizing scientist. But charged with *explaining* particular occurrences the historian appropriates and applies, as called for, generalizations served up by his colleagues in the generalizing sister sciences.[19] Furthermore, models of scientific explanation intended to establish the "unity of science" have made it appear that all causal accounts imply a law with retrodictive force, a law of the form "whenever E then $C_1, \ldots, C_n$."[20]

Since ordinary history does not resemble an applied science and since causal accounts in history are rarely covered by laws supporting retrodictions, the effect has been the opposite of that intended. Most historians and some philosophers have been more convinced than ever that historians account for occurrences in a way peculiar to themselves.[21] Surely many causal accounts are compatible with

17. *Ibid.*, pp. 458, 466.

18. "Applied science" as used here refers to the utilization of empirical generalizations in explaining or predicting particular occurrences. The application is cognitive rather than practical.

19. Carl G. Hempel is one such spokesman, as Maurice Mandelbaum has clearly pointed out: "Historical Explanation: The Problem of 'Covering Laws,'" *History and Theory*, I, No. 3 (1961), 233-36.

20. Retrodictive force means that it is possible to use the law to deduce the cause of an occurrence, reasoning backward from known effect to unknown cause.

21. E.g., Isaiah Berlin, "History and Theory: The Concept of Scientific History," *History and Theory*, I, No. 1 (1960), 18-19.

a "plurality of causes," i.e., they are accounts of occurrences that are "bound to happen" under any one of a number of different sets of sufficient conditions, so that retrodiction is not possible. Indeed most causal explanations in history are presumably of this latter sort, but they are no less adequate for being so—according to our conception of deterministic intelligibility. And although Dray and others rightly point out that the historian seldom finds ready-at-hand generalizations which relate precisely to his subject matter (that is, which "cover" exactly the events he wants to account for), they mistakenly construe this as one more indication of the inapplicability of any "scientific" model of explanation.

The lack of suitable, ready-at-hand generalizations, together with the prevalence of a "plurality of causes," contributes toward making ordinary historical thinking rather different from some applied sciences. We need to show that these differences do not place ordinary historical thinking outside the natural order line of questioning, with its ideal of deterministic intelligibility.

The historian who seeks to account for a particular occurrence typically has to engage in causal analysis. This means, in part, that *historians themselves often have to supplement ready-at-hand generalizations* (whether trivial common sense or scientific) *by formulating generalizations relevant to their subject matter.* Because of the "plurality of causes," the historian has the problem of ascertaining the determining conditions of *this* revolution, *this* migration, *this* business depression, etc. In addition, since he has *no* covering generalization ready at hand, he must formulate and verify one that covers the special combination of, say, revolution-determining conditions presupposed by the particular occurrence in question. Because the historian is not in the habit of revealing the logical structure of his explanations, what strikes us as we read his account is that he seems to be talking at length about specific events and circumstances but saying little or nothing about *kinds* of conditions. He *has* to attend closely to the particulars of the case before he can judge which were the determining conditions in this instance. But even in doing this he is concerned with the *kind* of event—the kind caused by one *kind* of set of conditions rather than another kind. Pertinent social, political, or economic laws, if there are any ready at hand, can rarely be applied as is, but they can serve as working generalizations. And, of course, nothing prevents the historian from combining available generalizations, scientific or otherwise, in formulating a nomological universal that meets the needs of his explanation problem.[22] In fact, this is what usually takes place in the course of causal analysis. We examine this process in greater detail in the sections that follow.

4. SINGLE LAWS AND CONCRETE OCCURRENCES

We have noted two reasons why the historian is not usually able to produce a natural order account in quasi-mechanical fashion, i.e., by simply noting what sort of event is to be accounted for, selecting from his stock of empirical generalizations the one which covers it, then asserting that "c_1 , . . . , c_n were the sufficient conditions presupposed by e." For one thing the historian may be confronted with a possible plurality of causes; for another he may not find ready at hand the generalizations he requires. Another reason, touched on earlier, is that the historian is often interested in accounting for occurrences which are not like anything else known to have happened before. The apparent incompatibility of this interest with an explanation model that requires a "covering" law is, as we said earlier, the Achilles' heel of the "unity of science" position.

Consider, for example, the Industrial Revolution in eighteenth-century Europe, or the military victory of the Union troops over the forces of the Confederacy which, in 1865, ended America's War between the States. Although other instances of the same kind are possible, the specific combinations of properties comprised in these occurrences are unique in human experience. It is impossible for the historian to account for them by subsuming them directly under a "covering" nomological universal. Presumably, *either* the historian establishes the determining conditions of these highly specific occurrences directly by independent judgment of the particular case, *or* he has to rely on experience of other relevant occurrences to shed light upon what caused what. We have denied that individual cases can be independently judged. We have argued that a natural order account presupposes at least the

22. See Carey B. Joynt and Nicholas Rescher, "The Problem of Uniqueness in History," *History and Theory*, I, No. 2 (1961), 158; Sidney Hook, "Some Problems of Terminology in Historical Writing," *A Report of the Committee on Historiography*, Social Science Research Council Bulletin 54, p. 113. A specific historical study which admirably illustrates many of the points in secs. 4 and 5 of this chapter is Charles Tilly's "The Analysis of a Counter-Revolution," *History and Theory*, III, No. 1 (1963), 30-58. See also Samuel H. Beer, "Causal Explanation and Imaginative Re-enactment," in *ibid.*, 6-29.

possibility of like occurrences. But how can natural order be ascertained if there have not *actually* been like occurrences? Opponents of "scientific" history sometimes ask this as a rhetorical question, as though for any regularity interpretation of causality actual like instances were a *sine qua non* of natural order accounts of particular occurrences. Because obviously there usually have not been like instances and because the historian seldom even attempts to state any nomological generalization—let alone show how he arrived at it—the validity of causal explanations in history, if they have any, appears not to be dependent upon "covering" generalizations and, accordingly, not deterministic.

In the same vein, it is often assumed that scientific generalizations are characteristically made about "simple" phenomena or about abstracted aspects of things and events. The abstractions of science are said to be "thin," and it is supposed that there is a connection between the simplicity of the scientist's subject matter and the very possibility of making generalizations about determining conditions. Because the historian as historian is committed to accounting for human occurrences in all their concreteness he cannot settle for simple phenomena or aspects, at least not "thin" ones, and therefore he cannot be presumed to explain in the same way the scientist does. The historian's accounts of particular occurrences, so the argument runs, do not imply confirmed nomological universals because they could not.

The counter-argument is that scientists, for their part, sometimes explain complex phenomena by breaking them down into components and by utilizing generalizations about these components. More than one nomological universal is utilized. And if scientific explanations never account for things or happenings in *all* of their concreteness, nonetheless, by bringing in more and more generalizations, explanations are developed which extend to occurrences of considerable complexity. Moreover, the historian himself never actually accounts for *all* that happens at any time or place; that would be an unending task. The historian, too, abstracts.

Obviously there is a *prima facie* plausibility to both argument and counter-argument. Assuming the plausibility of a nomological analysis of causality, and the correctness of our supposition that historians do engage in natural order thinking, arguments citing *either* the "uniqueness" of historical events *or* their generalization-resistant "concreteness" can be effectively countered by a more extensive formal analysis of natural order accounts of "complex," "concrete" events—and of the reasoning behind these accounts. In this way conceptual confusions can be disclosed and misunderstandings are cleared up. Partisans of the distinctiveness of history and partisans of the "unity of science" can then amicably continue to emphasize the respective features of history that interest them.

Our immediate task, then, is to show how there can be deterministic accounts, involving warranted generalizations relevant to events the like of which never previously occurred. This will involve disclosing what takes place in causal analysis, how it is connected with the formulation of relevant generalizations, and why it is natural for the historian not to state the covering generalizations explicitly.

Perhaps the simplest way in which the historian can account for a "unique" event is by disregarding certain features of his subject matter. He does not begin with a rough generalization that has to be refined; rather he begins with a highly specific, complex subject matter which he is quite prepared to simplify, deeming most of its features incidental. As accounted for, it has lost its one-of-a-kind quality. The process is well illustrated by the following example: The problem is to account for the fact that x, who is chairman of a certain philosophy department, year after year arranges the class schedule so that assistant professor z's course in logical positivism meets on Saturday morning, the most unpopular time of all with the students. Evidence in the case warrants the explanation that "Chairman x's discriminating action against assistant professor z is caused by his desire to minimize the spread of the doctrines of logical positivism."

It would, indeed, be odd if one were to demand that the motivational explanation be justified by citing other instances of the generalization "If a department chairman wants to minimize the impact on the students' mind of a course on logical positivism and believes that he will reach this aim by scheduling it at an unpopular hour, then he will do so." The point is that we all presuppose as a *truism* the vague and abstract generalization: If an agent desires an end E and believes that action A is likely to conduce to E and does not believe that the other consequences of A are so undesirable as to outweigh the desirability of E—i.e., does not believe that A will have other consequences he fears more strongly than he desires E—then he is likely to perform A. And since we presuppose this "law," we are completely satisfied that the proffered explanation of A in terms of motive E is correct once it has been established that the agent desired E, believed that A would lead to E, and did not believe that A would have consequences he feared more strongly than he desired E.[23]

In the example, having started out with the problem of accounting for "the scheduling of a course in logical positivism at an unpopular hour," the occurrence finally accounted for is "an action that is conducive to a desired end and that does not have consequences so undesirable as to outweigh the desirability of that end."

To account for a "unique" event without reducing it to an instance of a familiar kind calls for more complicated processes. We shall examine two of these. By no means mutually exclusive, they are often pursued concurrently. The first consists in making a single working generalization more specific (discussed in sec. 5). The second is the process of combining generalizations into composite nomological universals (discussed in sec. 6).

5. Working Generalizations

Patrick Gardiner quotes from Charles Seignobos' *A History of the French People*: "Louis XIV died unpopular . . . having caused France to lose . . . the incomparable position she had gained by the policy of the cardinals."[24] What, if any, would be the generalization implicit in this assertion? It might be the following: "Rulers are unpopular whenever their policies prove detrimental to the fortunes of their countries." But, as Gardiner comments, the historian would not regard this generalization as the warranting generalization implicit in an adequate account of the fact that Louis XIV died unpopular. He might regard it as having a bearing upon it.

But he does not regard it as *applicable* in the way in which it might be true to say, for example, that the law of chemical change is applicable. In the case of the chemical law, the chemist knows where he stands. Definite procedures exist whereby it is possible to decide with a considerable degree of confidence whether, for example, the chemical is of a given type, and whether the experiment is conducted under 'normal' conditions; and in these circumstances the applicability or non-applicability of the law to the particular case is comparatively easy to determine. But the historian does not conform to this mode of procedure: his explanations are not 'read off' according to formulae, and, if it were suggested that they should be, he might object that history is not a science.

23. Arthur Pap, *An Introduction to the Philosophy of Science* (New York: The Free Press, 1962), p. 264.
24. Gardiner, *Historical Explanation*, p. 65.

One is inclined to say that generalizations of the kind in question provide indications, and rough ones at that, of the sorts of factors which, under certain circumstances, we expect to find correlated with other sorts of factors; but that they leave open to historical investigation and analysis the task of eliciting the specific nature of those factors on a particular occasion, and the precise manner in which the factors are causally connected with one another. And, this being so, we may also feel that to talk in this context of 'laws', and of the 'application' of laws, is inappropriate, for to speak of 'laws' here may lead us to forget or neglect features that are important. And it is those that I wish to stress.[25]

But Gardiner does not go into any greater detail. The historian's problem is one of refining upon a working generalization. How does he proceed? What is distinctive about the way he proceeds?

We shall consider two sorts of working generalizations. The first of these are empirical generalizations formulated as relations between variables (in the mathematical sense), "the application of the law to particular situations being mediated" by assigning specific values to the variables.[26]

For example, Galileo's law for freely falling bodies ($s = gt^2/2$) might be refined so as to yield an explanation of the fact that a released body, falling freely, struck the ground at such and such a time. The refinement would involve specifying the value of the gravitational constant "g" for the latitude of the occurrence, specifying the distance "s" of the fall, and calculating the corresponding specific value of "t." These refinements and calculations could then be formulated as a nomological *universal* applicable to this *particular* occurrence; universal because it still applies to a kind of particular instances. The physicist who explains the time of impact is guided, in effect, by procedural rules governing the application of Galileo's law, and it makes no difference whether we think of these as built into the law or as attached to it. Note that the rules indicate how the law is to be formulated, i.e., refined, in order to apply to a specific case. Note also that the confirmed status of Galileo's law does not presuppose that any body at the same latitude ever previously fell freely the same distance in the same time. Such a previous particular occurrence of the same kind does not strike us as completely unlikely, perhaps,

25. *Ibid.*, pp. 89, 92, 93 (italics in original).
26. Ernest Nagel, *The Structure of Science* (New York: Harcourt, Brace and World, 1961), p. 463.

whereas the previous occurrence of another French Revolution does. But the principle is the same: we say that the falling body exhibited the regularity of natural phenomena; our readiness to say this is quite independent of the likelihood of antecedent occurrences of "just the same" sort.

Does the historian ever have at his disposal generalized quantitative laws which he can apply merely by carrying out the sort of refinement just described? On the whole, certainly Gardiner's comment applies: "the historian does not conform to this mode of procedure: his explanations are not 'read off' according to formulae. . . ."[27]

Another sort of working generalization is a law formulated in such a way that it assumes ideal conditions: it "states some relation of dependence which supposedly holds only under certain limiting conditions, even though these conditions may be rarely if ever realized." For example, Galileo's law is formulated for bodies moving in a vacuum and the law of the lever for perfectly rigid and homogeneous bars. "In consequence, when a concretely given situation is analyzed with the help of a law so formulated, additional assumptions or postulates must be introduced to bridge the gap between the ideal case for which the law is stated and the concrete circumstances to which the law is applied."[28]

Again we can ask: Does the historian have such laws at his disposal together with the "assumptions or postulates" required for specification? Perhaps the economic historian comes closest to this for, as Nagel observes, the 'ideal conditions' strategy has been favored by economists almost alone among social scientists. But as he remarks: "the discrepancy between the assumed ideal conditions for which economic laws have been stated and the actual circumstances of the economic market are so great, and the problem of applying the supplementary assumptions needed for bridging this gap is so difficult, that the merits of the strategy in this domain continue to be disputed." Still, it is quite another thing to contend that the strategy has some basic flaw.[29]

The way the "ideal conditions" strategy works in physics is suggestive of what the historian is often trying to do when he is refining a working generalization. The working generalization is not regarded as a tentative hypothetical explanation to be rejected

27. Gardiner, *Historical Explanation*, p. 92.
28. Nagel, *Structure of Science*, p. 463.
29. *Ibid.*, p. 509; cf. p. 464.

or adopted; it is a rough correlation which needs refinement. For example: "Rulers are unpopular when their policies prove detrimental to the fortunes of their countries. Louis XIV's policies proved detrimental. This apparently contributed to his unpopularity at the time of his death." The question may be whether or not in this instance the policies were a necessary condition of that occurrence, or it may be what other conditions, together with the detrimental policies, were the sufficient condition of the occurrence. Whichever the historian's question, he seeks to answer it by a more detailed inspection of the particular circumstances. Under the prevailing circumstances were the policies a necessary condition of the occurrence? Together with what particular circumstances did they constitute a sufficient condition?

The historian's working generalization does not tell him exactly what other conditions are relevant. He must find out. This is not a task of constructing a new generalization from scratch; it is a task of refining a crude correlation. But if we ask how the historian refines upon it, the answer is: by examining the particular circumstances in greater detail *and* by judging the relevance —or irrelevance—and the nature of the relevance of particular circumstances. How does he do this? If our question is about the logic, not the psychology, of the question, our answer must be that he does it (1) by examining *other* occurrences which shed light on his problem. They shed light because they have certain similarities to, together with certain differences from, the event in question. (2) Secondly, he does it by trying to think of sound generalizations which permit him to infer what effect, if any, such and such a factor would have in connection with certain other factors. (This is tantamount to improvising what we shall later call, following Bergmann, "composition rules.") Any "weighing" the historian does, any "judgment" he makes about this particular case, depend upon what he can learn directly or indirectly from other occurrences. Moreover, the basis for any judgment is a generalization. Correspondingly, the resultant assertion about the case in question ("*e* because c_1 , . . . , c_n") implies a generalization: "Whenever C_1 , . . . , C_n then E."[30]

30. Similarly, an assertion that "Under circumstances c_1, c_2, c_3, circumstance c_4 was a necessary condition of e" implies "Whenever C_1, C_2, C_3, then E if and only if C_4." In such cases, because of plurality of causes (and where the occurrence is not known to have been "overdetermined") one or more of the conditions mentioned in the first part of the generalization is likely to specify that alternative causes (i.e., other sets of sufficient condi-

Why are we not aware of these resultant generalizations? The historian does not formulate them. Why not? Because once he has reached his conclusion there is little point in casting it in general form. It is not likely to be useful in future explanations. It is not of obvious evidential force. He has already garnered his evidence in reaching his conclusion. The only way we have of knowing whether his conclusion is sound is to check on his account of *this* case, check the data on *other* cases, check the soundness of generalizations he employed, and check his reasoning from other cases and other generalizations. The upshot of his labors *is* discernment of a rule about occurrences, expressible as a nomological universal or subjunctive conditional, but he typically neglects to state it.

One objection to this analysis can be anticipated. It will perhaps be thought inappropriate to say that there is an implicit *generalization,* a nomological *universal.* The following example has been used to illustrate the objection. If we were to ask exactly what generalization "covers" the explanatory statement "Cleopatra's beauty caused Mark Antony to linger in Egypt," the answer might go something like this: "If a man exactly like Mark Antony falls in love with a woman exactly like Cleopatra, and in exactly the same circumstances and at just the same time that Mark Antony actually did fall in love with Cleopatra, then this man will linger in Egypt."[31] This latter statement does appear to be a disguised singular statement in the sense that there *could not be* more than one instance of the states of affairs described in the antecedent (the determining conditions). It is certainly not a nomological universal.

The analysis, however, is faulty. To have explanatory force the implied statement must resemble the following in form: "There is a set of traits $M_1, \ldots, M_n$ (which Mark Antony had and of which there could be an indefinite number of instances), and a set of traits $F_1, \ldots, F_n$ (which Cleopatra had and of which there could be an indefinite number of instances), and a set of circum-

---

tions for this kind of occurrence) did not obtain. On the nature of historical judgment, contrast Dray's remark (*Laws and Explanation,* p. 43) that "in typical historical cases, the evidence which could be assembled for 'law' and case may coincide." This is apparently another way of saying that all the evidence is found by examining the case itself—judging it independently. But how a historian or anyone else can manage that is the mystery.

31. Charles Frankel, "Explanation and Interpretation in History," *Philosophy of Science,* XXIV (1957), 143-44.

stances C_1 , . . . , C_n (which obtained at the time Mark Antony fell in love with Cleopatra and of which there could be an indefinite number of instances) such that if the entity characterized by traits M_1 , . . . , M_n falls in love ("falling in love" being defined in such a way that there could be an indefinite number of instances) with the entity characterized by traits F_1 , . . . , F_n, then the entity characterized by the traits M_1, . . . , M_n lingers in Egypt ("lingering in Egypt" being defined in such a way etc.)."

It may still be objected that although the latter is a statement about kinds of traits, kinds of circumstances, and kinds of behavior, nonetheless it is about such a special combination of kinds that we cannot seriously suppose there will ever be more than one actual instance. William Dray, for example, maintains that this suffices to undermine the claim that historical accounts necessarily imply corresponding generalizations, "for the notion of a generalization with but a single case would ordinarily, I think, be regarded as a self-contradictory one."[32] But this is to assume that in calling the implicit statement a generalization or universal we are committed to asserting that there is, was, or will be more than one *actual* instance of this combination of kinds. Dray even assumes that multiple instances are the only sort of evidence which would warrant the generalization. Neither assumption accords with our analysis of the logic of historical judgment. Why does the "disguised singular statement"-argument seem initially so plausible? Perhaps because it springs from contrasting historical explanations with *one* sort of scientific explanation, namely, explanations of the kinds of particular occurrences which do commonly occur and which can be subsumed more or less directly under a scientific law. It is mistakenly inferred that any warranted generalization *must* be about occurrences of that kind. Our discussion has shown how, in the best of sciences, "unique" particular occurrences can be accounted for nomologically as cases of a special *kind*.

The preceding analysis has not dealt with the wealth of qualifying phrases used by the historian to express the various types and degrees of incertitude with which he makes his generalizations and draws his inferences. We have said nothing about recognized, prevailing professional standards of evidence. What, for example, are the confirmation-criteria of a "sound" explanation? Do historians' evaluations and criticisms of works by other historians reveal the existence of generally accepted criteria? We have also

32. *Laws and Explanation,* p. 40.

not considered the obstacles which stand in the way of refining working generalizations about historical subject matter. In particular, we have said nothing about the criteria of relevant "similarity" (between occurrences) or about the details of the reasoning by which the historian judges, in the light of similar aspects of other occurrences, the nomological significance of some factor or circumstance in the case under investigation. We have certainly not maintained that the historian can always find other occurrences and working generalizations which facilitate causal analysis and permit him finally to judge how a multiplicity of factors co-determined an occurrence. These are all matters of great interest upon which little or no work has been done. Our remarks have been directed only to establishing the plausibility of a deterministic conception of historical intelligibility. For this purpose enough has already been said about the specification of working generalizations.

6. COMPOSITE LAWS

We have maintained that the nomological universal required for natural order intelligibility is a single generalization, even though in the process of formulating it many generalizations may have been considered. In some scientific explanations, however, we think of the implicit generalization as *composite,* as comprising several laws. Defenders of the "unity of science" have their answer ready when it is protested that no single law could "cover" events as specific as those historians often try to explain. Their answer is: these complex events are covered by a *set* of laws. But this answer has not proved convincing. We shall do well, therefore, to look more closely at this notion of a "set of laws." We shall begin, as before, with some distinctions that have their most obvious application in the more systematic natural sciences, and then examine their relevance to history.

In his book, *Philosophy of Science,* Gustav Bergmann uses the Newtonian law of "gravitational attraction" to elucidate composite law explanations.[33] The Newtonian law can be stated so as to show how the acceleration imparted to one body by another body depends upon their masses and mutual distance. The simplest possible occurrences to which the law applies are within a two-body system. Following Bergmann we shall call this an *elementary sys-*

33. Gustav Bergmann, *Philosophy of Science* (Madison, Wis.: The University of Wisconsin Press, 1957), pp. 131 ff.

tem. Mutual accelerations involving more than two bodies, however, can be explained using the two-body law, i.e., the law for elementary systems, together with a rule, called a *composition rule,* for calculating the several mutual accelerations of many-body systems. The Newtonian law itself is unspecified in respect to the number of bodies, their masses, and the distances between them. The law implicit in an explanation of the acceleration of a particular body due to gravitation would, if the body were part of a many-body system, be a complex version of the simple law worked out in accordance with the composition rule. It would still be quite natural to say that this implicit law (nomological universal) was a single law. It could be said to exemplify the specification process we discussed earlier. But we could also stress that the complex version of the simple law is a combination of applications of the law for two-body systems, for the composition rule calls for ascertaining the resultant acceleration due to mutual gravitational attraction by decomposing the many-body system into two-body systems. What we would finally have, then, is a number of laws (specified for each of the two-body systems) and a rule for *combining* the acceleration values of each two-body system. In formulating the "covering" law of an explanation of the gravitational acceleration imparted to any body as part of a particular many-body system, it is optional whether this "covering" law is stated by listing seriatim the laws of the several component systems together with the composition rules governing their interrelationships, *or* as a single law worked out by applying the composition rules to the laws of the component systems. The particular determining conditions of the occurrence to be accounted for would be expressed in different ways accordingly.

We have here an illustration, a very simple one, of an explanation which might be said to imply a "set of laws." It corresponds to what Dray calls the "complex version" of the covering law model. We see that (contrary to Dray's contention in his critique of the "complex version"[34]) there is no special problem as to how the several component laws are unified so as to "cover" the particular occurrence. This is taken care of by the composition rule which, strictly speaking, is part of the implicit law. The most obvious difference between the historian's problem of explanation and the problem faced by the scientist is that the latter has his composition rules ready at hand, while the historian often has to work

34. Dray, *Laws and Explanation,* pp. 52 ff.

them out for himself as best he can. The fundamental logical structure is the same. As Bergmann expresses it, the complete explanation apparatus comprises composition laws, or "rules," and laws for elementary systems. His comment is very much to the point:

> I called composition laws *rules* and I shall continue to call them so, at least occasionally; for the word comes quite easily when we refer to this sort of law. Yet 'rule' is confusing. (That is why I used it deliberately in order to get this point out of the way.) The source of the confusion is that 'rule' carries some of the connotations that are also carried by 'arbitrary', by 'convention', by 'way to proceed', and by 'man-made'. 'Law', used as in 'law of nature', has none of these connotations, a recent and right now very vociferous group of logical analysts to the contrary notwithstanding. A law states what is, or, if it is false, what is not the case. It is therefore not arbitrary, man-made, or a convention. Nor is it a way to proceed; nor perhaps, as some believe, a rule for "inferring" a statement of individual fact from some other such statement or statements. To avoid this mistake, one merely has to remember that the law itself is one of the premises of the inference. . . .[35]

Let us apply these distinctions to an example (adapted from Hempel[36]) of complexity: One cold night an automobile radiator cracked. Why? Because the iron radiator, of certain specifications, filled with water and tightly closed, was exposed for a certain number of hours under normal air pressure, to a temperature well below 32 degrees Fahrenheit. Several empirical laws are implied by this explanation, among them: a law relating the freezing of water to temperature, a law covering the change of water pressure (formulated as a function of temperature and volume), a law covering the expansion of water when it freezes, a law covering the pressure tolerance of iron containers, and a law covering the reaction of iron containers to internal pressure. One new feature of this example is that different kinds of component systems and processes are involved: e.g., cracking metal containers and freezing-expanding liquids. The explanation ascribes the occurrence to a combination of determining conditions which include these different kinds of systems. How is it possible to combine laws of different kinds of systems? Through the use of composition rules—rules which it is appropriate to call laws. And again it is possible to formulate the implicit covering law of the account of this oc-

35. *Philosophy of Science*, pp. 136-37.
36. *Aspects*, p. 232.

currence in two ways: either as a conjunction of the several laws and composition rules, or as a single law (the result of applying the composition rules to the various laws). Informally stated it amounts to the same thing: Whenever an iron radiator of certain specifications is exposed to such and such a combination of conditions, the radiator is bound to crack. We shall call the covering nomological universals in cases such as this *heterogeneous*, in recognition of the fact that they involve occurrence-determining relationships between different kinds of systems. In our previous example, the many two-body systems were all of the same kind; generalizations implicit in accounts of occurrences involving only one kind of system we shall call *homogeneous*.

We have distinguished between elementary systems, composite homogeneous systems, and composite heterogeneous systems. The relevance of these distinctions can be stated very simply. Knowing more about what goes into making historical explanations "complex," we can see that the differences between ordinary history and our formal analysis of natural order intelligibility are illusory. Historical accounts often involve composite heterogeneous systems. In this sense they are complex in form. We are frequently not able to specify just what the component systems are, how many are involved, and how they are interrelated, but the rudimentary logical structure is there. Even though historians are not in the habit of formulating the implicit generalizations of these explanations, we can nonetheless see what their character would be; in particular we can see how the generalization implicit in an account of a composite heterogeneous occurrence-determination can be a single nomological universal.[37]

We have already defended a conception of deterministic intelligibility that is not limited to occurrences within "closed systems."[38] Since the occurrences dealt with in ordinary history supposedly occur within closed systems only rarely if ever, it may be of interest to point out that one case in which a composite law is needed is in accounting for a particular occurrence that is jointly determined by the determining conditions operative in a closed system *and* by interfering contingent factors.[39] For example,

37. See Nagel's comparison of historical explanations of aggregative occurrences with the scientist's explanation of the behavior of a steam locomotive: both involve "a more or less integrated system of component parts" or "aspects" (*Structure of Science*, pp. 570-71).

38. Chap. II, sec. 7 above.

39. "Contingent" in sense (2): not necessary relative to selected facts and laws. Cf. chap. III, sec. 5 above.

suppose that during the past twenty-four hours our sun and its nine planets have constituted a closed system with respect to the positions of these bodies relative to one another. If there were to be no interfering factors, we could predict correctly, solely from our knowledge of the system, the relative positions during the next twenty-four hours. But suppose that during that period another sizable heavenly body passes close to our solar system and the predicted positions fail to materialize. We neither know of nor have we reason to believe that there is any law governing the total distribution of matter in space, from which this interference could have been deduced. But if we knew that an object of a certain size was going to pass close to our solar system and if we knew certain details about this occurrence, we could still predict the disposition of the bodies in that system. And if this knowledge only became available after the occurrence, we could use it to account for the difference between the actual and the (incorrectly) predicted positions.

When contingent factors interfere, the requisite explanation apparatus becomes more complex—more composite—but not different in kind. The differences between history and science in this regard, then, are only differences in degree. The scientist, in some fields at least, can ascertain laws more easily because he has a greater opportunity to study closed elementary systems, and the particular occurrences he has occasion to account for are more often explicable in terms of closed systems (elementary or otherwise). By contrast, regularities in the historian's subject matter are harder to detect due to the rarity of closed elementary systems, and even to the extent that he has reliable generalizations at his disposal he seldom finds occasion to use them in giving "closed system" explanations. He is continually faced with having to calculate the effect of interfering contingent factors. But we are certainly misled if we suppose that these differences extend to the fundamental presuppositions and over-all objectives of inquiry. Moreover, the dissimilarities between actual historical and unquestionably scientific accounts are sometimes grossly exaggerated. Scientists, too, have to allow for contingencies. On the other hand, all is not sheer chaos in the historical world. The historian finds plenty of occasions for distinguishing the accidental from the routine, normal on-going conditions from abnormal conditions caused by contingencies.

CONCLUSION TO PART ONE

In our discussion of the scheme of natural order intelligibility as one way of thinking about the world, we have tried to establish beyond controversy that it is proper to classify the historian—in some of his undertakings—together with the scientist in some of his. We have considered a number of counter-claims and reservations; it would be too much to say that we have covered all of them. We have considered at some length various features of ordinary historical works. The burden of the evidence is that when historical accounts are judged to differ from scientific explanations, "science" is being conceived in a way which obscures the kinship here at issue, or else the significance of familiar traits of historical works is mistakenly appraised.

That history has been thought to be peculiar is not surprising. Differentiating features in combination give the effect of radical dissimilarity. The unsuspecting are confident that there *must* be a fundamental difference somewhere in this array. When one difference is shown to be something less than fundamental—or to have its counterpart in some acknowledged science—another trait is siezed upon as fundamental. Hence the importance of examining with care a great many different facets of historical writing. Working with a carefully formulated conception of deterministic intelligibility, the allegedly fundamental peculiarities of history evaporate one after another into miscellaneous differences of secondary significance: the historian typically deals with heterogeneous systems; does not dispose of precise, already-confirmed generalizations; deals with topics so vast that they cannot possibly be treated thoroughly; mixes description with causal accounts so that we do not always know which is which; seldom attempts to state the sufficient conditions of occurrences; deals with distinctively human phenomena the description and causal accounts of which sound un-"scientific"; does not bother to be explicit about his use of general knowledge, which often takes the form of highly restricted generalizations; and deals with kinds of events that can have a variety of determining conditions or with particular events that we cannot seriously expect to recur ever anywhere again.

We have maintained, not that history properly speaking is science, but rather that one way of making the particular occurrences of history intelligible is deterministic, and that, in fact, historians do think deterministically. It is *one* of the things they do—even when they are confused as to the nature of their own undertaking and its kinship with what goes on in other disciplines.

It may still be objected that our analysis misrepresents historical practice. Most explanations in current historical writing seem to be different from what even our unusually elaborate analysis of deterministic explanations would lead us to expect. Many an historian seems to care little about precision in asserting a necessary condition; he cares still less about the set of sufficient conditions; and when it comes to universal determinism, far from being fired by a vision of pervasive natural order, he concedes in advance that determinism has its limits or else that the whole issue is purely academic. Historians tend to be unperturbed when someone calls attention to vagueness in their accounts of why events happened; unperturbed not because they are confident that historiography is progressing and in due course will produce accounts satisfying deterministic criteria, but because they consider the deterministic quest alien to themselves. The criteria of clarity, soundness, completeness, etc., for good *historical* explanations are, they suppose, simply different. Admittedly there is room for improvement, but this improvement is conceived to be relative to distinctive *historical* criteria, not to those of science. They assume that there is an *historical* scheme of intelligibility, relative to which ordinary historical accounts, or many of them, adequately explain why particular human events occurred.

Our reply is as follows. In his account of why in fact something happened, either the historian stops short of giving us the answer or he gives us a deterministic account. There are non-cognitive considerations—pragmatic, aesthetic, etc.—that influence what we expect of the historian. There are also conventional and contextual expectations that guide the historian. It may be that in fulfilling these the historian has satisfied himself, his colleagues, and his lay public. But we can always ask: Has he made the fact of the occurrence intelligible? Has he realized the ideal of the scheme of natural order intelligibility?

That the historian's particular problem can involve realizing this ideal in different ways is conceded. That there are good reasons why under certain circumstances the ideal should not be operative is conceded. That practical difficulties may prevent successful inquiry is conceded. Doubtless many accounts found in history books are expected to be no more than probabilistic, to do no more than establish a necessary correlation rather than a set of sufficient conditions, and to be presented as the result of intuitive skill rather than of a reasoning process employing generalizations that can be formulated and furnished upon request. Yet the way in which characteristics of peculiarly historical explanations are expressed, strongly suggests that historians and their readers presuppose the natural order scheme of intelligibility. How else are we to understand the meaning of "only a necessary condition and not a set of sufficient conditions"? Or the idea that "the generalizations upon which historical explanations depend are too complex to be precisely formulated"? Or the idea that a trained mind can discern why something happened without going through an elaborate process of reasoning? If this is the case, if the scheme of natural order intelligibility is commonly presupposed, even unwittingly, then it would not be surprising to find historians now and then becoming interested in perfecting their explanations in line with the ideal requirements of that scheme.

We have referred to the difficulties confronting those recent philosophers who have set their sights on what historians actually do. We have noted their predilection for "ordinary history." Symptomatic of their difficulties is the fact that just at the time they began to prick the conscience of philosophers for imposing preconceptions derived from "science" upon recalcitrant historians, more and more historians were joining in a critical examination of current historical practices and of their own professional preconceptions; more and more of them were feeling their way experimentally to closer ties with fellow-students of human phenomena, with behavioral and social scientists of all sorts. To the close observer of historiographical trends, the proposed revolution in philosophy of history looked suspiciously like a counter-revolution. There will be opportunity in Part Two for a positive evaluation of ordinary history. Here I wish to underscore the timeliness of the *formal* rapprochement between history and deterministic thinking envisioned in this first part of our study, by remarking on some recent developments in history and allied human disciplines.

We are told that historians typically just do not care to change their ways, that determinism is simply not a postulate of historical inquiry, and that even though the idea of a natural order may be somewhere in the back of the historian's mind, it does not function as an ideal or express his over-all objectives. We must take note, however, of the extent to which historians themselves are dissatisfied with "ordinary" historical explanations. The impetus to refine

on techniques of explanation and to impose more stringent requirements on historical writing has not come from philosophers
alone. Philosophical descriptions of what historians allegedly
actually do, which are guided by distrust of model-building executed under the spell of formal logic and the natural sciences,
consistently underplay the extent to which historians spontaneously
are moved to think more like the scientist, to shift the form of
historical accounts closer to systematic science, further from common sense.[40] If we were to judge by some analyses of ordinary
history we would never suspect how receptive to findings, to
adventurous explorations, in the human sciences, some historians
are. We would never suspect how extensively the scientific ideal
is consciously operative at the present time. Yet in the light of
intellectual history itself, the surprising thing would be if history
as a discipline were to remain rigidly ordinary and close to common
sense.

Impetus to change has come from still another source: the
social sciences. A recent observer of the past twenty-five years of
historiographical activity who detects an "increasing convergence
of history with the other social sciences," remarks upon the number of social scientists and representatives of related disciplines who:

have in recent years asked historians (often vainly) for their help,
offered their own, and sometimes poached on the historian's pre-
serves. Chief among them are economics, sociology, geography,
demography and several biological disciplines. Thus, for instance,
the theory of "economic growth" which looks like dominating the
academic economics of our age as the theory of economic fluctuations dominated the depressed 1930's, is little but economic history
based on theory and prolonged into the future (i.e., incidentally,
all that history is often supposed to be incapable of being). The
economist therefore turns to the historian, and if he will not help,
produces his history as best he can. This is often necessary. The
list of serious historical works by non-historians is already long
for this reason. Conversely, the non-historians have often recognized original departures in history before the historians: Lefebvre's
epoch-making *Les Paysans du Nord dans la Revolution Francaise*
was welcomed by the geographers, when the historians neglected
it. . . .

These tendencies have not merely changed the perspective of

40. Similarly, some historians have been led by the logic of deterministic
thinking to break down traditional barriers, following the clues of determining conditions wherever these might lead, rejecting the idea that history
comprises a very limited, somehow autonomously intelligible subject matter—
the human social past.

historical writing. They have also changed its technique. Certain parts of history (notably the narrowly economic) have approximated sufficiently to the method, and often—alas—the jargon of social science, to be extremely difficult to fit into the pattern of traditional historical prose, narrative or otherwise. But even in general history the mere widening of the historian's perspective has made it more difficult for him to maintain the old-fashioned flow from one event to the next. To explain the changing texture of a web is technically much harder than to trace a thread. . . .

The alternatives before the historian are to isolate and narrate or to synthesize and lose continuity. These, no doubt, are the growing pains of a maturing discipline. But those who will feel them most are not so much the expert historians as the intelligent lay readers who, in spite of the proliferation of first-rate popular writing—and the past fifteen years have been, in most countries of Europe, a golden period for "haute vulgarisation"—may find the history which is emerging today a very much more difficult subject than their fathers and grandfathers.[41]

Heightened sensitivity to the requirements of natural order intelligibility need not issue in a call for radical transformation of historiographical traditions. An instructive example is provided by the views expressed by J. H. Hexter in *Reappraisals in History*.[42] Hexter pleads for a "revolution" in historical thought, but it turns out that he is only urging historians to be more exacting, more consciously critical, more methodical in their use of language. The immediate result of this would be conceptual precision. In his description of the language of ordinary history, Gardiner reported that we find "absent the usage of concepts whose meanings can be expressed in exact terms."[43] Hexter agrees, and proposes that something be done about it. Gardiner, it will be recalled, went on to say that one of the consequences of the looseness of historical concepts is that historical generalizations must *inevitably* be vague. Were greater precision out of the question, historical explanations, too, would inevitably be vague. But Hexter, although he does not make the connection between conceptual precision and explanatory precision in exactly the same way, is clearly of the opinion that one greatly to be desired ultimate consequence of conceptual precision will be better explanations. Logical or linguistic reform will lead to "reappraisals" of hitherto accepted ex-

41. *The Times Literary Supplement,* October 13, 1961, p. 699.
42. J. H. Hexter, *Reappraisals in History* (Evanston, Ill.: Northwestern University Press, 1962).
43. Gardiner, *Historical Explanation,* p. 54.

planations.[44] In short, *Reappraisals in History* illustrates the process of self-criticism at work within the historical profession. It is self-criticism responsive to the criteria of adequate accounts of why particular occurrences in fact happened, criteria which derive from the scheme of natural order intelligibility.

44. As a perceptive reviewer of Hexter's book pointed out, linguistic and sociological confusions on the part of historians are interdependent (J. G. A. Pocock, *History and Theory*, III, No. 1 (1963), 133).

PART TWO

LIVING IN THE WORLD

Chapter VI.

The Standpoint of Living in the World

1. INTRODUCTION

The differentiated and refined ideal of natural order intelligibility discussed in Part One is one plausible framework of observation and judgment in our thinking about happenings; it answers to one sometimes consciously differentiated way of conceptualizing and relating what happens; it is, in retrospect, one outcome of man's collective, socially continuous—although individually sporadic—thinking about the world.

Our objective in Part Two is to depict a second fundamental standpoint of thinking—the standpoint of living in the world—and to discuss its relevance to history.

Confrontation of the world in such a way that a distinctive question arises is what we mean by a standpoint. The queries that give rise to critically differentiated lines of questioning develop from everyday encounters with the world. It is a philosophical error, however, to suppose that our everyday thinking has its own framework of intelligibility and provides the key to the intelligibility of the world.

Developing sophistication combines *refinement* in conception of standpoints of thinking with *differentiation* of these standpoints from one another. At the outset of man's thinking it is not apparent that there are fundamentally distinct question-posing ways in which the world is there for us, let alone what these are. To speak of the natural order question or the standpoint of natural order thinking, for example, is to view the process of differentiation and refinement from the vantage point of an understanding, arrived at by critical reflection, as to the sort of thinking appropriate to what is now seen to be a distinct way the world is questionable for us.

It is not that a certain stage of critical insight having been reached, the everyday cognitive activity of everyone now divides neatly into two types; it is rather that men can now distinguish two plausible fundamental standpoints for thinking about the world. These represent possible differentiations in the thinking of all of us, consciously made at times in the thinking of some of us, most obviously made in the thinking of those specializing in the rigorous pursuit of some line of questioning. Furthermore, just as the sceptic's philosophical doubts as to the existence of the external world appear ridiculous to those uninitiated in critical thinking and are ignored by the sceptic himself when he is engaged in the ordinary activities of daily life, so it is with such refinements as the ideal of natural order intelligibility or the ideal of rational action. Even after fundamental standpoints of thinking have been painstakingly differentiated, most persons continue to have confused notions of the presuppositions of the judgments they make about the world and are not ready to accept the idea that the world is intelligible in fundamentally distinct ways. The most self-consciously critical philosopher does not live completely absorbed in the single-minded quest for intelligibility. All of us sometimes relax our cognitive requirements, blur differentiations between one specialized way of thinking and another, and, in general, interpret the world in a manner bearing marked similarity to the only way in which happenings could be thought about before the process of refinement and specialization was well advanced. But there is this difference: for the person having critical insight into the duality of schemes of intelligibility and cognizant of their respective requirements, thinking about the world is not or need not be confused even when it is not thorough and even when there is a shifting from one standpoint to another. Such a person is aware of what he is about, or is at least able to clarify what he is about. In simplest terms, pre-critical thinking is marked by ignorance of the duality of standpoints and therefore by the impossibility of even occasional differentiated and refined thinking about the world; post-critical thinking is marked by casual disregard of the duality of standpoints and their requirements with the possibility of occasional or, in the case of specialists, extensive consciously differentiated and refined thinking from either of the fundamental standpoints.

The differentiated natural order standpoint with its refined scheme of intelligibility has much in common with what Dilthey distinguished as the "cognitive attitude," described by him as directed toward knowledge of objective reality. Similarly, the second fundamental standpoint, that of living in the world, can be seen as the standpoint of what Dilthey called the "emotional" and the "volitional" attitudes.

Our procedure in this chapter will be to outline the standpoint of living in the world and to make an initial differentiation between the two standpoints (section 2), then to discuss in general terms the relevance of the second standpoint to historical thinking, anticipating the detailed discussion of subsequent chapters (section 3).

2. DIFFERENTIATING THE STANDPOINT OF LIVING IN THE WORLD

To confront the world as living in the world is to confront it caringly. How the world is matters. Caring is a frame of mind, an attitude of concern, which poses questions about the world—questions as to the relative preferability of one or another alternative states of affairs. To care is to presume that one or another alternative might be preferable. Men care how the world is, but it is not always apparent to them what states of affairs are preferable. They have held various opinions as to what they can find out about this by thinking and what sort of thinking is appropriate to this end.

Ultimately what human beings care about is how human beings are—the condition they are in, or could be in if there were certain changes—or what human beings do. The human being cared about can be (surely often is), but need not be, the one who cares. Whoever is cared about is cared about as a human being, i.e., as one in the human situation. Whatever else this means it includes being a particular existence at (or during) a time and at a place in the bounded continuum of a lifetime, a continuum within that of the world.

Thinking from the standpoint of living in the world takes the form of ascertaining what is preferable. We shall distinguish between two sorts of judgments of preferability: evaluations and practical reasoning. Evaluations are judgments as to the comparative merits or shortcomings of a situation or aspect of a situation cared about. For example, we may evaluate the effects of certain events on our own human situation. What is evaluated can be past, present or future. Doubtless many, and perhaps most, evaluations are connected with practical considerations: they are made in connection with deliberating *whether* to take action, *what* to do, or when examining the consequences of choices already acted upon. It will facilitate discussion, however, if we deal with evaluation apart from practical reasoning, a procedure warranted by the fact that at least some evaluations of situations have no essential connection with rational actions.

The thinking we do from this standpoint reflects not only the particularity of situations but the multiplicity of ways in which a human being can fare well or ill, do well or badly, make things well or poorly. It reflects the diverse kinds of interrelationships we have with things human and non-human: the precarious combination of environmental conditions upon which survival depends; the physiological complexity of our bodies, which exposes us to a diversity of stimuli and gives us the ability to do countless things as well as to extend the range of possible activities by manipulating our environment; our involvement in numerous and varied cultural systems and correlated social organizations; and so on. Whence questions arise: Which of several possible actions or activities, which state of affairs, which product of our making is, in a particular situation or in general, the preferable one?

The questions we ask and answer from the standpoint of living in the world vary with the temporal perspective. We do not deliberate about an action already done; we do review and criticize past deliberations and compare the actual with the foreseen consequences. On the other hand, we do not criticize ourselves for a decision not yet made nor do we compare envisioned consequences with actual consequences of a decision we have yet to execute.

Judgments from this standpoint differ in generality. In one instance we may be deciding what action is called for in a particular situation; in another instance we may be generalizing about the kind of act appropriate to a kind of situation.

Judgments from the standpoint of living in the world, like natural order accounts, are themselves subject to appraisal as more or less adequate. They are not mere expressions of opinion or feeling. When on the basis of newly acquired insight I am no longer satisfied with my way of life, or when through deliberation I change my mind about what action to take, I have not merely changed my mind. My revised judgment is intended to be more adequate. The criteria of adequacy in the case of these judgments are no less complex than those of natural order judgments. Also like those, they are not our central concern in this study, and most of the characteristics just enumerated will not be discussed at length.

So much of our caring about the world is about our own situation that we can profitably generalize with this in view. To confront the world as living in the world is to be cognizant of a definite past and a future that is not definite, at least not absolutely so. We live with a sense of the continuity of our existence; with a version of our life in mind: our memorable past, a reckoning of our achievements, mistakes, failures and wasted opportunities; a sense of our situation here and now, our vocation and avocations; a sense of where we are headed, of uncertainties that sooner or later will be resolved in one way or another. Along with the notion of our life so far and expectations about what is yet to come, we have ideas about what would be desirable if it were possible and guidelines as to the action appropriate in certain types of situations. We have more or less stable loyalties, a sense of what roles we are expected to perform, an idea—crude or elaborate—of where we fit into various temporal continuities: the lifetimes of our friends and family, the history of our profession, our generation, our country, and, finally, world history.

As we go on living, we change and our perspective changes. New skills are acquired; old ones are lost. The premises of our appraisals and decisions change. We ridicule today what yesterday we took seriously. We come to know more about ourselves, about people, and about the world. With age we modify our projects and our expectations. In due course it is the prospect of our death rather than our life that shapes our plans.

The foregoing description has no claim to originality, being only a review of some pertinent and familiar features of concrete human experience. Before elaborating upon these in delineating thinking from the standpoint of living in the world, we can take note of one fundamental distinction between this standpoint and that of natural order thinking.

Evaluation and practical reasoning presuppose that there is a question of preferability (as to situations, institutions, courses of action, etc.) *for* one or more persons. There must be matters of concern, whether or not the person whose concern they are be actually consciously concerned. Only a matter for concern can raise the questions that lead into evaluation and practical reasoning, providing, in effect, intelligibility—the intelligibility of the world as lived in. Something is always judged preferable *for* someone; there is always, we shall say, a personal reference. This by no means implies that the *judgment* as to what is preferable for someone is personal, i.e., that preferability is a matter of personal judgment. The range of personal reference varies greatly. Some issues of preferability—in evaluation or practical reasoning—concern only one person, others concern humanity at large. What we are stressing here is the personal reference essential to questioning from the standpoint of living in the world. By contrast, there is no essential personal reference in natural order questioning. The natural order question poses itself irrespective of anyone's personal interests.

As a consequence, we have to distinguish between two senses in which occurrences involve distinctively human meaning. Natural order intelligibility is one way in which the world—including our own existence, behavior, etc.—is intelligible *for* human beings. Relations of natural order *are* in this sense one mode of distinctively human meaning.[1] But there is nothing essentially human about natural orderliness itself as there is, by contrast, about preferability. The personal reference essential to preferability is a reference to persons *as human beings,* as in the human situation. In so far as there is nothing essentially human about natural orderliness itself, the natural order relatedness of the world (being related in terms of natural order) resembles neutral meaning relations and *differs* from the other distinctively human modes of meaning: being satisfactory for someone (evaluations), and being the appropriate thing for someone to do or the appropriate way for someone to proceed (practical judgments).

3. RELEVANCE TO HISTORICAL THINKING

How does the standpoint of living in the world relate to historical thinking—thinking about particular human occurrences?

1. One must be cautious then about designating only one kind of intelligible account as "humanistic." See, e.g., William Dray, *Laws and Explanation in History* (London: Oxford University Press, 1957), p. 139; and "The Historical Explanation of Actions Reconsidered," in *Philosophy and History,* ed. Sidney Hook (New York: New York University Press, 1963), pp. 132-33. There is a sense in which logical analysis as well as academic conventions support this description, but it risks being misleading and being construed invidiously.

The difference between the ways in which it and natural order thinking enter into historical thinking is largely a reflection of the difference noted in the preceding section. Our discussion of historical thinking from the standpoint of living in the world will accordingly differ in form from Part One.

Judgments of preferability are personal in reference. *For* persons living in the past—past relative to the present in which the historian sets about making the past intelligible—there were questions of preferability. Some questions of satisfactoriness for them (matters of evaluation) were actually posed by them. Some of these questions they answered thoughtfully, using generalization and judgment. An indefinite number of questions of satisfactoriness for them could have been posed. Similarly, there were an indefinite number of questions for these persons as to what to do and how to proceed (practical questions), of which some were actually posed and some were answered thoughtfully by them. Even when no question was explicitly asked or answered, they engaged in activities and viewed happenings with the understanding—sometimes resulting from previous thinking—that what was being done was appropriate, or that what was happening was satisfactory (or unsatisfactory). The historian can *describe* the questions asked, the thinking done (or the manner in which the questions were resolved, whatever it may have been), and the temper of mind, mood, or outlook with which activities were carried on and happenings regarded. This is *descriptive* understanding, i.e., description of meaning relations; in this case, description of distinctively human meanings concretely experienced or objectified. But, as we shall have occasion to point out, the historian can also *identify* with the standpoint of living in the world of those persons in the past; in so doing he regards the questions as universally human. It is this latter way of regarding the lived experience of the past which distinguishes *identifying* understanding from mere description, *descriptive* understanding. Identifying understanding presupposes descriptive understanding though doubtless these are rarely, if ever, two distinct and sequential operations. The historian does not first describe and then regard what he has described identifyingly. Yet the distinction is valuable; it reminds us that there is another way of regarding lived experience and objectified meaning relations, namely, as manifesting natural order. An historian's description can be ancillary to both standpoints of thinking; it can serve two ultimate aims: identifying understanding or natural order thinking. It may be impossible for the reader of an historical work to ascertain whether the historian regarded the human experience he describes in his account identifyingly or not. Only rarely will an historian explicitly state his interest in so regarding the past. In any case, given a description of distinctively human meaning the reader can himself regard the latter identifyingly, even, indeed, when it is apparent from the historian's account as a whole that *his* way of regarding the described material was from the contrasting standpoint of natural order.

Are we to say that when the historian (or reader) regards past experience identifyingly he is *thinking* about the past and making it *intelligible?* We might balk at saying so in cases where the past experience under consideration did not itself involve thinking: where questions about things that mattered were not thought about by those directly concerned; where the caring confrontation of the world was not rationally developed. But in cases where thinking was done by the persons themselves and issued in evaluational or practical judgments, it seems plausible to say that in regarding the past identifyingly we not only know *what* human meaning relations were experienced and objectified (and in this sense understand them), we not only know *that* they were experienced and objectified, but we also find the past intelligible. It is intelligible to us as having been intelligible to them, as having been thought about and judged by them *as fellow human beings.* The kind of intelligibility that the world had for them is recognized as one of the *kinds* of intelligibility that "our" world has for us, a kind we ourselves at least sometimes pursue, the goal of one form of our own questioning. Intelligibility by means of identifying understanding is a matter of degree, comparable in this respect to the intelligibility of the world relative to our own confrontation of the world: the less our own confrontation is rationally developed, the less intelligible is the world for us.

Of particular interest here is identifying understanding of the natural order questioning and answering of other persons in the human past. It strikes us as less appropriate to regard this as a distinct way of making that past intelligible. This is because what was in question (i.e., natural order) lacked essential personal reference. The questioning about natural order by past persons was not about the world as questionable for them only, but as questionable for mankind in general. Their questions at that time are, or could be, our questions now. All occurrences pose the natural order question for all persons. Natural order intelligibility is impersonal. Not so the intelligibility of the world from the standpoint of living in the world. To be sure, some questions from that standpoint are of broad human concern. Questions thought about by the persons he is dealing with are occasionally matters of personal concern for the historian himself. But many are not of this sort, and to the extent that they are not, what was going on in the past becomes distinctively intelligible to us only when we know how it was intelligible to the persons in the past and only when we regard this intelligibility as human in *kind*.

We have suggested that although it may be inappropriate to characterize identifying understanding as such as a way of *thinking* about the human past, it is nonetheless plausible so to characterize identifying understanding *of past thinking from the standpoint of living in the world*. This, then, is one way (a) in which the standpoint of historical thinking is the standpoint of living in the world. Another way (b) is for the historian, still identifying with the concerns of others in the past, to make judgments of preferability based on the concerns of others, judgments which those concerned did not make but which they would have made had they raised certain questions of preferability and clearly and cogently thought out the answers. In other words the historian can make judgments for them as to what would have been preferable for them. Finally, there are those cases (c) in which, thinking having been done by other persons about their concerns, the historian criticizes that thinking. All of these are ways in which the historian can be said to think about the past and to make it intelligible from the standpoint of living in the world. They have in common that there is personal reference to the past concerns *of others* (past relative to the present time of the historian's account).

Doubtless the conventional subject matter of history is comprised of past particular occurrences in the lives of others: their past existence and activities, including whatever thinking they may have done—*their* thinking, not the historian's own. It will seem natural enough, therefore, that the chapters immediately following deal with thinking about the human *past* with reference to the past concerns of others. We should note, however, that there is no essential difference between the thinking we do about the past concerns of *others* and the thinking we do about our own past when we identify with *our* past concerns. The essential differences are between standpoints from which we think, not in the subject matter about which we think. Our own past, like the past of others, can be merely described, or we can attempt to give natural order accounts of it or view it from the standpoint of living in the world with some past personal reference, whether to ourselves or to others.

An obscure appreciation of this underlies the ambiguous status of autobiography relative to the conventional view of history. Autobiographies, like histories, are very commonly accounts of the past written from the standpoint of living in the world in terms of past personal concerns. If, on the one hand, there is hesitancy about accepting autobiography as history, history being conventionally conceived of as dealing with the past of *others*, there is also a tendency to regard autobiography as history; a plausible tendency in the light of the identity of the standpoints of thinking. Moreover, generals or statesmen occasionally do turn historians, or historians, having played important roles in public events, reconstruct them from the standpoint of their past concerns as thoughtful participants. Such cases serve to underscore the arbitrariness of a restriction of history to the past of others.

Having duly emphasized unity of standpoint over against the distinction between our past concerns and the past concerns of others, we shall simplify our discussion of historical thinking about the human past from the standpoint of living in the world, restricting it to the past with reference to the past concerns of others and thus preserving on grounds of convenience a superficial accord with one conventional idea of history.

So far we have spoken only of thinking about the human *past* and of thinking about it in reference to *past* human concerns. But just as natural order thinking was found in Part One to have no essential limitation to past occurrences, so thinking from the standpoint of living in the world has no such limitation. And just as natural order historians, breaking through the conventional restriction of explaining only the past, sometimes explain the present and predict the future, so we find that the idea of history as the study of the human past is not the only idea of history current today germane to the standpoint of living in the world. Another conception of history and historical thinking embraces present and future. We conceive of ourselves as being in the stream of history: as living *now* in an historical period, phase, or stage of history, and as *making* history. There is such a thing as living history, which is not the past revivified but our existence "here and now" with its continually changing foreground, its background of the past, and its future prospects.

Historical thinking, in accordance with this conception, may be simply an *evaluation* of our own or some contemporary's situation—an evaluation infused with historical consciousness, a sense of the temporality of existence; or an evaluation of the present compared with the past, or even of the future compared with the present or past. In these cases, as evaluation, the thinking is *not* geared into a deliberation about steps to be taken to improve a situation or a criticism of action already taken. Or, still in accordance with this broader conception of history, historical thinking can take the form of *practical reasoning*: deliberation infused with historical consciousness. The conventional associations of history with the human past are strong, however, and even when history is conceived of as a process now under way in which we —historians and readers alike—are taking part, the tendency is to conceive of historical thinking restrictively as thinking about the *past* in connection with present or future concerns. This bias makes little difference in the case of evaluation but can be misleading as regards practical judgment. In treating the latter we shall indeed discuss the distinctive way in which the *past* is thought about when the orientation is that of prospective action, but we shall be careful not to assume that historical thinking about present and prospective concerns is limited to this alone.[2]

Whereas the conventional idea of history as the study of the human *past* tends to exclude as historical subject matter those events in which the historian himself (i.e., the person thinking about the past) played a prominent part, the principal focus of philosophical controversy about history with a *present* or *prospective* orientation has been precisely the *thinking done by persons*—plain men or generals, statesmen, etc.—*about matters of concern to themselves*, i.e., where the personal reference is to themselves. Our subsequent discussion will adopt this focus although it is not essential to the kind of thinking involved. Specific personal reference does not dictate by whom the thinking can be done. Just as the historian can think about situations and actions from the standpoint of living in the world with personal reference to the past concerns of others so he can think about them taking what is of *present* or *prospective* concern to others as the requisite

2. Chapter IX below, esp. secs. 2 through 5.

personal reference. In the latter case, let us make it quite plain that we are speaking of "present or prospective" relative to the time when the historian engages in thinking, and the "others" referred to are his contemporaries in the strictest sense of that term.

It is worth noting two developments that have contributed to the idea of historical thinking as thinking done with present or prospective concerns in mind rather than as essentially disinterested thinking about the past. Refinement in the observation of past human occurrences disclosed the temporal perspectives that permeate man's thinking about happenings. Wilhelm Dilthey's influence in this regard was considerable, not only through his historical studies but through his generalizations about the temporal structures of lived experience, generalizations drawn from the perceptions of historians, poets, playwrights, and other acute observers. This disclosure of temporal perspectives suggested novel lines for historical inquiry. It also heightened awareness of features present in one's own thinking about happenings of personal and broad social significance alike. What began as an attempt to discover the living past, to make historical reconstructions more lifelike, yielded insight into certain characteristics of all living experience, our own included, and gave a new meaning to "history." Broadened to take in the reconstruction of the temporal structure or time-consciousness immanent in the on-going lived experience of others at some past time, "history" came to be used more and more to refer to the time-consciousness universal in human experience: lived experience as permeated by consciousness of time.

A second influential development derived from critical reflection on historical thinking, in particular from reflection upon the nature of objectivity in historical reconstructions. Disinterested, scientific objectivity having been a conscious aim of many historians in the nineteenth century, it was noticed that their present interests and personal circumstances often influenced not only the selection of areas of study in the past but also the interpretation of the material selected. The profound observation was made —at first, not surprisingly, with exaggerated claims as to its significance—that the framework of these interpretations was itself practical. The adequacy of such historical accounts could only be judged by viewing them as practical in orientation and by taking cognizance of their hidden link with practical reasoning about some *present* problem—a connection unsuspected by the historians themselves. To ask whether an interpretation was objective or not, or which was more objective, was conducive to wholesale historical scepticism when "objectivity" was construed in terms appropriate to natural order thinking. This recognition of the way practical considerations having to do with the present shaped historical reconstructions of the past encouraged a change in the concept of history itself. "History" now could mean, among other things, essentially practical thinking about the past from the standpoint of problems in the historian's present.

The two developments referred to were complementary. Together they opened the way to description or identifying understanding (and criticism) of past historiography *as* thinking from the standpoint of living in the world, the reference of which is to concerns then present or prospective. And they have reinforced critical awareness of the interdependence of temporal perspectives in those of our own historical studies which proceed from the standpoint of living in the world and have our present and prospective concerns as their frame of reference: in such historical thinking, thinking about our past is essentially connected with thinking about our present and future.

We may remark here finally upon another and somewhat special variety of historical thinking. History, we said, is sometimes thought of as embracing past, present, and future. "Human history" signifies the entire temporal course of human existence—including what is to come—or the temporal aspect of any human existence. It has sometimes been supposed that the spectacle of the whole of history or the temporal aspect of the existence of human individuals, societies, institutions, etc., poses special problems from the standpoint of living in the world: How can *any* human condition or achievement be truly valuable when all are ephemeral? How can any reliable evaluations be made of parts of history when the significance of the whole of history is not known? Can it make any appreciable difference which alternative action we choose, in view of the confusion, the cross-purposes, the transiency, the pointlessness that appear to characterize the over-all course of human history? It has been held that the solution to these problems is provided by a form of historical thinking: discovery of the underlying significance of transient existence through discovery of the meaning of history. Most historians today dissociate themselves from so ambitious an undertaking, yet we are told that it is impossible to do any kind of historical thinking at all without a "philosophy of history," and this is often taken to include a conception of the meaning of history. It is only appropriate, therefore, that we consider the contribution of this particular form of historical thinking to evaluation and practical reasoning, and that we examine its claims as a contribution to the intelligibility of particular occurrences.[3]

3. See below, chap. IX, sec. 6.

Chapter VII.

Evaluation

1. INTRODUCTION

We have provisionally characterized the standpoint of living in the world as viewing the world caringly. Some distinctive features of this standpoint as a standpoint for thinking are dealt with in this chapter, some in the chapter that follows. All thinking from the standpoint of living in the world is directed towards making judgments of preferability. We distinguish, however, between judgments of preferability in which we are *not* choosing a course of action and those in which we are. The former we are calling *evaluations;* it is these alone that we examine in this chapter.

Whether the historian transgresses the limits of professional propriety when he makes evaluations is not at issue. We are interested solely in differentiating evaluations from descriptions of an occurrence and from natural order accounts—all of which are in fact found in works classified as history.

We have spoken of evaluations as judgments as to the "merits or shortcomings" of situations, etc. We have also used the terms "satisfactory" and "satisfactoriness." This terminology is not intended to imply a criterion of evaluation. To employ "satisfactoriness" as the basic concept in a theory of valuation is not tantamount to endorsing this or that conception of "the good." Thus "satisfactory" is not assumed to be equivalent to "affording pleasure" or "affording a feeling of satisfaction." Nor does our terminology signify disregard of different types of value or of the peculiarities of rights, duties, and obligations. The expression "merits or shortcomings" has the advantage of not suggesting specific criteria of judgment, but the disadvantage of not conveying anything of an attitude of concern. "Satisfactory" and "satisfactoriness" will be used here because they are least misleading and are sufficiently indefinite not to obscure the identity of a certain fundamental line of questioning, notwithstanding differences in the way it has been carried out in various cultures and by various philosophers.

In refining upon the nature of evaluations, it will not be our purpose to indicate precisely what human conditions, ways of life, institutions, etc. are most satisfactory. Our analysis here contrasts with our handling of natural order thinking. In Part One we carefully defined natural order and made only passing reference to procedures and canons of inquiry appropriate for ascertaining natural orderliness. We shall leave the concept of "the satisfactory" indefinite and shall consider briefly (section 2) the process of thinking that leads to adequate evaluations, with particular regard to their objectivity—a major point of controversy.

In section 3 we shall consider evaluations as comparative judgments of alternative possibilities. We shall maintain that evaluation, as a fundamental way of viewing the world, involves conceiving of alternative situations, comparing these as mutually exclusive possibilities, and making a judgment about them which is intended to be objective. This will give us an opportunity to differentiate between evaluations and natural order thinking, by contrasting their respective presuppositions regarding determinism. Pressed for a provisional definition of evaluation, we could say that it is a process of thinking about occurrences from the standpoint of living in the world, a process in which intentionally objective comparative judgments are made ascribing to occurrences predicates such as "more satisfactory" or "less satisfactory," the occurrences being conceived as mutually exclusive possibilities.

2. POSSIBILITY, SCOPE, AND REQUIREMENTS OF OBJECTIVE EVALUATIONS

How are objective judgments as to the merits and shortcomings of world happenings possible?

Pre-critically, so to speak, evaluation consisted in the application of a fixed body of unquestioned principles to particular cases. By contrast, critically refined evaluation calls for continuous inquiry and re-examination with the aim of improving principles, adding new principles, rejecting old ones, reworking the relationships among principles, and so on. Principles of evaluation formerly tended to comprise relatively specific criteria as to what was preferable. The good life was formulated in one or more specific ideals: the sage, the saint, the knight, the gentleman, the financier-philanthropist. There was presumed to be a fixed scale of preferability. Such principles and assumptions were more obstructive than constructive when it came to making sound appraisals of particular situations, and especially of novel circumstances (such as those attending fundamental social, economic, and political changes). Critical principles of evaluation tend to be less specific. They are looked upon as tools for analysis of specific situations rather than as formulations of categorical criteria of the good and the bad. No rigid hierarchies of goods are acknowledged; no paradigm of the good life.

The thinking that is done in connection with reaching an evaluation can be relatively crude or elaborate, but if there is any thinking done at all it will include analysis of the situation being evaluated and application to it of warranted principles of evaluation. Refinement in valuational thinking—aside from the all-important process of developing individual insight and sensibility—takes the form of improvement in techniques of analysis and in the principles utilized. The findings of modern psychology, for example, suggest ways of ascertaining what we or others actually need or desire in particular situations—ways superior to mere introspection.[1] As to principles, methodical utilization of the various sciences of man has already yielded significant results supplementing and modifying conventional ideas of miscellaneous origin. Some principles are universal generalizations about conditions having merit in respect to fundamental human needs and goals (e.g., physical health, mental health, and maturity); others are restricted generalizations reflecting the particular forms of those fundamental needs and goals which happen to prevail at a certain time and place. All are evaluative principles.

Some generalizations employed in the process of evaluation involve no direct reference to human concerns but are used in judging what would happen under such and such conditions. These can be anything from precisely formulated deterministic generaliza-

1. Cf. Abraham Edel, *Ethical Judgment: The Use of Science in Ethics* (Glencoe, Ill.: The Free Press, 1955), chap. II. I substantially agree with the position developed by Edel. He presents arguments in support of many of the points summarily treated in this chapter. I have also adopted some of his terminology.

tions to crude rules of thumb. In combination with our ideas about what in general has merit from the standpoint of caring, these non-evaluative generalizations yield more concrete principles of evaluation. The latter take cognizance, for example, of the incompatibility under certain circumstances of two or more conditions, each having individual merit, or of the disproportionate cost under certain circumstances of attaining an otherwise "satisfactory" condition owing to the negatively evaluated "means" upon which its attainment depends deterministically or probabilistically.[2]

Principles of evaluation, as distinct from evaluations, neither constitute nor imply evaluations of any particular state of affairs. They serve to guide our thinking about particular states of affairs, helping us to judge what is, will be, or would have been satisfactory. Together with non-evaluative generalizations, they function as rules of observation, directing our attention to specific features of situations, to specific consequences of actual or contemplated circumstances, actions, policies, institutions, etc.; they function as rules of judgment for determining what is satisfactory in the light of what observation discloses. They are "principles" of evaluation in the sense that we can proceed from and according to them in making evaluations proper. Problems of evaluation which otherwise would be bewilderingly complex and therefore "indeterminate," are thereby rendered less indeterminate. Can a rational evaluation ever completely and conclusively determine what is satisfactory? The complexity of evaluation makes this more an ideal to be aimed at than a practical touchstone of the adequacy of our judgments. These principles, in combination with observations, do not usually allow us to pinpoint with certainty the relative merits or shortcomings of alternative situations, but we can nonetheless be confident that methodological evaluation and all that this implies is indispensable in reducing the indeterminacy of comparative preferabilities. In other words, it is indispensable in reducing the arbitrariness of evaluations and makes more objective our judgments of the merits and shortcomings of world happenings from the standpoint of living in the world. Not forgetting that sensitivity to values and self-understanding are likewise essential, let us make explicit that in speaking of methodological evaluation we envision

2. Included among these non-evaluative generalizations are those dealing with what Edel terms "central necessary conditions" and "critical contingent factors" (*Ethical Judgment*, pp. 302-5).

the full scientific perspective which embraces the lessons of the
human sciences from biology to history, and applies them to the
contemporary life of society and the individual, to help us fashion
a general outlook on our world and ourselves. This does not mean
that "Science gives us values." Science does not create values, only
men create values. . . . Science does not give us goals, but men use
their knowledge to broaden and refine and increasingly to achieve
their human aims. And they use their growing knowledge of
themselves to work out what their aims are and to distinguish increasingly the spurious from the genuine. A full scientific understanding thus molds their way of looking at the world. They see
themselves at every point as active creators out of the past and into
the future.[3]

Statements in historical works employing valuational terms can
obviously be very different in intent even when apparently alike
in form. They can be merely descriptive. They can be intended
to produce a certain response on the part of readers, a response
having nothing to do with the intelligibility of the human past
(e.g., to stimulate loyalty toward an institution whose role in the
past is praised by the historian). Or the historian may intend to
make an evaluation in a sense approximating our use of the term.
Our analysis incorporates the view that an historian aware of the
requirements of critical evaluation can lay claim to making objective judgments of preferability, a goal made meaningful by
tested rational procedures for reducing the indeterminacy of such
judgments. Evaluations which do not aim at objective validity are
essentially inadequate.

3. DISTINCTIVE PRESUPPOSITIONS: "POSSIBILITY" IN EVALUATIONS

By contrast with principles of evaluation, evaluations proper
are judgments of the merits and shortcomings of particular occurrences (i.e., situations, aspects of situations, effects on situations
of persons, things, institutions, etc.). They are essentially comparative judgments. Evaluations assert that such and such specific conditions are, will be, would be, were, or would have been
the most (or least) satisfactory, or more (or less) satisfactory.

3. Edel, *Ethical Judgment*, p. 339. See also John Dewey, *Theory of Valuation* (International Encyclopedia of Unified Science, Vol. II, No. 4 [Chicago,
1939]). For an example of the formulation of principles of evaluation, see
Nevitt Sanford, "What is a Normal Personality?", in *Writers on Ethics*, ed.
J. Katz, P. Nochlin, and R. Stover (Princeton, N. J.: D. Van Nostrand, 1962),
pp. 615-29.

Comparison may be tacit but it is nonetheless essential. The occurrences compared in these judgments are thought of—tacitly or explicitly—as *possibly actual* and *not necessary*. Clarifying these latter notions and their distinctive status and function in evaluation will give us an opportunity to emphasize the distinctiveness of the presuppositions of thinking from the standpoint of living in the world vis-à-vis the presuppositions of natural order thinking.

We begin by noting that *what* is more or less satisfactory must itself be a state of affairs that is, was, or will be possibly actual. One requirement of conditions that are "possibly actual" is that they be compatible with known nomological universals. Consider, for example, the following judgment: "How bad living conditions were in ancient Sparta can be judged from the fact that not a single Spartan citizen, to the best of our knowledge, was able to live a hundred years without food or water." This judgment implies that it would have been more satisfactory for certain human beings to have lived a hundred years without food or water, and compares an actual state of affairs with this hypothetical state of affairs. To such a judgment, however, we would make the retort: "More satisfactory? But such a thing is not even possible!" The "impossibility" in this case derives from established generalizations about the nourishment essential for human survival.

Evaluations proper also presuppose, however, that certain specific conditions be viewed as actual, i.e., actually actual; conditions which *are* or *were actual* or, in the case of evaluations of future occurrences, are plausibly expected *to be actual* occurrences at some future time. What we are asserting, in effect, when we evaluate, is that "For certain persons at that time and place and under certain conditions (or kinds of conditions) not only possible (in the sense indicated) but actual or presumed to be actual, it would have been more or most satisfactory if. . . ." An evaluation proper is a comparative judgment of the relative satisfactoriness of two or more different states of affairs as alternative possibilities, any of which could occur (or have occurred) under certain specified actual or predicted circumstances (viewed as actual). In making the evaluation the latter are assumed constant; the alternative possibilities constitute the terms of the comparison. The different states of affairs are evaluated *as occurring in* the situation defined by the viewed-as-actual circumstances.

To say that any particular occurrence is "possibly actual," then, means that it is a state of affairs the actual occurrence of which is consistent with warranted nomological universals *and* with those circumstances which are viewed as actual. One—or even both—of the alternative possibly actual occurrences can be an actual state of affairs past or present. Consider, for example, the evaluation "We are better off today than we would have been if antibiotics had not been developed." What is judged better (and we shall assume that "better" can plausibly be analyzed as "more satisfactory") is, in this instance, an actual state of affairs. But like the state of affairs with which it is being compared (antibiotics not at present developed), it is viewed as possibly actual relative to certain actual circumstances viewed as actual (together with nomological universals).

Evaluations proper, as expressed in everyday language (and commonly in historical writing), are superficially diverse. "We would be better off if we stayed out of the affair entirely." "We did the best possible thing under the circumstances." "Their situation at that point was about as good as they could have hoped for." "We can thank our lucky stars when we think what might have happened!" And so on. What we maintain here is that, when such statements and their intention are analyzed, we often discern a form of human thinking, appropriately termed evaluation, which is essentially a comparative judgment involving possibly actual conditions.

Evaluation is never simply a comparison of two or more actual conditions, although it often seems to be so. We do compare actual situations and judge one more satisfactory than the others. Upon closer inspection, however, we discover that possibly actual conditions are being considered in all such judgments. A judgment of satisfactoriness is about a specific situation (or kind of situation). When we compare the satisfactoriness of two or more actual conditions we are considering these as alternative possible conditions occurring in a specific situation (or kind of situation). For example: "We are certainly better off now in this seaworthy lifeboat than we were a few minutes ago, close to drowning, far out in this cold, stormy sea, poor swimmers that we are." What do I mean when I say that we are better off now than we were then? I mean that of the two conditions, both of which are possibly actual with respect to "being non-swimmers far out in a cold and stormy sea" (a specific situation), our actual condition now is better than our actual condition then. Although both are actual, i.e., one is actual and the other was, they are thought of as alternative possibilities. They are possible in the sense that their occurrence is compatible with the viewed-as-actual circumstances defining the specific situation and with natural order. The comparative judgment is meaningless apart from the concept of "possibly actual."

There are both restrictive and indeterminate aspects of the conditions that we compare in making judgments of satisfactoriness. They *must be possible* conditions. Any evaluation that is not purely speculative or hypothetical must conform to the limitations imposed by the concept of possibly actual as analyzed above.[4] On the other hand, the so-to-speak indeterminate status of the terms of comparison is implicit in the fact that evaluations are comparative judgments of the satisfactoriness of *two or more* possibly actual occurrences. Comparison requires that there be more than one. If more than one is conceived of as possible, neither can be viewed as necessary. In other words, I do not conceive of any of the alternative possibly actual states of affairs as having sufficient conditions for its occurrence. The conditions viewed-as-actual restrict what states of affairs qualify as possible, but they cannot be so restrictive as to eliminate the very condition of comparison: at least two alternative possibilities. The conditions viewed-as-actual cannot be sufficient conditions of any one "possibly actual" occurrence.

Are there or are there not sufficient conditions for the occurrence of one of the alternatives under appraisal? This is a question independent of the line of inquiry we call evaluation. There is no essential connection whatsoever between evaluating a state of affairs and judging whether or why it was necessary or impossible. This is so whether the state of affairs is one that actually happened, one that could happen, or one that is expected actually to happen. It makes no essential difference to the nature of evaluation as such which possibly actual occurrence is, was, or will be actual, and upon what sort of reasoning or evidence an assertion happens to be made to the effect that one or another possible actual occurrence is, was, or will be actually actual.

The following example will illustrate the restrictive as well as

4. Initially disregarding these limiting requirements can, to be sure, have heuristic value, opening our eyes to entirely possible actual conditions which would not readily have occurred to us as possibilities had we maintained a scrupulous regard for what we supposed was possibly actual. But even then, unless the conditions which are compared are ultimately conceived of as possibly actual, we do not have an evaluation proper.

the indeterminate aspects of states of affairs viewed-as-actual. "How satisfactory was the situation of the Mayflower colonists after their first year in the New World?" Are we to assume, as actually actual, the location of the colonists in New England, and that "satisfactory" means satisfactory under the climatic conditions and other circumstances to which they were exposed once they decided to settle there? Or are we allowed to compare their actual condition with their possibly actual situation if they had settled anywhere else along the Atlantic Coast, perhaps finding a welcome from friendly Indians to the south where the climate was also more benign? If the former, then the possibilities for satisfactory conditions are more limited. They become still more limited if we view as one of the actual conditions the attitudes of the Indians actually encountered by the New England settlers, but we could just as well compare the relative satisfactoriness of the colonists' actual situation with what it might have been—still in New England— had the Indians been much friendlier or, as the case may be, more actively hostile than they in fact were. Wherever the lines are drawn as to which actual conditions are to be regarded as actual, *some* possibilities must remain in order for an evaluation to be made. Any judgment as to how well off the colonists actually were presupposes such possibilities.

These possibilities, considered within the framework of the standpoint of evaluation, are equally possible. Reckoning with the sufficient conditions (or even the probability) of the colonists' *actual* choice of a site, their *actual* mode of administering the colony, their *actual* encounters with Indians, disease, and so on, is quite irrelevant to the logic of evaluation. *All* that evaluation presupposes is that any of at least two conditions be judged possible relative to certain conditions viewed as actual. Working with these possibilities in applying techniques and principles of evaluation, the thinking that issues in a judgment of satisfactoriness at no point involves a judgment as to whether or why one thing or another was bound to happen (or was likely to happen). The coming about of one of the alternative possibilities is never judged to be or presumed to be necessary; whether it is necessary or not is a question that does not even arise—from this standpoint.

It may be remarked that the idea of actual states of affairs as limiting (i.e., restrictive) conditions and the idea of alternative possibilities are ideas common to deterministic thinking as well as to evaluation. This tends to obscure essential differences between the two standpoints: natural order and living in the world. The distinctive status and function of the concept of "possibility" in evaluational thinking should therefore be stressed.

To begin with, we may recall that evaluation presupposes some orderliness in the way some things happen. Specific empirically grounded knowledge of natural order controls our acknowledgment or our rejection of a state of affairs as *possibly* actual; a state of affairs that is judged nomologically impossible under the viewed-as-actual circumstances is rejected accordingly. But we have seen that with regard to occurrences acknowledged to be possibly actual, evaluation involves no implicit claim or presupposition to the effect that one or another of these will or did necessarily come to pass. Nor, certainly, is an explicit assertion called for to the effect that one or the other will or did necessarily come to pass. Natural order thinking, by contrast, postulates the necessity of particular happenings—past, present, and future—and the corresponding impossibility of alternative occurrences. The natural order line of questioning fulfills its goal in disclosing the necessity of occurrences.

Deterministic thinking does make use of the concept of alternative possibility, but we must note carefully how it is used. For example, in trying to ascertain the sufficient conditions of a particular occurrence which in fact occurred, I may ask myself whether the occurrence would have occurred in the absence of a certain circumstance which I know to have been a fact. This device is intended to help me conclude whether the circumstance in question was or was not among the sufficient conditions of the particular occurrence. In using it I must think of alternative possibly actual occurrences, i.e., of what did happen and what would have happened under different circumstances. It is to be noted, however, that in *this* consideration of what might have happened under contrary-to-fact circumstances, my intention is to disclose a deterministic relationship among states of affairs. Evaluation, by contrast, does not presuppose possibilities as a device for disclosing why what in fact happened necessarily happened; it presupposes possibilities in view of judging satisfactoriness. At no stage of evaluational thinking is this presupposition of possibilities abandoned. From the standpoint of living in the world, thinking of occurrences as alternative possibilities is an *ultimate* presupposition.

A particular occurrence or state of affairs evaluated as more or less satisfactory is, *so judged,* neither necessary nor impossible.

From what has been said we might be led to assume an absolute incompatibility between the presuppositions of deterministic thinking (i.e., thinking from the natural order standpoint) and evaluation (i.e., thinking from the standpoint of living in the world). Determinism is a presumption of deterministic thinking. Is not indeterminism a presupposition of evaluation? Is not my thinking of two or more occurrences as alternative possibilities tantamount to judging that either one of them (though not of course both) could have happened or could happen *all things considered?* By no means. In evaluating I do not presuppose that if we were to inquire after the sufficient conditions of what actually occurred—the actually actual—our inquiry *must* fail. I do not presuppose that, as regards future occurrences, it is impossible to make deterministic predictions as to which of the "possibly actual" occurrences will come about. I do not so much as raise a doubt about the appropriateness of determinism as a regulative principle of inquiry into why particular occurrences happen. We conclude that in evaluation some occurrences are neither thought about deterministically nor regarded as subject to the general presumption of determinism.

Broadly speaking, the whole issue of universal determinism lies outside of the scheme of intelligibility of thinking from the standpoint of living in the world, at least as far as evaluation is concerned. This allows for the compatibility of the two schemes of intelligibility: the presumption of determinism being integral to the natural order scheme of thinking; indifference to the issue of universal determinism being an essential characteristic of the scheme of evaluation. But compatibility, we must remind ourselves, is not equivalent to interrelatedness. When someone asserts that a certain state of affairs would have been highly satisfactory but was impossible owing to such and such circumstances, we overlook the disparity in the presuppositions of the two parts of the assertion. The evaluation "highly satisfactory" presupposes alternative possibilities under certain circumstances and is systematically independent of the necessity or impossibility of those alternatives—"necessity" or "impossibility," that is, in respect to *all* determining conditions. That we do blithely make assertions of this sort, juxtaposing evaluations with natural order accounts, only testifies to the fact that we do unwittingly think about the world in fundamentally distinct ways.

Only compatibility then, but at least that. There is no vexatious problem for philosophy in the fact that we find it plausible to think of the world in ways which intercross, which borrow from one another, but which diverge when pursued single-mindedly, imposing their distinctive presuppositions.

Chapter VIII.

Rational Action

Past Concerns of Others

1. INTRODUCTION

In Part One we argued that all occurrences of the human past are subject to natural order inquiry. From the inexhaustible wealth of possible subject matter of natural order historiography we selected rational actions for particular attention. The main point of our discussion of rational action in Part One was to establish that natural orderliness extends no less to rational actions than to the physiological processes of the human body or the transformations of energy in a steam engine. In this Part our interest is in the relevance to historical thinking of rational action viewed from the standpoint of living in the world.

Chapter VIII begins with a description of rational action as viewed from the agent's own standpoint as living in the world (section 2). The difference between this and natural order thinking is then treated, providing further evidence of the distinctiveness of the two standpoints of human thinking (section 3). The remainder of the chapter deals with historical thinking of past rational actions where the personal reference is to the agent's own concerns at the time of the rational action (the agent in question conventionally being a person other than the historian himself). Although this is a common form of historical thinking, the standpoint involved is seldom made explicit and the presuppositions of the standpoint are not clearly apprehended and not clearly differentiated from those of natural order thinking—circumstances conducive to controversy.

2. RATIONAL ACTION FROM THE STANDPOINT OF THE AGENT

What interests us initially are the presuppositions and structure of the thinking that a person does when he is deliberating about *what* to do or *how* to proceed, or criticizing his decision to act in a certain way. Our analysis applies to deliberations and criticisms which are so matter of course, so condensed, so fleeting that persons are scarcely aware of them. Our analysis also applies to deliberations and criticisms which, although conscientiously elaborated, are judged by competent observers to be out-and-out rationalizations. Provisionally we shall identify the person deliberating with the agent himself, and consider him as deliberating about an action *to be done* by him (perhaps in conjunction with others). Thus we shall be considering practical judgments in which a person concludes as to the appropriateness of a particular course of action in which he will be engaged at or during a specified time in the future. Correspondingly we shall identify the critic as the agent himself re-examining the wisdom of a choice already made, retaining the reference to his concerns as the agent of that intended rational action (whether it was executed or not). Criticism of rational action, however, presents some special complications which we shall deal with separately in a subsequent section (section 5); our principal focus here will be on deliberation.

Questions about what I should do and judgments about what should be done arise for me as living in the world, as caring about what happens, caring questioningly: What shall I do? How shall I proceed? Was that what I should have done? For convenience, when these questions are being asked from the standpoint of living in the world, we shall speak of the "standpoint of the agent" and of its correlate, the "practical world." The world is "practically" intelligible as comprising times and places for me to do or not to do something, to go on or to stop doing, to change or not to change myself or my relationships to things and others. I am the center of my practical world. I view it in terms of the *possibility of my* doing, acting, making. I am going to be the person who did this and not that. I think of the world as organized with reference to the effects of my possibly doing or not doing, etc. Whether or not I do something makes a difference in how the world will be.

I face this possibility with a retrospective view of what the relevant world has actually been like up to now.

Of my many concurrent practical relations to the world, some are brief and fragmentary, some long-standing and continuous. Some are in the forefront of my field of attention, some are peripheral. In a larger sense, the practical world is not confined to things with which and persons with whom I am now or have been or expect to be practically related. Much of the world having no direct practical relevance, it does not figure in my practical considerations. But even this "making no practical difference" is itself a practical relation, presupposing that *other* things in the world *are* practically significant, *are* matters of practical concern.

Who am I? From the standpoint of practical awareness I think of myself as something "in" the practical world, conscious of it as having the features we have been describing and conscious of myself as having definite characteristics as well as indefinite possibilities. Uncertainties I may have, but I am not totally confused about my situation in the practical world. A person who does not know some of his definite characteristics—who he is, where he is, what time it is, what he is doing—is more than practically disoriented; he is not "in" the practical world. He cannot even pursue the line of questioning that constitutes practical reasoning. His experience can make no practical sense; it is void of practical intelligibility.

A presupposition of the intelligibility of my practical world, then, is that I, aware of myself as a being with certain physical qualities, structural and behavioral characteristics, find myself in the spatio-temporal world of things and persons, viewing it in the light of my possibilities—the things I can do to make a difference in myself or in the world.

An extensive survey of the many things I can do would be pointless. We shall only make a few comments. Situations which we think about practically need not, of course, be "ours" alone. When I express practical interest in the deplorable situation of others, their situation becomes mine; it centers upon me in the sense that I am considering what I shall do about it. Often the action I judge appropriate is an action by someone else, my only problem being to find the best way to get him to do it. In such cases the deliberate persuasion which I exercise, my use of force or my having recourse to legal counsel in order to get him to do something, is my rational action. Doubtless most of my activities are social; either they are carried on co-operatively or they involve a concern with the effects on others. But the fundamental idea that the world of our own rational action is centered about us as individual human beings is not qualified by these social aspects of our doing. Similarly, our practical world is pervasively institutionalized, but the characteristic formality and impersonality of institutions does not qualify the self-centered character of the practical standpoint.

Finally, the concept of "doing" or "action" is comprehensive; it is intended to encompass all modes of activity which can be viewed in terms of feasibility, a concept to be clarified shortly.[1]

Whether deliberation is explicit or implicit, perfunctory or elaborate, crude or precise, rational action from the standpoint of the agent involves intending to act consistently with a judgment in which a particular course of action is apprehended as fulfilling the requirements of a practical principle. By practical principle we mean any rule or set of rules for determining what to do or how to proceed. The form of a practical principle is as follows: "The thing to do or the way to proceed in situation S is that one which satisfies requirements R_1 , . . . , R_n." The judgment—we shall call it a practical judgment—in which deliberation (ideally) terminates, takes the form: "I am in situation s; e uniquely satisfies requirements R_1 , . . . , R_n of the relevant practical principle P; therefore, the thing to do is e." Where a practical principle (or composite of several principles) leaves us with alternative courses of action, we are obliged to supplement the principle until we decide rationally what to do. In a "toss-up" situation, "winning the toss" may even be incorporated as one of the requirements of the practical principle by which we choose; or, following some other appropriate principle for handling such problems, we may judge it better to refrain from action, doing nothing for the time being.

So conceived, deliberation and criticism can be said to take place in connection with a great many different kinds of action, many of them trivial. I can be said to deliberate about when to do my shopping, about which step to take next in the process of putting together a Chinese wood-block puzzle, about whether to

1. We thus exclude many things our internal organs "do." On the other hand, we include not only coping with the environment in direct and obviously life-serving ways (seeking food, shelter, protection from physical danger, and so on) but such activities as education, therapy, playing games, making and enforcing laws, and engaging in deterministic historical thinking. These activities, we say, can be viewed in terms of feasibility.

go to my destination on foot or by bicycle, about whom to vote for in an election, about the best way of setting up a scientific experiment, about whether to accept or refuse a job, about how to commit suicide, about whether or not to launch a nuclear attack. Innumerable examples offer themselves from the activities of artists, engineers, farmers, soldiers, bankers, athletes, etc.

The practical principles utilized in deliberate actions can be of the most diverse sorts. They can be rules of neutral meaning systems (such as natural and artificial languages), of institutionalized culture systems (in such areas as public law, education, the military, banking and stock marketing, organized athletics), or rules of organizations and formalized activities of lesser scope (anything from the by-laws of corporations to rules about permissible behavior at the family dinner table). They can be concerned solely with the selection of a means to an unquestioned end-in-view. Ends-in-view can be theoretical or practical, "moral" or "immoral." A principle can require that we take the consequences of our prospective action into account, or can direct us to act irrespective of consequences. Thus the categorical imperative "Thou shall not lie!" can function as a practical principle (provided it is not a command obeyed under duress), but so can the "utilitarian" maxim: "Act so as to maximize the happiness of the greatest number of living creatures." Some principles are essentially auxiliary in that their function is to guide the agent in interpreting, applying, or constructing other principles. Finally, principles of these diverse sorts may be more or less systematically and consciously interrelated.

The soundness or unsoundness of the practical principles employed in deliberation is for the moment not germane. All that is essential, formally speaking, is that a person intend to ascertain what course of action is the thing to do, i.e., the one particular course of action satisfying the requirements of the practical principle applicable to the given situation. And if an action is done *as* "the thing to do," in accordance with a judgment, tacit or explicit, by way of a practical principle, we shall call it a *rational action.*

"Action" includes occurrences sometimes called "mental acts." It would be a mistake to suppose that as agents we only deliberate concerning overt behavior. I can deliberate, for example, about how to solve a quadratic equation, how to determine the volume of a cylinder, or how to solve a mathematical puzzle, provided that I work out the solution (and this, in these instances, is the action) by applying mathematical principles and general rules of procedure. Obviously, in working out problems in pure mathematics or formal logic the practical world, or at least the foreground, that part of it that "matters," narrows to my train of thought—to the occurrence of my getting the solution. Even though I regard my solution to such problems as having extensive practical applications, these need not matter in the context of the mathematical or logical problem-solving.

"Caring to do the appropriate thing" does not imply that we enjoy doing what is appropriate, let alone that "what is appropriate" is tantamount to "what we enjoy." In mathematical puzzle-solving, for example, strictly speaking the aim of the practically oriented caring, the object of the practical deliberation, is getting the right answer. We need to distinguish between this object of caring and "caring for" in the sense of "liking to do" puzzles. The right answer, the answer cared for, is the one that "satisfies" the requirements of the puzzle that a person is engaged in doing. Why it is cared for or whether satisfaction will ensue upon getting the right answer, are irrelevant to the rational action of "solving the puzzle." As rational agents we can be emotionally indifferent to the action to be done; we may even look upon the action as unpleasant. Nor does caring imply that any vital interests, any convictions about what is worthwhile in life, any considerations or feelings of moral responsibility or obligation are involved. We often reason concerning what to do within a certain problematic situation without first making sure that it is really worth bothering about.

Rational action need not be a response to a felt perplexity or uncertainty. Assigned to work out a problem which obviously requires practical reasoning, I may see straightaway what practical principles to apply and how to apply them. Where there *is* uncertainty, it can derive from quite different circumstances: I may be pricked by my conscience, criticized by another person, advised to do something obnoxious to me or at odds with my principles. Having committed myself to do something I may encounter obstacles; or an obligation may conflict with my inclinations. Perhaps I have just discovered a new and appealing "experience," a different style of living or an alternative way of doing something: I must think whether to pursue this or not. I feel an urge to experiment, to broaden my horizons, to seek my fortune: How shall

I set about this? I feel sympathy for someone in trouble, resentful, or vengeful: What should I do about it?

There are important differences between those instances of deliberation in which the only question is "In situation s what occurrence e satisfies the requirements of principle P?" and cases in which preliminary stages of deliberation are required wherein, always proceeding in accordance with practical principles, a person ascertains which among various already known and accepted practical principles applies or from which accepted practical principles a practical principle can be constructed that is applicable to the specific situation.

What is deliberated about is *something that is to happen*—something that is to occur at a certain time and place, namely, my action. Deliberation is a thinking about occurrences. *This* thinking about occurrences, however, is not directed at ascertaining what is to take place by referring to nomological universals and determining conditions. Instead, as we have seen, it is directed at ascertaining which happening (an action on the part of the agent deliberating) is *appropriate*.

We shall now look more closely at the agent's view of rational action, keeping in mind our conception of deliberation as issuing in a judgment to the effect that "e is the thing to do or the way to proceed because it alone satisfies the requirements of the relevant practical principle P." From the standpoint of the agent, the *reason* for e's being the thing to do is that e alone satisfies the requirements of that principle which is judged relevant. What he is to do is intelligible from the agent's standpoint as that action, selected from among various alternative courses of action, which he intends to do because, thinking about the world caringly, he judges it the appropriate thing to do.

3. "Could do otherwise" from the Standpoint of the Agent

The intention of deliberation is to ascertain what we shall do by ascertaining what we should do, i.e., what action is appropriate. In deliberating, the thing we shall do—an occurrence at a particular place, at or during a particular time—is not thought of deterministically. This means that in deliberating we do not pursue the kind of thinking we have called natural order thinking with regard to that particular occurrence—our future specific action; nor do we incorporate into our thinking any available natural order account (i.e., prediction) of that occurrence. It is an essential characteristic of deliberation that it not include any natural order account whatsoever of the agent's specific action. A corollary of this is that in deliberating, the agent's own specific action is not among the circumstances which the agent thinks of as necessarily or probably actual at a future time, namely at or subsequent to the time when he will be acting; nor is it thought of (except hypothetically) as a determining condition of any of these predicted circumstances. The agent thinks of himself as going to do a certain *kind* of action, but he does not think of himself as necessarily or probably going to do this or that *specific* act.

From the agent's standpoint the question is: What course of action is *appropriate*? He seeks to ascertain a characteristic of a course of action which natural order thinking could not possibly establish. The deliberating agent can only answer this distinctive question by, as it were, filling in the concept of what he will actually do (the *specific* act) on the basis of a consideration of appropriateness. If he is to engage in practical reasoning at all, the concept of his specific action must be indefinite, must be partially "open," because at least some descriptive predicates delimiting the specific act to be done are to be ascertained by practical reasoning, namely, the predicates describing those features of the act by virtue of which it—rather than any alternative course of action—is the thing to do.

Clearly then, there are two distinct ways in which we think about what is to happen. One: on the basis of our knowledge of circumstances and relevant nomological knowledge we think about what will necessarily or probably occur. The other: on the basis of a practical principle we think about what it would be appropriate to do in a given situation. Obviously if my concept of "what I shall do" completely specifies my action, I cannot deliberate, i.e., I cannot engage in practical reasoning directed toward establishing which specific action meets the requirements of appropriateness. Indefiniteness is systematically required of the concept of the act to be done in order for there to be thinking about "the thing to do," in order for us to think deliberatively about what is to happen.

Consideration of what *can* be done is, however, also essential. Deliberation directed to action *requires* that "the thing to do" be judged *feasible*. In the context of deliberation, the agent must think of himself as actually able to carry out the action if it should be judged in all respects the thing to do. (Retrospectively, he looks upon it as something he could have done had he judged it appropriate). To consider an action feasible is to judge that its occurrence is consistent with certain actual states of affairs, environmental and personal, and with established nomological universals pertinent to the future of these states of affairs. What circumstances the agent takes into consideration vary, of course, from case to case. Speaking generally we can say that an agent judges what is feasible on the basis of what he considers relevant environmental factors—available resources and obstacles—and what he thinks he is personally capable of doing as determined by such factors as his health, strength, knowledge, fortitude, financial resources, political influence, etc. In any case, for an agent to judge an action feasible he must not merely judge that the requisite resources are available and that there are no external hindrances, not merely that *if* his attitude (or any other personal trait) were such and such, he then could manage to do the act; rather he must consider that he could actually carry it out *providing only* that it be judged the thing to do.

If I were to ask: "What specific actions can I do in this situation, *all things considered?*" I would institute a line of questioning which, in principle, would issue not merely in a judgment about what is possible but what is necessary. Every specific trait of what I will actually do would be judged necessary. In pursuing that line of questioning, peculiar to natural order thinking, it would be presumed that if we knew enough about the circumstances and about natural order, our inquiry would terminate in a judgment as to exactly what I am bound to do. In deliberation, by contrast, inquiry into or judgment about what is feasible is restricted. For an agent seeks to ascertain not simply what actions would be feasible but which feasible act is appropriate. Appropriateness is never equivalent to feasibility alone. And, as we have seen, judging which action is appropriate requires that the agent work from an indefinite concept of the act to be done. The specification of the concept is effected by reference to a practical principle, not to natural order. In practical reasoning, feasible necessarily means possible; it never means necessary. Whenever the issue of feasibility is raised from the standpoint of the agent—and it is by no means always explicitly raised—consideration as to what I can or cannot do logically *ex-*

cludes taking cognizance of all determining conditions of my action.[2]

We conclude that the rational agent thinks that he could do the appropriate thing *or do otherwise* than the appropriate thing. Essential restrictions upon deterministic thinking stem from the nature of practical reasoning: choosing among feasible alternatives on grounds of appropriateness. The presuppositions of thinking from the standpoint of living in the world, whether evaluations or practical reasoning, thus differ from those of natural order (or deterministic) thinking; but they differ in such a way as to allow for compatibility. Compatibility, however, as pointed out above, is not equivalent to interrelatedness within a unifying scheme of intelligibility. It is just this lack of unifying scheme that makes it plausible to speak of the radical pluralism of historical thinking.

4. The Historian and the Standpoint of the Agent

The viewpoint of the agent toward his rational action is not that of an historian who accounts for it in terms of determining conditions, i.e., in terms of natural order. In the latter case, the aim of the historian's line of questioning is a natural order account of the type discussed in Part One. For the agent, the act was "the thing to do."

In the context of thinking from the natural order standpoint, presenting the agent's reasons for doing what he did, and tracing any practical cogitation involved in the agent's discernment of the course of action meeting requirements of the judged-to-be-relevant practical principle, constitute *description* of *what happened*—description that is requisite to giving an account of the determining conditions of the course of action. It constitutes what we called the ancillary function of *descriptive understanding*: a description of meaning relations in the service of (in this case) a natural order account of an occurrence. "Understanding the reasons for the action" only sets the stage for a natural order inquiry. The natural order account discloses why this particular occurrence took place (or could have been expected with a certain probability) then and there; it makes the described occurrence intelligible.

Descriptive understanding of meanings (here: the meaning

2. In practice, deliberation seldom proceeds by *first* establishing which acts are feasible, *then* establishing which among them is most appropriate. But even though commonly carried out concurrently, the two operations—judging feasibility and judging appropriateness—have the relationship indicated.

relations in a process of practical reasoning) can serve natural order thinking, but in saying this we do not give an adequate account of the significance of "understanding an agent's reasons" for the intelligibility of particular occurrences. What we have neglected to consider is *identifying understanding* of rational action. And closely related to (a) identifying understanding of rational action as a way in which the historian thinks about past occurrences, are (b) the historian's thinking about what *would have* constituted sound practical reasoning on the part of a person who was confronted with a choice but resolved the situation in some way other than by practical reasoning, and (c) the historian's *criticizing* an agent's practical reasoning. Of the latter two, (c) presupposes identifying understanding of practical reasoning and (b) presupposes identifying understanding of the personal concerns of the person who, even if he did not think his way to a decision about what to do, nonetheless confronted the world as questionable from the standpoint of living in the world: the world posed for him the question "What shall I do?" or "How shall I proceed?" We shall confine our attention here largely to (a). The special problems involved in the criticism of rational agents will be dealt with later (section 5). Since (b) presents no difficulties once (a) and (c) have been discussed, we shall not treat it independently. Agents often criticize their own actions. The historian's identifying understanding of such criticism also presents no particular difficulties. The focus of our discussion of identifying understanding will be the historian's understanding of the agent's *deliberation,* i.e., his practical reasoning with the intent to act, rather than his self-criticism.

Descriptive understanding, in the form of understanding an agent's thinking, can serve natural order thinking about rational actions *or* it can serve identifying understanding of rational actions. It is convenient to distinguish "finding out what happened" as a preliminary phase of natural order inquiry, a phase to which descriptive understanding belongs. Once the historian knows what happened (what action was taken by the rational agent and—descriptive understanding—what his reasoning process was in deciding to do what he did), he looks for natural order in these occurrences. The latter phase is natural order inquiry properly speaking. By comparison, in the case of identifying understanding as a way rational actions are intelligible, the "second phase" is not one of further questioning or inquiry, but consists simply in the historian's taking a distinctive view of what happened. The latter makes all the difference. It is easy to miss the significance of this "taking a distinctive view" and to confuse descriptive understanding and identifying understanding. The essential difference is that in the latter we—historian or reader—regard the agent's *way* of thinking about the world and making it intelligible as the same *way* in which particular occurrences of *our* respective practical worlds can be intelligible to us and similarly for all human beings. Not that all men always act rationally, but that whenever a human being does act rationally the occurrence of that act is universally intelligible as the thing he thought to be the appropriate thing to have done.

Why did just that occur then and there? Answer: It was thought to be the thing to have done. We regard the rational actions of others as "accounted for," as "intelligible," when we know what mattered to them, what their reasoning was, and when, as fellow human beings, we *identify* with the way a person confronted and thought about the world. When these conditions are fulfilled it is plausible to say that we not only understand what went on, what happened, but we know why it happened. When reasons are cited with identifying understanding, the citing of reasons is not merely descriptive in import nor is it to be confused with the descriptive content of a deterministic account. It constitutes a distinctive form of intelligibility. "Citing reasons" *can* thus be a distinctive way of establishing why something happened—why precisely that action precisely then and there.

Identifying understanding of rational action does not presuppose that the standpoint of the agent as a way of thinking was consciously and accurately differentiated by the rational agent himself, any more than it presupposes that the agent's practical reasoning was sound. Actual practical reasoning is like actual natural order thinking in that it is mostly neither consciously differentiated nor adequately carried out by persons thinking about happenings of the world in these ways. The way of thinking is recognizably in operation even when the thinker was confused about standpoints, even when it seems obvious to us that mistakes were made as to what was the thing to do.

It has generally been supposed that there is but one characteristic way in which historians make occurrences intelligible. It has also been supposed that this historical way of viewing occurrences is peculiarly close to that of everyday life.[3] What light does our discussion shed on these notions?

To begin with, our analysis has taken note of a special ambiguity about "describing" what happened in those cases where the happening is a rational action. Depending upon how the description of rational action is intended and interpreted, a description *can* be a way of accounting for what happened. Unless the difference between descriptive and identifying understanding is grasped, it is impossible to assess the claim made in some monistic analyses of historical thinking that historians characteristically disclose the *why* of occurrences *by describing*, i.e., by providing a detailed account of *what* happened. Whether this claim is correct or not depends upon the meaning of "why," upon what sort of phenomena the historian is describing, and upon the viewpoint assumed by historian or reader toward the description. Only in the case of a description of thinking (here: practical reasoning) regarded identifyingly from the standpoint of the agent is the description a disclosure of "why" in the sense that, beyond merely stating what happened, the account presents the agent's action as the subject of a judgment (here: the agent's) that terminates a fundamental line of human questioning about the world.

We have now seen that there are two ways of accounting for particular occurrences. No one will dispute that both ways are encountered in the works of historians. Is one or the other of these to be singled out as "history proper"? Even if this were done on some pretext, it would still be important to bear in mind that historians actually do both sorts of thinking, important to avoid inferring that particular occurrences of the human past *can* only be accounted for in one way, or that one way is intrinsically more appropriate, more adequate. Taking these precautions, one finds it easy to understand why occasionally historians come forth fired with the idea of pursuing single-mindedly one or the other of these ways of thinking. Such specialization may not be common, but it has a firm foundation in the distinctions between the two ways.

It is common practice these days to show how people come by their ideas, including their practical principles, and how various

3. See, e.g., William Dray, *Laws and Explanation in History* (London: Oxford University Press, 1957), pp. 124, 138; Isaiah Berlin, "History and Theory: The Scientific Concept of History," *History and Theory*, I, No. 1 (1960), 20, 30; John Passmore, "Explanation in Everyday Life, in Science, and in History," *History and Theory*, II, No. 2 (1962), 106-10.

internal and external influences shape their practical decisions. In opposition to this approach, there are some thinkers sensitive to the violation of the standpoint of the agent that is involved when remarks about the determining conditions of an agent's deliberations are introduced into an account of his decision even in the most casual way. To be sure, there are many interrelationships between practical thinking and deterministic thinking. Not infrequently one takes place within the context of the other. The very principles of action utilized by the agent in practical reasoning may call for him to be on guard against his own blind prejudices and unruly passions. Remarks by an historian regarding determining conditions of the agent's deliberation are alien to identifying understanding, however, when they are intended to account for the latter's practical reasoning in natural order terms. They are alien because cognizance of determining conditions of his practical reasoning enters into the practical reasoning of the agent only in the form of judgments made by him about the possible distortion of his practical reasoning by his prejudices, passions, etc., and about how to avoid this. Deliberation does not consist in a natural order accounting for itself; neither then does identifying understanding. We have seen that inquiry into the determining conditions of a rational action is not merely not of interest at the time to the agent who is deciding what to do; a limitation on natural order accounting is an essential requirement of practical reasoning. The natural order thinker presumes that the agent must decide to do and must do a specific action. The agent thinks of himself as able to do otherwise.

Our analysis discloses that there is a basis for distinctive specialized accounts of particular human occurrences corresponding to the fundamentally different ways the world is questionable for us. We have noted that thinking from the standpoint of living in the world presupposes personal reference whereas natural order thinking does not, and that the presumption of determinism characteristic of natural order thinking is not applicable to evaluation or to practical reasoning. The extraordinarily interesting fact remains that we find the same historian sometimes adopting the standpoint of the agent and sometimes that of natural order. This is one way in which the historian's thinking resembles our thinking in everyday life. In everyday life we are not specialists. We pass from one standpoint to the other a thousand times a day without any hesitation or sense of discontinuity. Like many an historian, we use both.

The actions of those around us are rendered intelligible just as indiscriminately as many historians combine deterministic-type assertions about rational actions with identifying understanding. In short, one could say that the thinking we do in everyday life and the thinking of many historians manifest the same incoherence; incoherence in the sense that the presuppositions of the respective schemes of intelligibility differ: they cannot be derived from one another, and they cannot be shown to complement one another within the unifying perspective of a still more fundamental way of thinking. This incoherence is not naive; quite the contrary. Instead of being resolved by philosophical reflection, it is revealed and affirmed by the latter.

Another way of looking at the matter is that the indiscriminate thinking of some historians, in common with the thinking of everyday life, is more adequate than specialized thinking, more adequate in the sense that it embraces both of these human ways of accounting for particular occurrences. We have seen that the frequently-made allegations to the effect that natural order thinking (usually under the rubric "science") is characteristically abstract, does not stand up when construed to mean that there can be no natural order explanation of particular occurrences. It is defensible, however, when duly reinterpreted: natural order intelligibility *does* leave something out. But the corollary would not be the one proclaimed by many partisans of historical "understanding," namely, that it is the latter which, by contrast with "science," avoids abstraction and affords intelligibility of human existence in all its concreteness. Our analysis emphasizes limitations of *both* ways of thinking; affirmation of the inadequacy of either one as *the* intelligible account of a rational action is justified by recognition that the other is just as fundamentally human.

There is, finally, another respect in which historical thinking often resembles our everyday thinking about happenings: both are prone to be vague. In both, statements that are made about particular rational actions are vague as to intended meaning and, consequently, in what they are understood to mean. Even when there is awareness of the difference between two ways of accounting for occurrences, the specific intention of a given statement is not always successfully communicated. Vagueness only becomes a liability, however, when a question arises which calls for critical awareness. A prime example is the question with which we are dealing: What is the nature of historical thinking? But there are other questions that call for critical differentiation of our ways of thinking, questions which straddle historical practice and life-situations; notably, the questions about freedom and responsibility that we shall discuss in the following section.

If, indeed, coherent accounts of rational actions are of two distinct sorts, and if historians combine these indiscriminately, there is little to wonder at in the conflicting claims regarding the nature of "history proper." The fuzziness of language and the conventionally relaxed logical demands that characterize so much historical writing do have their counterpart in everyday thinking. But this in no way alters the fundamental diversity of standpoints. This diversity underlies the logical incoherence readily discernible in historical works, once we know what to look for, and dooms to futility all efforts to discover the essence of what historians ordinarily do.

5. "CRITICISMS" AND STANDPOINTS

In actual historical writing identifying understanding is often conjoined with criticism, but not all of the critical judgments made by historians of the actions of others have the orientation of identifying understanding. With differences in orientation go differences in presupposition; when these differences pass unnoticed, the result is controversy among historians about the appropriateness or soundness of this or that particular critical judgment, and controversy among philosophers of history about the appropriateness of any or all critical judgments in historiography.

Our topic here is the historian's criticism of rational actions or of persons as agents involved in particular occurrences. One of the principal issues to be discussed is whether or not agents are morally responsible for their actions. We shall find that the "indeterminism" presupposed in some criticism of rational actions has the same form as the "indeterminism" presupposed in evaluation and deliberation, i.e., a restriction upon deterministic thinking essential to the standpoint of living in the world. It is not a characteristic of occurrences in themselves, but rather a qualification of that presumption of determinism which regulates natural order inquiry. We shall find, furthermore, that although criticism of various sorts is appropriate, moral praise and blame, as these are often construed, are not appropriate.

In discussing criticisms of rational action it will be helpful to distinguish different senses in which actions are judged "reasonable" and in which persons are deemed "responsible" for what has happened, as well as some different types of criticism. We can begin by noting that some judgments to the effect that a person did or did not act reasonably (judgments which would not usually be called criticisms) are *descriptive* in intent. They are characterizing judgments, neither providing a natural order account, nor an evaluation, nor—as we shall maintain—a criticism from the standpoint of rational action.[4] I can be said to *describe* a person's action as reasonable when my judgment "*x* behaved reasonably" answers the question: "Is the way *x* behaved an instance of reasonable behavior?", i.e., does it meet the requirements of a certain concept of reasonable behavior (for example, the person's own concept or the prevailing view at that time)? Similarly, a judgment to the effect that "*x* was responsible" is descriptive when it is intended to assert solely that his behavior, status, or circumstances being what they were, the person was responsible in a sense of the term defined, for example, by the concepts and application rules of a certain legal system. If, according to the latter, "being responsible" is equivalent to "being a determining factor of an occurrence," then it suffices to know that the person was in some way a determinant: the description applies. The descriptive judgment does not assert that *x* was a determining factor of an occurrence; it presupposes this. A similar type of descriptive judgment, not to be confused with evaluation proper, characterizes an act or its consequences as "satisfactory" in relation to a certain concept of "satisfactoriness."

Other judgments to the effect that persons were responsible—judgments which probably also would not be termed criticisms—assert precisely what some descriptions of "reasonable" or "responsible" behavior presuppose: they assert that the persons were determining factors of an occurrence. These are natural order accounts. In these judgments, "being responsible for an occurrence" may or may not be used in a narrower sense, i.e., so as to apply only to persons who acted deliberately and whose deliberation determined the occurrence.

Of the judgments so far mentioned—descriptive judgments in which "behaved reasonably" means "acted deliberately," "evaluative" characterizations of the consequences of actions, and natural order judgments in which "responsibly" implies "having been a

4. See Ernest Nagel, *The Structure of Science* (New York: Harcourt, Brace and World, 1961), pp. 492 ff.

determinant"—all obviously can apply to rational action. None of these types of judgments, however, is criticism from the standpoint of living in the world. The judgments we shall now consider also assert a person's reasonableness, unreasonableness, or responsibility; they are more likely to be called criticisms, and they *are* plausibly analyzed as criticisms from the standpoint of living in the world. We shall distinguish three types: evaluations (*Ce*); criticisms from the standpoint of the agent (*Ca*), and praising and blaming (*Cpb*).

Irrespective of whether the deliberation was sound or not, we evaluate how a deliberate action turned out: Were the consequences satisfactory or not, judged by objective criteria, compared with the consequences to have been expected had other courses of action been taken? To ask "How satisfactory were the results?" or "Was the choice a happy one considering how it actually turned out?" is to ask for an evaluation, i.e., a judgment from the standpoint of caring but not one that involves essential reference to the practical reasoning of the agent. Unsound practical reasoning can lead to actions that turn out well. Sound reasoning may be nullified by freakish eventualities. That the result of our rational action was satisfactory or unsatisfactory may be immensely significant in subsequent practical reasoning, but an evaluation of the consequences, or even of the decision as leading to those consequences, does not constitute a criticism of the decision-making carried out from what we have called the standpoint of the agent.

We may recall here our earlier conclusion[5] that although evaluations do not presuppose indeterminism, the presumption of determinism that is plausible in thinking from the standpoint of natural order has no application to evaluation as such. But, on the whole, there is little occasion for controversy about freedom and responsibility in connection with criticisms of type *Ce;* it suffices to have differentiated them.

By criticisms from the standpoint of the agent (*Ca*) we mean judgments as to *whether* the agent's deliberation was sound or faulty and judgments *specifying the strong or weak points.* If the practical reasoning was faulty, in what respects was it faulty? If sound in all or in certain respects, what were these? Judgments of this sort differ depending upon the assumptions made. For example, a decision based on practical reasoning can be criticized

5. Chap. VII, sec. 3, above.

on the basis of knowledge—factual and nomological—that was available (whether utilized or not) to the agent at the time of the decision, or upon the basis of knowledge available at the time the criticism is made. The same applies to principles of action and methods of problem-solving. But it should be noted that whatever the knowledge, principles, and techniques presupposed in making the criticism, the decision of the agent is regarded as intentionally *objective*. The critic asks what would have been a sound decision for the agent as a human caring to choose the appropriate course of action. In judging the faults or merits of the decision, the critic identifies with the standpoint and intention of rational action. This identification with the standpoint of the agent is a feature common to Ca criticisms, irrespective of differences in assumptions as to knowledge, principles of action, and techniques of decision-making. It should be added that many of these Ca criticisms pertain to *how* knowledge and principles of action were utilized, *how* techniques of problem-solving were implemented: to details of utilization rather than to what was utilized, to details of execution rather than to the general character of the approach to a problem. For example, the agent may have reasoned faultlessly except for an obvious oversight, having failed entirely to consider as an alternative a course of action which certainly would have been feasible and which certainly would have been the thing to have done, had the agent only thought of it.

In what sense, if any, do Ca criticisms presuppose indeterminism? In our discussion of deliberation from the standpoint of the agent we said that deliberation from that standpoint, although it did not presuppose an assertion of the form "there is an occurrence e which had no sufficient conditions," did presuppose an essential restriction on natural order thinking. We now affirm that, like deliberation, Ca criticisms presuppose a restriction on natural order thinking without presupposing any absence of natural order in the happenings of the world. This must be so because Ca criticisms are directed at the practical reasoning of the agent. To be sure, the decision to act having been made, anyone aware of this occurrence *can* think about it in terms of the presumption that it had sufficient determining conditions and that, all things considered, the agent could not have decided to act otherwise. But Ca criticisms cannot be made in accordance with this presumption. They must be made in accordance with the assumption that various alternative courses of action were feasible. The difference between deliberation and

Ca criticisms is this: In deliberating, the question is: "In situation *s*, which feasible course of action is appropriate?"; in making *Ca* criticisms, the question is: "In situation *s*, which feasible course of action should have been judged appropriate?" The ascertainment of the thing to do as the thing to do must be regarded, in *Ca* criticism as well as in deliberation, as depending on a judgment of appropriateness, i.e., practical reasoning. The standpoint of *Ca* criticisms, then, is not the natural order standpoint. It shares with *post hoc* evaluation the standpoint of caring, i.e., of living in the world.

The *Ca* critic—whether the agent himself or another person—can view a decision with the benefit of hindsight. He knows something about how the decision in fact worked out (or about how a different decision would have worked out if it had been carried out). But this knowledge is not used to make an *evaluation* of the decision: Was it the best thing to have decided to do in the light of all presently known facts and eventualities (*whether or not* these could have been taken into consideration by the agent in faultless deliberation)? Rather, in *Ca* criticisms knowledge of how things actually turned out suggests ways in which the deliberation as deliberation could have been better, or calls attention to merits in a process of practical reasoning that might otherwise be overlooked.

The significance for a study of historical thinking of this differentiation of *Ca* criticism will emerge as we go on now to consider the third type of criticism (*Cpb*) and its presuppositions, especially as regards determinism. We shall devote particular attention to two contrasting interpretations of judgments, commonly termed criticisms, which we associate with praising and blaming. To simplify matters we assume that praising and blaming pertain to persons as agents. Judgment enters in as a discernment of the praiseworthiness or blameworthiness of the person. The questions to be kept in mind are these: Do *Cpb* criticisms presuppose indeterminism? If so, in what sense?

We begin by examining a popular interpretation of *Cpb* criticisms—one which has recently been defended by Isaiah Berlin, whose presentation is conveniently centered upon history and historical thinking.[6]

Berlin maintains that to be subject to praise or blame, a person must not only have performed an action causing certain conse-

6. Isaiah Berlin, *Historical Inevitability* (London: Oxford University Press, 1954).

quences, he must himself have been an *ultimate* determining condition of the specific action done, i.e., of *what* he chose to do. These qualifications being met, the person is said to be "morally" responsible, i.e., subject to "moral" praise or blame.

It is Berlin's opinion that this interpretation is not only philosophically sound but is embedded in ordinary ways of thinking and talking, and accepted by most historians as well as by mankind generally. He calls judgments of praiseworthiness or blameworthiness "moral" criticism; the historian, so judging, is said to engage in "moral" praising and blaming. Like Berlin, we are not particularly interested in the grounds according to which this or that person is praised or blamed. We are interested, as he is, in the presuppositions of these judgments.

In his discussion of responsible action Berlin speaks frequently of the agent's choice or decision, but he does not stipulate that to be responsible an agent must have made his choice by deliberation. "Chose what to do" may mean only "was an ultimate determining condition of the specific action done." But if we can show that the requirements of responsible action stipulated by Berlin cannot be supposed *ever* to be satisfied in fact, and if it is obvious that the addition of any further requirements would not alter this state of affairs, we will have shown that *Cpb* criticisms of *rational* actions, interpreted as Berlin would interpret them, are uniformly lacking in plausibility. They lack plausibility because their presuppositions are untenable.

According to our analysis of natural order thinking, it is not plausible to presume that any occurrences do not have sufficient conditions, i.e., are undetermined, unless the weight of scientific opinion supports such a view, a qualification which applies at present only to sub-atomic occurrences.[7] Arguments purporting to establish the indeterminism of any human actions will not have validity within the framework of natural order inquiry unless they cite empirical findings that serve as evidence of indeterminism from that standpoint. Does the position which Berlin represents assert that praising and blaming presuppose that some human actions—those subject to praise and blame—are undetermined? Utilizing our definition of "being determined" as it applies to particular occurrences, we shall argue in the affirmative. Therefore,

7. Note that there is no reason to suppose that disorderliness in sub-atomic occurrences would have any bearing on whether human decisions and actions are determined or not. See, for example, Nagel, *Structure of Science*, p. 316.

according to our analysis and in the light of present empirical scientific knowledge, no judgment of moral responsibility, no praise or blame, is warranted—in terms of the interpretation of praising and blaming defended by Berlin.

Berlin's requirements for morally responsible action are tantamount to a presupposition of indeterminism. A moral action, he maintains, presupposes a choice. The choice must have the agent himself as one of its determining conditions and, in this instance, as an *ultimate* determining condition. In other words, the choice could be (and presumably would be) *partially* conditioned by such factors as antecedent events (heredity, education, influences of the physical or social environment) or dispositional characteristics of persons or things, whether physical, biological, or psychical (for example: character, habits of thought, feeling and expression, and "compulsive" motives).[8] Indeterminism enters the analysis in connection with the notion that the agent himself is also one of the determining conditions, and indeed—the crucial point—an *ultimate* determining condition. In other words, nothing independent of or other than the agent determines this determining condition of the choice and thus, indirectly, of the act. Berlin's idea is that a person is not to be held responsible nor praised or blamed for something that he did not freely choose to do. The other determining conditions must leave him *some* latitude of choice, *some* freedom of action; hence the requirement that some element of his nature be a determining condition of his decision and not be itself determined by anything, at least not by anything other than the agent himself. As Berlin puts this, the decision to do this rather than that must be "within the individual's control."[9]

At first glance this might appear to imply no indeterminism. Berlin himself sometimes speaks as though his position does not base responsibility on indeterminism but solely on a rejection of one version of determinism, the version according to which, as he phrases it, occurrences are accounted for "by the *kind* of causal explanations which are accepted in, say, physics or biology."[10] His position does entail an assertion of indeterminism, however, in either one of two ways. The self-controlled self is either empirical, a part of the world, or it is non-empirical. If the self-controlled self is part of the world it is an occurrence, or bundle of

8. Berlin, *Inevitability*, pp. 26-27, 32-33, 35.
9. *Ibid.*, p. 26n.
10. *Ibid.*, p. 33 (italics added).

occurrences, neither determined by other occurrences nor taking place according to any rule (as would be the case if the self were a closed deterministic system). From the standpoint of natural order, it would have the status of an ultimate feature of the world, determining other occurrences but itself undetermined. It would be an instance of disorder comparable, presumably, to sub-atomic behavior. Because Berlin does not explicitly identify the self with anything empirical it is perhaps unfair to doubt that there is any evidence for the claim that whatever it is he is referring to actually is undetermined. All one can say is that nothing empirical that ever has been identified as a self or personal agent has ever been shown to be undetermined. The general presumption of determinism operative in natural order inquiry bids us doubt a claim of this sort in the absence of very considerable evidence, and evidence is lacking. Our presumption is, then, that if the self-controlled self is empirical it is not undetermined. The stipulated necessary condition for moral praise and blame is not fulfilled.

If, on the other hand, the self-controlled self is non-empirical, then a morally responsible human action would presuppose a particular occurrence (the decision) which did not have sufficient conditions. The reason for saying that it did not have sufficient conditions is that, on our terms, a determining condition must be empirical and the determining conditions that remain after the self is disqualified are not sufficient, for they are said to leave a margin of indeterminacy. A moral choice, being only partially empirically determined, would from the natural order standpoint be only partially determined. As far as natural order inquiry is concerned, it would be as unpredictable in detail (what the agent chose within the range of alternatives open to him) as the behavior of an individual electron.[11]

To sum up: The position we have been considering, represented by Berlin's formulation, asserts in one way or another that praise and blame together with moral responsibility presuppose indeterminism. On the basis of our analysis of thinking about particular occurrences, together with current knowledge regarding

11. Without precisely identifying the self-controlled, choice-determining self, Berlin does suggest that it is extra-empirical when he describes it as not "an object in nature," thus setting it apart from any "physical, or psychical, or psycho-physical chain of events" (*Ibid.*, pp. 33, 35). But perhaps this is only a way of saying that, unlike most other worldly things or occurrences, this one—or these—is undetermined. See Nagel's criticism of Berlin's concept of the self, in *Structure of Science*, p. 601.

the determining conditions of human action, it is plausible to presume that all human decisions and actions are determined, and ultimately determined by causes none of which is accurately described as within the control of the agent. Therefore, praising and blaming, as interpreted by Berlin, are never warranted.

We now consider a second widely held interpretation of *Cpb* criticisms. This second interpretation, explicitly rejected by Berlin, is also purported to be in accord with ordinary usage of praising-blaming terminology. According to this second view, in order to be held "morally" responsible, i.e., subject to "moral" praise and blame, the person's decision must have been a determining condition of his action: had he chosen to act otherwise he could have done so. Whereas Berlin seems to hold that to praise is to let it be known that a person has chosen well in carrying out an (undetermined) action called "choosing," in this second interpretation to praise is to intend to perpetuate a way of responding to or handling a certain kind of situation, it being assumed that praising the kind of thing a person decided to do or the way he decided to do it tends to result either in the agent's repeating his performance under similar circumstances, or in other persons—who seek praise—imitating what he did. Assuming this latter conception of the function of praising and blaming, it is obvious why the second interpretation of *Cpb* criticisms is indifferent to whether there were or were not sufficient conditions of the choice, let alone whether the sufficient conditions were or were not in part ultimately "under the agent's control."

Even if this second interpretation of praising and blaming did not actually accord with ordinary linguistic use, it would recommend itself to anyone who believes that neither conventional assumptions of moral discourse, whatever they may be, nor "feelings" of responsibility, nor a "sense" of moral freedom, can appropriately be invoked to support the claim that certain occurrences (namely, rational actions) are undetermined. There is also no doubt of the plausibility of the distinction between behavior in which the making of a choice is a determining factor and behavior in which it is not. This difference is found in human behavior. The idea persists, however, that there is something more to being responsible than having been able to "do otherwise" *if* one had chosen differently, something more to the indeterminism of rational choice than merely the contextual irrelevance of the determining conditions

of the choice when what we are interested in, as critics, is perpetuating or discouraging similar choices in the future.

Berlin correctly judges it a weakness of the second interpretation that it provides no account at all of "could have done otherwise" from the standpoint of the agent. But lacking an adequate
differentiation and analysis of the standpoint of the agent, he and
numerous others who have been prompted by an intuitive sensitivity to affirm a "stronger" sense of "could have done otherwise"
have been misled into defending an absolute human freedom by
specious arguments. They reason that if "he could have done
otherwise" means "he could have done otherwise if he had so
chosen," if the agent's choice is an event like any other, and if it
is assumed that, all things considered, the agent's choice is sufficiently determined by factors not within his (the agent's) control,
then human agents have no "freedom" at all. To safeguard "freedom" they argue that the agent must be a non-natural agent capable of affecting the course of nature, or an (in part) absolutely
indeterminate empirical self.

The inadequacy of the second interpretation of praising and
blaming consists, however, not in its failure to take cognizance of
absolute self-determination as a requirement of moral praise and
blame, but rather in its failure to differentiate and specify characteristics of the standpoint from which a rational agent thinks about
what he is going to do, a standpoint with its own correlated concept of responsibility. Correspondingly, it fails to take cognizance
of this as the standpoint from which certain types of criticism
are made. Thinking from the standpoint of a rational agent involves a special conception of alternative possibilities,[12] which does
not have the radical indeterministic implications of Berlin's concept of "free agent" but which might well be termed "stronger"
when compared with the freedom of "could have done otherwise
if he had so chosen." Our analysis of standpoints of thinking thus
goes to the heart of the free will-determinism controversy, affording a resolution of disputed issues that remarkably corroborates
some major contentions of both parties to that controversy.

Let us bring our analysis to bear on the second interpretation.
If praising and blaming have the functions ascribed to them by
this interpretation, then *Cpb* criticisms, i.e., judgments of praiseworthiness or blameworthiness, are conclusions of practical reasoning. The rational agent in these instances is the critic. The

12. See above, sec. 3 of this chapter.

critic's problem is whether it is appropriate to blame or praise a person's decision to act in a certain way. The appropriateness in question is that of the consequences of the praise or blame: Would it be appropriate to perpetuate or to discourage decisions to act in that way? The critic's own decision, regarded from what we have called the standpoint of the agent, is itself essentially excluded from being thought about deterministically. The interpretation we are examining, however, says nothing about *his* decision, but is concerned solely with the decision of the agent whose action is being judged praiseworthy or blameworthy.

Does it say that the agent's decision was determined? No, for there is said to be no necessary presupposition as to whether there were or were not sufficient conditions of the choice. There are, nonetheless, different ways in which the agent's choice might in fact be thought about by the critic, and there are significant differences in the presuppositions of these ways of thinking.

In judging praiseworthiness or blameworthiness it may be deemed relevant to think about the decision deterministically: What were its sufficient conditions? Whether or not to encourage or discourage the perpetuation of this sort of decision may be regarded as depending upon what sort of determining conditions the decision had. In this case the critic's deliberation requires natural order thinking—on his part—about the agent's decision. Or it might be deemed relevant in judging a person praiseworthy or blameworthy to evaluate the consequences of his decisions, making a comparative judgment of satisfactoriness (i.e., a *Ce* criticism). In still other cases it might be deemed relevant to criticize the practical reasoning by which the agent reached his decision (i.e., a *Ca* criticism).

Evaluations, as we saw, are not partial or incomplete natural order accounts, which could, in principle, be developed into adequate natural order accounts in accordance with the presumption of determinism peculiar to the natural order line of questioning. In making evaluations the presumption of determinism is simply not applicable. When, therefore, the critic, in the course of making a judgment of praiseworthiness or blameworthiness, *evaluates* the agent's decision, he is not merely contextually disinterested in whether the decision had sufficient conditions and what these might be; rather, because he is evaluating, these considerations are essentially alien to his line of questioning.

The same thing applies to cases in which the critic is criticizing the practical reasoning of the agent. But there is a difference. We are more sensitive to restrictions on deterministic thinking in the case of rational action, a sensitivity reflected in our use of the term "responsible." "Acting responsibly" is obscurely linked, for us, with "acting deliberatingly *from the standpoint of the agent.*" We therefore sense the inadequacy of an analysis of "he could have done otherwise" as equivalent to "he could have done otherwise if he had so chosen." The latter analysis accords well enough with natural order thinking about the decision; it is compatible with the presumption that the decision had sufficient conditions. But from the standpoint of the agent, the standpoint of acting "responsibly," there is an *essential* restriction on deterministic thinking: filling out the indefinite concept of "the thing to do"—the action to be done—by practical reasoning requires thinking of various alternative courses of action as feasible, and this requires that the choice not be thought of as sufficiently determined.

We have used the two interpretations of judgments of praiseworthiness and blameworthiness as a foil to underscore the complex assumptions of criticisms of rational actions. The position for which Berlin has been taken as spokesman derives whatever credibility it has from its sensitivity to the essential restriction upon deterministic thinking involved in rational action. But it errs in misconstruing this as a restriction of natural order intelligibility, as presupposing that some human behavior is indeterministic. The second position incorporates a conception of praising and blaming which is sustained by philosophical criticism, but it vastly oversimplifies the presuppositions of judgments of praiseworthiness and blameworthiness. In particular it errs in assuming that "acting responsibly" has the same meaning in all praising and blaming, losing sight altogether of the distinctive concept of "acting responsibly" correlated with criticisms from the standpoint of the agent (Ca). From the standpoint of the agent, the critic and the rational agent himself—who may be one and the same person— think of the agent as being able to do any one of various things; in acting responsibly, from this standpoint, the agent confronts the future as a future in which he is to do something, and regards what he is to do as depending not on the natural order conditions of his choice but upon what feasible course of action he thinks appropriate in the light of applicable principles of action.

The distinctiveness of the standpoint of the agent is reflected— but not always clearly—in the questions we ask about actions.

Prospectively the agent deliberating asks: What would be the appropriate thing to do? By contrast, thinking prospectively in terms of natural order, one asks: Circumstances and natural order being what they are, what will happen? The question "What shall I do?" is ambiguous out of context and invites confusion; it can mean either "What would it be appropriate to do?" or "What can I be expected to do?" It is no doubt an important step toward recognizing the independence of the standpoint of the agent when we become aware of this ambiguity. But sometimes, even when these distinctions are acknowledged, it is maintained that *retrospectively* considered there is only one question to be asked about an action in making it intelligible: "Why did I do what I did?" or "Why did he do what he did?" and only one answer: a reply in terms of determining conditions. It is supposed that the heterogeneity of deliberation is merely apparent and that the agent's peculiar way of thinking about what is to happen is due to his inadequate perspective, caught up as he is in deciding, attending to what he "should" do instead of making his deliberation an object of natural order inquiry. But rational action is viewed distinctively *in retrospect* from the standpoint of the agent. The retrospective question from that standpoint is: Was the decision sound? as distinguished from the natural order question: What were the determining conditions of the rational action? Here too, the distinctiveness of thinking from the standpoint of the agent is obscured by ambiguity, the ambiguity of "Why did I do what I did?" and the corresponding question historians ask about the rational actions of others, "Why did he do what he did?" But whenever an historian views a rational action with identifying understanding and does so consistently with the presuppositions of the standpoint of the agent, he aims to make it intelligible in a way that is not assimilable to natural order thinking.

In maintaining the independence of the standpoint of the agent over against natural order thinking we are not overlooking that nomological universals and natural order accounts of certain particular occurrences are often formulated in response to practical considerations and often utilized in practical reasoning. For practical purposes we sometimes ask for a natural order account of our own rational actions; we ask why—in natural order terms—we made a certain decision. It makes no difference whether or why we ask for this account; that it is to serve a subsequent practical purpose does not alter the natural order character of the account as such. It is noteworthy, however, that we cannot ascertain whether our rational action was preferable solely by reference to this or any other knowledge of natural order; such critical judgments—Ce or Ca—as we have seen, require either principles of evaluation or principles of action, or both. The principles of action that we employ in the future may be modified in the light of natural order accounts of past rational actions, but the presuppositions of future deliberation utilizing that natural order knowledge will still be different in kind from those of natural order thinking.

6. The Historian as Critic of Rational Action

There is a class of expressions which we constantly use (and can scarcely do without) like 'you should not (or need not) have done this'; 'why did you make this terrible mistake?'; 'I could do it, but I would rather not'; 'why did the King of Ruritania abdicate?', because, unlike the King of Abyssinia, he lacked the strength of will to resist'; '*must* the Commander-in-Chief be quite so stupid?' Expressions of this type plainly involve the notion of more than the merely logical possibility of the realization of alternatives other than those which were in fact realized, namely of differences between situations in which individuals can be reasonably regarded as being responsible for their acts, and those in which they can not. For no one will wish to deny that we do often argue about the best among the possible courses of action open to human beings in the present and past and future, in fiction and in dreams; that historians (and judges and juries) do attempt to establish, as well as they are able, what these possibilities are. . . . It seems superfluous to add that all the discussions of historians about whether a given policy could or could not have been prevented, and what view should therefore be taken of the acts and characters of the actors, are intelligible only on the assumption of the reality of human choices.[13]

What Berlin is claiming to establish in the quoted passage is the reality of human choice as he conceives it: choice involving an element of absolute self-determination; in effect, indeterminism. But it is now apparent that affirmation of the reality of human choice pertains to the standpoint of rational action. Contrary to Berlin's view, this standpoint is *not incompatible* with the standpoint of natural order thinking; it is *independent* of the latter. It entails a restriction upon deterministic thinking but does not entail even partial indeterminism. The "reality of human choice" is upheld in the sense that the restriction is essential to a fundamental way of making the happenings of the world intelligible.

13. Berlin, *Inevitability*, pp. 31-32.

In rejecting the indeterminism of human choice we have also rejected the plausibility of ascriptions of responsibility and judgments of praiseworthiness and blameworthiness which presuppose that indeterminism. Berlin is certainly justified in believing that many historians do make allegations of responsibility and bestow praise or blame in the belief that these judgments are appropriate only on his (Berlin's) terms, i.e., only if the agent is free in his (Berlin's) sense of the term. But *these* ascriptions of responsibility and any attendant moral praise and blame are incompatible with the scheme of intelligibility presupposed in natural order inquiries. The burden of evidence falls squarely upon the historian who ventures to praise and blame men of the past on the assumption that their actions were to some extent *ultimately* self-determined and that the agents therefore deserve credit or blame—assumptions not rendered a whit more plausible by the fact that they generally pass unchallenged by his peers and his public.

We have seen that some criticisms of rational actions are evaluations (Ce) and some are from the standpoint of the agent (Ca). The objectivity of both sorts of criticisms when made by historians is a point of controversy. There is nothing to add here to our previous remarks about the possibility, in principle, of objective evaluations, but it is fitting that we comment on the possibility of objective Ca criticisms.

Criticism of the agent is directed at the reasonableness of the decision. The parallel between criticism from the standpoint of the agent and thinking about occurrences in terms of determining conditions is noteworthy. The canons and criteria of adequate judgments from the standpoint of the agent that come into play when criticism of the reasonableness of a decision is undertaken are, like the canons and criteria of natural order judgments, the fruit of a long process of experimentation and reflective analysis and are continuously subject to revision. Their only warrant is that, having been tested and critically worked over, they are the best available at the time. They are not self-evident or definitive. Accordingly, the only general characterization that can be made of appropriate actions is that they accord with sound principles of practical judgment soundly applied, with the understanding that today the discipline of reasonable action aspires to be an experimental science. It has not always been held that the way to establish "the thing to do" is by an appeal to reason; certainly the appeal to reason has not always taken the form of an appeal to experimental science. The concept of reasonableness has emerged and evolved in the course of reflection upon practical thinking.[14]

The importance of these remarks might be missed if we were to choose our examples selectively from modern times and from areas of decision-making where (a) reasonableness strikes us as the obvious criterion and where (b) the practical principles are often not notably controversial—areas such as engineering or public health. In many cases that confront the modern historian, engineers and public health officials base their decisions on experimental science, not on conscience, taboo, or revealed moral law. The historian and his readers take the appropriateness of this for granted. Moreover, it is often relatively easy to see, especially with the advantage of hindsight, where an engineer's or health officer's practical reasoning went wrong. But we do not have to look far afield for complications. Already we find a difference in economic policy-making. Reasonableness is called for by all parties, but what policy is reasonable? There is anything but consensus as to the principles of economic policy-making, and the contrasting appraisals of specific policies by disinterested experts reflect this disagreement. Still more controversial situations abound in the domain of "moral" conduct, where the appeal to reason is variously interpreted or rejected outright in favor of diverse alternative foundations of moral judgment.

To say at the outset, therefore, that neither conscience, nor moral law, nor any other criterion or sanction other than reason is the basis of criticism of the agent, is already to take the position that sound criticism by the historian from the standpoint of the agent is not always or necessarily based on the assumptions of the particular agent whose decision is being appraised. For example, an agent who resorted to astrology at some stage of his deliberation may be adversely criticized for this. The extent to which the historian invokes techniques of deliberation and practical principles which *he* regards as the best available, and truly appropriate to making a decision in the situation in question, *but which the agent did not*, can obviously vary considerably.

The simplest cases for analysis are those in which the historian invokes no practical principle that the agent would not himself have endorsed. Even though the historian does not consider *all*

14. See Abraham Edel, *Ethical Judgment: The Use of Science in Ethics* (Glencoe, Ill.: The Free Press, 1955), chap. II, and Carl G. Hempel, *Aspects of Scientific Explanation* (New York: The Free Press, 1965), pp. 463 ff.

of the agent's practical principles sound, he may appraise the reasoning of the agent relative to *some* practical principles that do have objective status for historian and agent alike. Thus both might subscribe to the practical principle that one should choose a course of action that achieves one's goal without jeopardizing some other value more highly cherished than the goal itself, and even should the historian consider it unreasonable of an agent to have been pursuing a certain goal he can still say the agent chose his course wisely or unwisely in terms of this practical principle. It is generally regarded as "practically" unreasonable—objectively so—not to perceive which of one's practical principles apply to a situation under consideration. Or again, it is deemed "practically" unreasonable—objectively so—to make formal errors in the course of deliberation, e.g., in making inferences about a particular case from a general rule. Many criticisms by the historian are based on commonly accepted "objective" practical principles such as these. The historian will remark that the agent displayed a foolish consistency, an extreme rigorism, a lack of circumspection or thoroughness in sizing up the situation and considering alternatives; that he decided too quickly in a situation calling for caution, or too slowly in a situation where almost any action would have been preferable to delay. These traits are objectively judged to be shortcomings in practical reasoning, although there may be disagreement about their bearing upon a particular case. It is easy for us to imagine the agent criticizing himself for these faults; indeed, he may actually have done so when the results of his decision drew his attention to them.

At a more complex level, criticisms may be directed at the unreasonableness of the principles or the unreasonableness of the technique of utilizing the principles. Thus the historian may judge that a principle was unreasonable because based on faulty knowledge of cause and effect. "Spare the rod and spoil the child" is a practical principle once widely accepted in Western societies, but which has been discredited as child development became better understood. In criticizing the decision of an agent a century ago to discipline a child with a good whipping, the enlightened critic probably does not imagine that the agent would have found the criticism acceptable. The critic maintains that some principles are objectively sound, and others unsound, *whether or not the agent thought likewise*. The underlying assumption of the claim to "objectivity" is that *if* the agent had had the requisite knowledge, insight, and experience, and possibly had not had certain deep-seated habits of thought and feeling, he would have agreed with the historian's criticism.

The critic who maintains that the agent *should have chosen otherwise* does not abandon the standpoint of the agent. He judges that the agent's practical reasoning was faulty: the agent should have deliberated otherwise in respect to the latter's own intention of choosing the appropriate course of action. The critic does not maintain that the agent should have decided to do something that the agent was not capable of carrying out. The course of action that, according to the critic, the agent should have chosen, must be one of at least two feasible actions, one of the things the agent could have done. Not that the agent could have done it all things considered, but that he could have done it considering the world selectively in the manner of agents.

Is it proper, however, for the critic to charge the agent with mistakes in practical reasoning which, all things considered, the agent was bound to make (since, presumably, there were sufficient conditions of the impulsiveness, carelessness, errors in inference, etc. which characterized the agent's reasoning)? The critic's judgment is legitimate in relation to the agent's own intention in deliberating. The agent sought the answer that the critic presumes to have found: In that situation, what course of action satisfied the requirements of the relevant practical principle and thus was the thing to have decided to do? The critic's strictures would only be inappropriate if they presupposed that the agent could have chosen otherwise (and thereby could have done otherwise) all things considered, something that criticisms from the standpoint of the agent do not do.

In the preceding section we emphasized the variety of types of criticism and the differences in underlying standpoint. It remains only to comment on the motley character of the criticisms encountered in historical writing. Commenting earlier on the similarities between the historian's thinking about the past and our everyday thinking, we remarked that in both of these the two standpoints of thinking are haphazardly combined; in both we find judgments being made which are so vague in intent or in which the intent is so vaguely communicated that we cannot be sure from which standpoint of thinking they are made. To this we can now add that, scattered among judgments from the standpoint of living in the world and mingled with natural order accounts are criticisms of all sorts (*Ce, Ca,* and *Cpb*). Then, there is a host of judgments so vague that we cannot be sure whether they are *descriptive* characterizations of persons as "reasonable" or "responsible," *criticisms* from the standpoint of living in the world, or *natural order* accounts. Even when we are quite certain that a judgment is a criticism, we may be unable to establish whether it is an evaluation, a criticism from the standpoint of the agent, or praise (or blame) with efficacious intent.

This haphazard mingling and vagueness presents no serious problem most of the time, either in everyday life or when we are reading historical works. But, as we have said, it can become a source of controversy when, in the absence of the relevant critical awareness, a question arises involving differentiation between standpoints and discrimination among various types of judgments from the respective standpoints. Whether or not a certain historical personage is to be blamed for something can never be settled until we are in clear agreement about the presuppositions of the judgment of blameworthiness. Our main purpose in making distinctions and tracking down presuppositions has been to terminate sterile controversy.

❋   ❋   ❋   ❋   ❋

In concluding this chapter it may be instructive to comment on some similarities and differences between the position we have been developing and views set forth by William Dray. He distinguishes between history written from the standpoint of the agent and history written from the standpoint of a spectator, recalling our distinction between the standpoint of natural order and what we too have called the standpoint of the agent. There are, however, some important differences, which should be noted.

Dray's main theme is historical *explanation.* Consequently, when he comes to discuss the "standpoint of the agent" he treats the distinctive thinking by the historian from this standpoint as "rational *explanation.*" In his earlier work (*Laws and Explanation in History*) he did not make it entirely clear that a rational explanation was *not* an explanation of an occurrence in terms of determining conditions. Subsequently, however, Dray has clarified his conception of rational explanation: in tracing the agent's reasons the historian does not account for the action in terms of determining conditions; he merely ascertains the reasons on the

basis of which the agent judged the action to be the thing to do.[15]
But nowhere does Dray take cognizance of the difference between
descriptive and identifying understanding, nor does he deal, as we
shall presently, with thinking about particular occurrences from
the standpoint of the agent where the personal reference involves
present or prospective concerns. Moreover, even if it were
plausible to maintain, as he does, that historians typically give
"rational" rather than "covering law" explanations, this would not
render any less important our criticisms of his own non-"covering
law" analysis of causal explanations of particular occurrences.

On the issue of determinism, it might appear that our positions
are in fundamental accord. This is not so, although there is at
least one significant point of agreement: an account of a rational
action from the standpoint of the agent (Dray calls this a "rational
explanation") does not presuppose that there were sufficient conditions of the agent's action. Dray, however, has not shown why it
does not, whereas I have tried to show *how* a restriction on deterministic thinking is essential to practical reasoning.[16]

In addition, Dray (1) has stated that he holds a "libertarian
metaphysical position"; (2) has conceded the possibility, in principle, of explaining rational actions in terms of sufficient conditions
(characteristic of all "covering law" explanations); and (3) has
stated that he cannot see that "rational explanation" and explanation
in terms of sufficient conditions (he calls it "explanation on the
covering law model") are incompatible.[17] Rather, he suggests,
since they belong to "different logical and conceptual networks,
within which different kinds of puzzlement are expressed and
resolved," both types of explanations *of the same particular occurrence* would be compatible. In maintaining (3) he appears to
overlook the fact that (1) and (2) would be contradictory if
asserted of the same particular occurrence. That is to say, if a
particular action were explained as having sufficient conditions,
this assertion would contradict the assertion that it was an instance
of metaphysical "liberty."

15. William Dray, "The Historical Explanation of Actions Reconsidered,"
in *Philosophy and History*, ed. Sidney Hook (New York: New York University
Press, 1963), pp. 108-9, 113 ff., 129; also William Dray, *Philosophy of History* (Englewood Cliffs, N. J.: Prentice-Hall, 1964), pp. 14-15.

16. Our analysis incidentally also shows the *point* of the historian's thinking of action from the standpoint of the agent even if he is able also to
explain it deterministically. Cf. A. Donagan, "Explanation in History," *Mind*,
LXVI (1957), 153, and Dray in *Philosophy and History*, p. 131.

17. *Ibid.*, p. 131.

There are various ways in which this paradox might be resolved. Our analysis accomplishes this as follows: it (a) specifically eschews "metaphysical" pronouncements (as distinct from the conclusions of critical reflection); (b) identifies one line of questioning (one of Dray's "logical and conceptual networks") as the quest for natural order; (c) establishes that from this latter standpoint there is at present no confirmation of disorder (i.e., no indeterminism) in human action; and (d) discloses that another line of questioning, namely, from the standpoint of the agent, involves a restriction on deterministic thinking. In rejecting (1)—interpreted in any relevant manner—and agreeing with (2) and (3), no contradiction arises. Our notion of distinctive fundamental types of thinking about world happenings precludes our having to defend incompatible metaphysical positions. Our position is that when we are thinking from that standpoint from which all things (i.e., all determining conditions) *are* considered (namely, natural order), the evidence supports a presumption of the determinism of human behavior, rational as well as non-rational; on the other hand, from the standpoint of the agent's thinking about the most appropriate course of action, "all things" are necessarily *not* considered. Both types of thinking pass critical scrutiny. Their divergencies admit of no higher synthesis.

Chapter IX.

Rational Action

Historical Thinking and Present Concerns

1. INTRODUCTION

Conventionally the field of history is limited to particular occurrences of the human past. We have seen that one way in which some of these occurrences can be thought about, and made intelligible, is by identifying understanding of the evaluational or practical thinking done in the past by others about the world in reference to their concerns. In so far as they thought about actual particular occurrences, those occurrences were intelligible to them —either as evaluated or, in the case of actions, as the appropriate thing to do. We recognize this kind of intelligibility as human. It is plausible to say that occurrences become intelligible *to us* when, identifying with the standpoint of others as living in the world, we understand how they thought about those occurrences. This kind of historical intelligibility is perhaps most strikingly exemplified by the intelligibility of rational actions, intelligibility afforded by identifying understanding of the thinking of other rational agents. To the extent that others merely had preferences and did not make judgments of preferability, to the extent that they merely did what they were told without thinking about the appropriateness of what they did, the meaning relations manifested in their subjective experience and its objectifications can, perhaps, be understood identifyingly; but just as we would hesitate to say that their world and their actions were intelligible to them, so we would hesitate to say that their world and their actions are intelligible to us through our comprehension of those not-rationally-developed meaning relations.

Judgments of preferability—as judgments from the standpoint of living in the world—are essentially personal in reference. The concerns can be our own. Since our specific matters of concern often change as we change and as circumstances alter, there would be nothing unusual about the past being intelligible to us through identifying understanding of *our own past* concerns. But not only is the conventional subject matter of history what others did and what happened to them in the past, the conventional personal reference is to concerns *they* had *then*. An autobiography in which the personal reference is to the author's relatively personal past concerns (as contrasted, e.g., with a public functionary's impersonal account of his activity on behalf of public concerns) is thought to be not quite "history proper." Although it deals with the past it does not deal with it primarily in terms of others' past concerns. Still less conventional is our thinking about the world when the focus of thinking is *our present concerns*. Should this be called "historical" thinking? Does it yield intelligibility from the standpoint of living in the world or is this thinking perhaps altogether distinctive?

Let us make it clear that by "present" we mean contemporaneous with the time of the historian's thinking. In regard to the presentness of the concerns we should note that a thinker can, to be sure, identify understandingly at time t_1 with the thinking done by someone else in reference to this other person's concerns at t_1, just as well as he can think about the world in reference to *his own* concerns at t_1 (including those he shares with others). To simplify our analysis, however, we shall concentrate on the latter.

We shall reserve comment on the distinctiveness of this thinking and on the appropriateness of calling it historical thinking, until we have considered just how thinking about particular occurrences of the human past is involved in the thinking a person does about the world when thinking in reference to his present concerns from the standpoint of living in the world and, conversely, how the latter influences the former. We shall restrict our discussion to practical reasoning, omitting reference to evaluation. We do so because there is nothing remarkable about evaluational thinking in reference to present concerns; it raises no special problems for reflection, and to analyze it would contribute little or nothing to a clarification of the nature of historical thinking.

2. PAST PARTICULARS AND PRESENT CONCERNS

Particular occurrences of the human past can serve as the *basis for* generalizations, or we can make judgments about past particulars which *presuppose* independently established generalizations. The past particulars (and their relations to each other) that serve as the *basis for* generalizations used in practical thinking need only have significant similarities with (and may, of course, have significant differences from) traits of persons and things that make up the present problematic situation: such past particulars (and relations) we shall say comprise the *past in general.*

It is illuminating to differentiate from the *past in general* a second category of past particulars—which we shall call the *specific past*—comprising past occurrences that are existentially or causally connected with the agent's present situation and future prospects. Judgments about *these* past occurrences are made from the standpoint of the agent using generalizations based on the *past in general.* The *specific past* comprises past states of specific persons and things in the present situation, past relationships among these, or determining conditions of past, present, or future states and relationships of these persons and things.

The following relevant kinds of generalizations are based on the *past in general:* (1) nomological universals (fulfilling to a greater or lesser extent the requirements specified in Part One); (2) principles of action; and (3) principles for making predictions (having the orientation of *predictive science*). Keeping practical thinking always in view, we may observe that nomological universals and predictive principles include generalizations about abilities, overt responses, feelings, etc.—the agent's own as well as those of others. Principles of action, in the broad sense in which we have used this expression, include, e.g., ideas about circumstances under which we should trust our intuitions, when experimentation is called for, what form it should take, when risks should be taken, when we should stop worrying and let matters take their course, when to persevere, the extent to which we should restrain our passions and mask our feelings, what kinds of things we should bear in mind as matters of concern, and what forms of activity and modes of human relationship are preferable under what circumstances.

From the standpoint of the rational agent, generalizations of the three kinds referred to put the past into a form in which it can be utilized in practical thinking. They make the past useful to persons thinking about what to do. Let us note first how principles of action and nomological universals are employed in making judgments about the *specific past*.

Rational action does not always have a clearly defined beginning. I have been continuously acting and am presently engaged in many rational actions. What I am now—at any time—engaged in doing rationally, reflects my working commitments, plans, projects, and so on; these, in turn, in conception and manner of execution represent judgments based on knowledge derived from the *past in general*, together with factual knowledge of particular happenings —past and present—of my practical world. I may not at every moment actually be thinking about what I am doing as what I *should* be doing. Even so, if I *have* thought about it and if I am always ready to reconsider its appropriateness this activity is plausibly described as intelligible to me. At times, however, I do actually think about the appropriateness of what I am and have been doing, or about what future action would be appropriate. It may be that I am simply interested in keeping track of my activity which, as rational, carries with it certain assumptions about feasibility, expected consequences, etc. Or I may be moved to engage in practical thinking by specific circumstances of various sorts. The practical thinking may be about situations of greater or lesser urgency and immediacy. Which questions we ask about the past depends in part upon which type of situation our practical thinking is all about.

Sometimes we know in general terms what is to be cared about, without being able to see clearly what is specifically to be cared about—or cared about most—in a given situation. Using principles of action as tools of analysis, we seek to identify the specific form in which matters of general concern are at stake in particular circumstances. Or we seek to judge according to principles of action what the order of priority is among identified specific matters of present concern. The continuity of past and present and the elusiveness of the present state of things as an object of inquiry combine to make it possible as well as necessary that we look to the *specific past* for insight into the present and future. Thus, one phase of practical thinking consists in a scrutiny of the (usually recent) *specific past*, bringing to bear principles of action based upon the *past in general*. Concurrently, using nomological universals as tools of analysis, we seek to identify certain states of affairs as determining conditions of other states of affairs. Ultimately what interests us in this causal analysis are the determining conditions of states of affairs that are matters of concern: circumstances that have to be endured, however deplorable; circumstances that we intend to modify; circumstances upon which the successful pursuit of a course of action will depend; and so on. The determining conditions are variously called means and resources or obstacles and hindrances; they are variously described as positive, favorable, helpful, and friendly, or negative, hostile, and destructive—indicating that matters of concern are at stake in manifestations of natural order.

The way in which available nomological universals—whether deriving from scientific inquiry or from the fund of trivial common knowledge—function as tools of analysis in thinking about the *specific past* from the standpoint of rational action is very similar to the function of available nomological universals in disinterested natural order inquiry. The available generalizations are often loose working generalizations that undergo refinement as analysis proceeds. This refinement of nomological relations can only be supported by direct or indirect evidence, or a combination thereof. In practice this means that determining conditions in the particular case are more precisely ascertained—and more confidently established—by comparing the case at hand with other known cases. Thus use is made of particulars comprised in the *past in general*. A similar procedure is involved in utilizing nomological universals which state "typical" or "ideal" conditions. Still another facet of causal analysis is likely to be the construction of "composite" generalizations out of "simple" ones. Whatever the combination of logical steps involved in a decision-oriented causal analysis of the particular human past, when we speak of judgments about particulars "presupposing generalizations" it should not be assumed that the thinking referred to has the form of a simple subsumption of a particular under a precise, tight "covering law" ready at hand.

The interdependence of identification of concerns (utilizing principles of action) and causal analysis (utilizing nomological universals) is readily apparent. What it matters to me to achieve or to preserve in a particular situation will depend upon what is at stake. General principles of action may direct my attention to a situation and lead me to find out whether something I am concerned about is at stake; conversely, causal analysis disclosing that a certain concern is at stake will suggest to me that supporting or safeguarding whatever is at stake is a requirement of the thing to do. Thus, a concern for national survival may prompt me to ask whether my country's policy of augmenting and perfecting defensive armaments is proving conducive to national security or is increasing the risk of war. What a causal analysis reveals on this score affects what I require in a candidate for public office and, in due course, what action is appropriate on my part when I step inside the voting booth. My caring that a candidate with sound views on national defense is elected is, in this example, the specific form taken by my concern with national survival.

Another interdependence important in clarifying the nature of historical thinking is that between generalizations based on past particulars (*past in general*), and judgments about past particulars comprised in the *specific past*. First, as regards natural order thinking, to the extent that the judgments about particular events of the human past involved in practical thinking assert or imply causal relationships, these judgments presuppose *generalizations,* for the causal relation is a special type of nomological relation and the nomological relation implies *generality*. It does not matter whether the implicit generalization of the causal assertion is ready at hand and already precise enough or is worked out and refined by the person thinking about the *specific past*. Where specialization develops, the rational agent looking for causal relations in the *specific past* may draw upon the findings of some other person who makes a specialty of generalizations based on the *past in general*. Because a nomological relation is a relation between particulars *as instances of kinds* and cannot be directly established by inspection of a single instance, and because the scope of world happenings and natural order is so vast, there is occasion for a close working relationship between the specialized quest for generalizations based on the *past in general* and the causal analysis of the *specific past* by rational agents. In other words, if there is a division of intellectual labor, the specialist in useful generalization cannot be altogether oblivious of which areas of investigation are pertinent for causal analyses oriented toward rational action. When the working relationship is close, the way he formulates his generalizations will depend upon what form of generalization is best adapted to the techniques of causal analysis found most suitable in clarifying certain types of practical problems. Intellectual division of labor is carried still further when causal analysis of the *specific past* also becomes a speciality. The rational agent who utilizes the thinking of specialists in deciding upon a course of action in reference to his concerns, may not himself be a specialist in either sort of thinking about the past. The specialists, for their part, may or may not share the concerns of a particular rational agent. A professional political analyst, for example, may or may not share the concerns of a particular voter. In any case, the working relationships between the generalizing, the causal analysis, and the decision-making can be more or less consciously exploited and coordinated.

What we have said in regard to causal analysis about the interdependence between generalizations based on past particulars (*past in general*) and judgments about particulars (the *specific past*) applies, *mutatis mutandis,* to the formulation and utilization of principles of action. To cite one parallel, utilizing principles of action (based on the *past in general*) as tools of analysis in order to identify our concerns and determine requirements of an appropriate course of action, often consists in refining and combining general principles which are "loose" and "simple." Just as in a causal analysis we look over the *past in general* for particulars that afford significant comparisons, so also in the process of identifying concerns. Thus we do not utilize the *past in general* only in the form of completely formulated principles of action. We generalize in the course of identifying our concerns, converting recollected or reported past particulars into instances of a kind relevant to our present concerns.

We have confined our attention so far to generalization and judgment about *past* particulars, indicating only that often it is the recent *specific past*—"current events" or "contemporary history" —of which a causal analysis is most illuminating to the rational agent, and in regard to which identification of concerns is most pertinent. These recent particulars and their interrelationships reveal most about the particular conditions under which our actions will take place and the specific form in which our concerns are at stake. But it is important that our discussion include thinking about the *future,* and deal with the interdependence between decision-oriented thinking about past and future.

The future is nothing less than the ultimate focus of practical thinking. Which alternative action is appropriate is so in respect to judgments about what can be expected to happen. We anticipate the future rationally by utilizing generalizations based on the *past in general*, and by close observation of actual states of affairs at or during certain times (usually recent). It is in this connection that we call on principles for making predictions, the third kind of generalizations based on the *past in general*. The intention of these generalizations-for-making-useful-predictions is not natural order intelligibility. Difficult as it may be to ascertain whether a generalization based on the *past in general* was intended *as* a nomological universal (which *can* be used predictively) or as a generalization for making useful predictions, the distinction between these orientations of our thinking is fundamental. We have already noted that *predictive science* has distinctive presuppositions. No one familiar with computer theory and prediction techniques will contest this. Thinking about the *past in general* with these presuppositions yields distinctive generalizations, notably prediction-oriented probabilistic correlations of specific empirical data. These prediction techniques and correlations—crude or sophisticated—are used in making judgments about what the future will be like no matter what course of action we choose, as well as in predicting the probable effects of alternative courses of action under the anticipated circumstances.

But the point to be emphasized here is the interdependence of our view of the future and our thinking about the past. What we look for in our causal analysis of the *specific past* and in our identification of concerns will depend upon the envisioned future. For example, expectations regarding future developments which our choices will not affect one way or the other, direct our attention to the need or the possibility of counteracting any adverse effects of those anticipated developments or of capitalizing on attractive opportunities which we judge to be in the offing. In order to decide what to do we need to find out more about what is going on right now and why; also more about what is at stake for us in this situation. *Conversely,* what we discover in thinking about the *specific past* directs our attention to predictable future developments of concern to us which might otherwise have been unforeseen, or to possible attainments which we might otherwise have overlooked. Thus, familiarity with the *kind* of thing that was done in the human past might open our eyes to unsuspected and otherwise "unbelievable" possibilities of human existence; it can materially enlarge our conceptions about what a person can do or become, i.e., about what might be feasible for ourselves as agents.

The kind of experience he had I might have; the kind of hardship he endured I might be able to endure; the way in which he solved his problem might work for me. Knowing what someone was able to do, I try to find out whether that kind of thing would be feasible under the present circumstances. If I anticipate that it would be, I may go on to judge appropriate a kind of action that would not otherwise even have been considered as an alternative, let alone as the thing to do.

3. ILLUSTRATIONS OF INTERDEPENDENCE

The interdependences that we have been considering are logical interdependences in thinking oriented toward rational action. Three of these are of paramount interest to us: (1) the interdependence between identification of concerns and causal analysis; (2) the interdependence between generalizing judgments and judgments about particulars; and (3) interdependence in thinking about past, present, and future occurrences respectively.

Studies of the *past in general* and of the *specific past* are often geared in with practical thinking, and depend upon assumptions about the future, even though this is not made explicit. Studies of the future, intended as a contribution to practical thinking, characteristically assume generalizations based on the *past in general* and on conclusions derived from studies of the *specific past* that are never systematically set forth. Explicit interdependence of generalization and judgment about particulars in practical thinking —especially in the works of professional historians—is exceptional. To illustrate our remarks in section 2 we shall mention here (without commenting on their intrinsic merits) a number of studies that do clearly exemplify the more important interdependencies.[1]

Many economists who have directed their attention to the study of past business cycles (*past in general*) have assumed the preferability of a stable economy, and have consequently been eager to find out how recurrent, severe depressions might be avoided. They have studied the strategy of controls and have advised policy-makers as to appropriate policies under specific conditions. Which measures they have judged appropriate on a given occasion has depended in part upon a causal analysis of the *spe-*

1. Suggestive remarks concerning the practical import of historical studies are found in Abraham Edel, *Ethical Judgment: The Use of Science in Ethics* (Glencoe, Ill.: The Free Press, 1955), pp. 272-82, and J. H. Randall, Jr., *Nature and Historical Experience* (New York: Columbia University Press, 1958), pp. 56-57, 68-69, 99, and *passim*.

cific past using generalizations (correlations of variables) based on the *past in general*. Their work abundantly illustrates how thinking about particulars of the *past in general*, in so far as it leads to a formulation of generalizations useful as instruments of causal analysis or prediction, can be an important contribution to deciding upon the best course of action. Describing the aims and methods of his pioneering work on business cycles, the following remarks of Wesley C. Mitchell stress the interdependence between generalizing from past particulars—including those of the recent past—and the use of these generalizations in causal analyses of particular currently on-going systems.

We shall seek to find what features have been characteristic of all or of most cycles, and to concentrate attention upon them, paying less attention to features which have been peculiar to one or a few cases. In this respect, our aim will be like that of economic theorists, and different from that of economic historians, commercial journalists, and business forecasters, who are concerned with particular cycles. But our way of finding what is typical and what is exceptional will be the way of the statistician and the historian who ventures to generalize. . . . We must be ready to consider concrete events such as historians treat; but we must array them in groups after the fashion of statisticians, and interpret them in the light of what we know about economic behavior, after the fashion of economic theorists. Similarly, we must be ready to apply the mathematical technique of statisticians; but we must guide our statistical investigations by rational hypotheses and eke out our statistical observations by recourse to historical records. So, too, while we must be ready on occasion to analyze imaginary cases with the theorists, these cases should be arranged whenever possible with an eye upon the historical and statistical data by which speculative conclusions may be tested.

And with regard to the use of history:

Of course, there is no logical opposition between the theoretical and the historical viewpoints, any more than there is opposition between causation and analytic description. On the contrary, history and theory supplement each other. The theorist who wishes to analyze the workings of current economic institutions needs a vivid, objective view of their characteristics. That view he can obtain most effectively by a study of their evolution. Nor is current history less important to him than history of the past. It is only by historical observations that he can determine what features of business cycles are common and what are occasional, a matter upon which he should satisfy himself before he devises his imaginary experiments. So, too, the statistical worker appeals to history for help in performing the most difficult of his technical tasks—separating "irregular" from cyclical fluctuations. And by whatever methods a theorist works, he may—and should—check his explanations by seeing how far they account for the cycles of history.[2]

The same interdependences are apparent in studies that have been made of past wars with the intention of finding causal factors that might be controlled in response to a concern for preserving international peace. These studies have yielded generalizations about the "causes" of war, generalizations applicable both in causal analysis of *specific pasts* and in forecasting the consequences of actual or alternative policies. The forecasts, in turn, would be expected to influence policy decisions as to appropriate courses of action. All of this is illustrated many times over in Quincy Wright's *A Study of War*, illustrated all the more clearly because of the author's explicit methodological considerations, his avowed intention of making the *past in general* useful to the statesman, his own utilization of both available descriptive material and generalizations of the social and behavioral sciences, and, finally, because of the systematic form of the work, which terminates with a discussion of principles (including techniques) of "social" action relevant to "the control of war."[3]

The French sociologist and political scientist, Raymond Aron, has said that the only worthwhile battle is for "the mastery of nature and the well-being of mankind."[4] Guided especially by the latter of these general concerns, Aron has conducted numerous causal analyses of the particular past of Western society, with the conscious intent of discovering the conditions—both obstacles and resources—that confront anyone today who is trying to forge reasonable social, economic, and political policies for the foreseeable future. Owing to the acceleration of revolutionary developments during the last few decades,[5] Aron assumes that for practical purposes it is, above all, the recent *specific past* that deserves study. He has analyzed international relations and the development of our industrial society with this focus. Concurrently, to provide generalizations instrumental for causal analysis and prediction

2. Wesley C. Mitchell, *Business Cycles: The Problem and Its Setting* (New York: National Bureau of Economic Research, 1927), pp. 469-70, 57.

3. Quincy Wright, *A Study of War* (one volume abr. ed.; Chicago: Chicago University Press, 1965).

4. Raymond Aron, *The Dawn of Universal History* (London: Weidenfeld and Nicolson, 1961), p. 53.

5. *Ibid.*, pp. 15 ff. and 22.

Aron has carried out generalizing studies of the *past in general* (the "sociology of industrial society"), and has used these studies to gain insights into current conditions, to anticipate consequences, to identify specific concerns, and to formulate specific principles of action. Aron has endeavored to place his expertise in decision-making at the disposal of statesmen and the public at large, in accordance with the practical principle that theoretical and historical inquiry are fulfilled in rational action. His *Paix et Guerre entre les Nations*[6] explicitly combines generalization (*"sociologie"*), analysis of the recent past and present (*"histoire"*), and formulation of principles of action (*"praxéologie"*). It is assumed that anyone today who is concerned about the fate of humanity is faced with the problem of translating this concern into requirements of appropriate action under specific circumstances. In the book referred to, the central problem, one presumably faced by citizens and statesmen of major Western powers today, is the possible justification of a commitment to use thermonuclear weapons against other countries under specified circumstances.

W. W. Rostow is another contemporary social scientist who has carried out both ambitious generalizing studies and causal analyses of the recent *specific past,* as the basis for an identification of specific matters of general concern and for specific recommendations.[7] Rostow, too, has been active on the political scene, making recommendations on appropriate public policy in the light of his own (and others') interdependent methodical inquiries into past, present, and future.

The Brazilian economist Celso Furtado based his activity as Minister of Planning in the Brazilian government in the early 1960's on his own causal analysis of recent Brazilian social-economic history. Holding that the sole objective of an analysis of social-economic processes is to provide guidelines for action, Furtado concluded from his scrutiny of the relevant *specific past* of Brazil, and from comparisons with developments in other countries confronting similar problems of economic development, that violent revolution was not a *sine qua non* of significant progress in his country, but that prospects for peaceful change were slight unless a co-ordinated economic plan was promptly instituted—a plan

6. Raymond Aron, *Paix et Guerre entre les Nations* (Paris: Calmann-Lévy, 1962).
7. See W. W. Rostow, *The Stages of Economic Growth* (London: Cambridge University Press, 1962) and *The United States in the World Arena: An Essay in Recent History* (New York: Harper, 1960).

which could effect comprehensive changes by concentrating on a few factors identified as "strategic."[8] Furtado has also endeavored to clarify the status of economic development as a matter of concern: it is a means only, an essential means for achieving what he declares to be the ultimate concern of most Brazilians, namely, the implementation of authentically "humanistic" ideals.[9]

Another economist who has studied the process of economic development in South America, Albert O. Hirschman, has specialized in making generalizations based on the *past in general.* Concerned that economic development should take place without senseless violence and suffering, Hirschman has studied the recent and most relevant *past in general* of "underdeveloped" countries with a view to making this past "usable" for all who share his concerns and who are (as Furtado for a time was) in a position to take constructive action. In one research project Hirschman examined the ways in which selected social and economic problems have been handled in three South American countries during approximately the last hundred years.[10] Having reconstructed three "problem histories," combining description and causal analysis, Hirschman concludes with a number of tentative generalizations (nomological or predictive) about the "dynamics" of problem-solving in South America, and formulates some tentative principles of action based on these generalizations.

Turning to professional historians, one does not have to look to doctrinaire Marxists for illustrations of action-oriented historical thinking. We cite first an example drawn again from the area of South American studies and having social-economic development as its concern. We mentioned that in the course of a causal analysis of the *specific past* the inquirer will sometimes turn to particulars of the *past in general,* particulars which permit significant comparative judgments and enable the inquirer to work out nomological relations or to confirm his hypotheses. This working-out may take

8. See Celso Furtado, *A pré-revolução brasileira* (Rio de Janeiro: Fundo de Cultura, 1962), pp. 9-32; part of the preceding book appeared in English translation under the title "Brazil: What Kind of Revolution?," *Foreign Affairs,* XLI, No. 3 (1963), 526-35. See also Celso Furtado, *The Economic Growth of Brazil: A Survey From Colonial Times,* trans. R. W. de Aguiar and E. C. Drysdale (Berkeley, Calif.: University of California Press, 1963).

9. Cf. Rostow, *Economic Growth,* chap. X, "A Statement of Values."

10. Albert O. Hirschman, *Journeys Toward Progress: Studies of Economic Policy-Making in Latin America* (New York: The Twentieth Century Fund, 1963). See also his earlier work, *The Strategy of Economic Development* (New Haven: Yale University Press, 1958).

the form of refining loose generalizations, finding out how to combine "simple" generalizations, and taking cues from generalizations
of limited universality (i.e., those which, as formulated, are applicable to *other* times and places). In such cases the line between
the generalizing orientation of social and behavioristic sciences
and historical judgments about non-duplicable particulars all but
disappears. Generalizing and causal analysis go hand in hand;
the *past in general* and the *specific past* are thought about concurrently. This interdependence and its practical bearing are
recognized in a proposal for a research project outlined in the
bulletin of the Center for Historical Studies of the University of
Brazil. The project is in line with an action-oriented editorial
statement in the same publication: "It is necessary that historians
in Brazil become aware of the important role of historical study in
Brazilian society. It is imperative that they comprehend the necessity of situating contemporary problems in their historical context—
the only way in which they can be truly understood and
solved...."[11]

In the words of the authors of the proposal: ". . . the principal
task of Brazilian historians is to contribute toward an understanding of the social-economic process, an understanding indispensable
for social reforms, such as agrarian reform."[12] Specifically they urge
research into the connections between agrarian conditions in
Brazil and her economic relationships with European countries
since colonial times. How is the historian to discern the determining factors of change and continuity in this complicated course of
events? An important tool of analysis would be the comparison
of the Brazilian experience with that of other regions in colonial
America and with analogous yet quite independent particular developments in other continents, utilizing insights from studies of
contemporary social-economic structures and developments that are
in some respects comparable. Since no generalizations presently
available are entirely suitable for carrying out the causal analysis
upon which, in turn, an appropriate agrarian reform program can
be based, they propose, in effect, that nomological relations be
worked out by comparisons utilizing selected past particulars together with various sorts of working generalizations. Some of
the latter may be gleaned from causal analyses by historians of

11. Editorial in *Boletim de História* (Centro de Estudos de História,
University of Brazil, Rio de Janeiro), V, No. 7 (1963), 11.
12. Eremildo Luis Vianna and Guy de Hollanda, in *ibid.*, p. 113.

other *specific pasts,* some from generalizing studies—studies methodically carried out by specialists in generalization. Some of the past particulars (*past in general*) that provide illuminating comparisons may belong to current events. Present as well as past states of affairs could be studied in the course of formulating generalizations sufficiently refined to assist the historian's researches into the *specific past.*

In the field of diplomatic history, George F. Kennan's *American Diplomacy: 1900-1950* was inspired by uncertainties that developed in his own thinking at a time when he shared responsibility for forming the foreign policy of the United States of America, uncertainties regarding appropriate policy objectives and working assumptions. In quest of relevant general "principles of action" he examines the *past in general.* A number of diplomatic episodes are scrutinized, the selection being influenced by the aim of the inquiry. The analyses of these episodes combine (a) identification and criticism of the principles of action that guided American foreign policy on those occasions—in so far as there was an intention to act rationally, and (b) identification of the causes of occurrences connected with those episodes. In Kennan's words:

This is not an attempt to recount a sequence of events, to report the development of new historical fact, or to give a rounded picture of America's diplomacy over fifty years. It is an attempt to look back from a present full of uncertainty and controversy and unhappiness, to see whether a study of the past will not help us to understand some of our present predicaments.

What is saddest of all is that the relationship between past and present seems to be visible to so few people. For if we are not to learn from our own mistakes, where shall we learn at all?

What lessons, in other words, does the record of the external relations of the United States over the last fifty years hold for us, the generation of 1951, pressed and hemmed in as we are by a thousand troubles and dangers, surrounded by a world part of which seems to be actually committed to our destruction and another part to have lost confidence either in ourselves or in itself, or in both?

These are the questions which have taken me back, in the past few months, to a review of some of our decisions of national policy in these fifty years.[13]

To cite one example of the general principles of action that issue from his analysis, Kennan concludes negatively that in dealing

13. George F. Kennan, *American Diplomacy: 1900-1950* (Mentor paperback ed.; New York: New American Library, 1952), pp. 10, 55, 56.

with a conflict of national interest, it has proved unsound to choose courses of diplomatic action on the premise that there is a "formal criterion of a juridical nature by which permissible behavior of states could be defined"; a sounder alternative requirement of appropriate courses of action is that they be "least unsettling to the stability of international life."[14]

Another type of study of the *past in general* is exemplified by Herbert J. Muller's book, *The Uses of the Past: Profiles of Former Societies*. It is an attempt to formulate and justify a number of basic principles of action (and evaluation) together with the requisite supporting attitudes—principles and attitudes often associated with scientific or naturalistic humanism. In a series of informal case studies we are shown the quality of life, the principles of evaluation and action, the successes and failures of former "societies." "We are confronted by societies embodying radically different ways of life, but it remains our business to judge the historical consequences of those ways. We can hope to make more intelligent judgments if we are aware of the many ways, and do not take for granted that our own is necessary or necessarily superior to all others."[15]

Relying heavily upon the generalized descriptions and causal accounts of these past societies (Greece, Rome, Byzantium, etc.) available in the works of historians, Muller concludes that the evidence points to the wisdom of solving problems and responding to uncertainties by adventurous experimentation based on the best available knowledge. That this is the best way to face the future constitutes a general principle of action applicable to countless diverse problematic situations.

Muller's book is intended for a wide audience; argument and evidence are often sacrificed to literary effects calculated to incite reflection and to gain a hearing for a comprehensive body of attitudes, values, and ideals which few people today live by. But the book is relevant because in it the author does explicitly what is often done implicitly: concerned with the future, he looks to the *past in general* for guidance, seeking primarily not natural order or predictive generalizations but insights that can function as principles of action. Moreover, the relevant *past in general* is the human past as available in works conventionally classified as his-

14. *Ibid.*, p. 94.
15. Herbert J. Muller, *The Uses of the Past: Profiles of Former Societies* (New York: Oxford University Press, 1952), p. 43.

tory. Muller's own use of the past is thus an illustration of the principle he espouses: a sound approach to the problems and incertitudes of today calls for learning from past experience about how to confront the future. His turning to the past as *past in general* (even though our ideas and institutions are causally dependent upon the selected former societies, so that these could be studied as the *specific past* of our present situation) and the way he approaches it exemplify another direction of dependence which we have stressed: not only have present concerns led Muller to survey the past, but *how* he surveys the past and *what parts* of it he selects for study reflect the dependence—as regards practical reasoning—of thinking about the *past in general* upon one's view of the present and future prospects. Muller is only somewhat more explicit than most authors of similar studies when he formulates—as a sound principle of action—a principle that he has followed himself: Where one looks and how one looks to the *past in general* for guidance, even for a general approach to problem-solving, should be guided by thinking about the future, i.e., by as reliable and clear a view as possible of the kind of problem-solving situations that lie ahead and the kind of resources that will be available to meet them.[16]

4. "History Proper" and Useful History

Thinking about particular happenings of the human past can, as we have shown, be involved in practical reasoning, i.e., in rational action: We think about past particulars in connection with deciding upon an appropriate course of action. But is this thinking about the past truly *historical* thinking?

If we seek enlightenment from what professional historians say and do or from theories about the nature of historical thinking, we are again confronted with controversy. One group of historians and theorists maintains that history is properly "present-minded" and action-oriented; "present-minded" in the sense that its point of departure is present-day problems and a concern for the future. Historical thinking essentially serves rational action. Its function is to clarify our concerns, the resources at our disposal, and the obstacles that confront us. The historian keeps track of how action based on decisions already made is working out. He points out emergent features of our present situation that might warrant a reassessment of priorities among our concerns, a re-allocation of

16. E.g., *ibid.*, p. 360.

our efforts or a reappraisal of our chances of succeeding. In opposition to this view, another group of historians and theorists of history maintains that present concerns regarding practical problems have no essential relationship to historical thinking. Our discussion thus far strongly suggests that this is another groundless controversy; further exploration of the disputed issues leaves no doubt that this is indeed the case.

On one side of this controversy it is claimed that historical thinking *can* have no relevance to decision-making because human existence is comprised of unique occurrences. Past particulars can therefore shed no light on the present or the future. But we have noted that the characteristics that constitute the non-duplicability of happenings do not preclude nomological relations. Similarly, as regards principles of action, the non-duplicability of happenings does not preclude working generalizations about the thing to do, which can serve as tools of analysis and reduce the indefiniteness of our concept of the appropriate course of action in a given situation. By combining and refining these generalizations we can, in principle, achieve in deliberation what we can, in principle, achieve in natural order thinking: a judgment based on experimental observation and analysis as to the "sufficient conditions" of an occurrence. The sufficient requirements of appropriate action are logically analogous to the sufficient conditions of an occurrence in terms of natural order. Clear recognition that any causal assertions about non-duplicable particular past occurrences presuppose a generalizable relation between particulars *as instances of kinds* should facilitate recognition of the plausibility of looking to past (or comparable present) experience for insights into causal factors of practical import. Similarly, clear recognition that criticisms of the reasonableness of a past rational action of another person presuppose objective principles of action should facilitate acknowledgement of the plausibility of looking to the past for insight into the appropriate course of action in respect to present concerns.

Again, it is claimed that "history proper" *can* have no essential relation to practical thinking *and* that the way to discover the nature of historical thinking is to scrutinize the actual work of professional historians. But some professional historians profess a contrary view of "history proper," and some of these (as is evident from examples in the preceding section) practice as well as profess thinking that is action-oriented.

Historians often speak as though any concern with the utility of their thinking inevitably compromises its objectivity. Only interest-free history can be objective, and historical thinking is least exposed to interest-distortion when it chooses a subject matter remote from sensitive present problems. Critics have countered by disclosing the unconscious controlling assumptions of historians who have given lip-service to a conception of "history proper" stripped bare of practical implications. Not only in what they have selected to describe or make intelligible by an explanatory narrative but also in tell-tale remarks about the significance of what they deal with, "pure" historians have disclosed their involvement with present concerns and their advocacy of certain principles of action.[17] It has often been pointed out that the doctrine of professional indifference to contemporary practical problems has operated to leave the historian himself unaware of practical commitments implicit in his "disinterested" reconstructions of the past. E. H. Carr observes that the contemporary historian who is wary of contributing as historian to the making of history, and who argues the impropriety of allowing the writing of history to become entangled with historical action, is with striking frequency one committed to the *status quo*.[18] In the same vein, it has been adjudged more than a curious coincidence that the "uniqueness of human phenomena" argument against the utility of history has been favored by conservative historians.[19]

Yet these disclosures do not establish conclusively that historical objectivity absolutely depends upon the historian's consciously assuming the role of specialist assisting his contemporaries with their practical reasoning. There is evidence of self-deception on the part of historians, but advocates of disinterested historiography argue persuasively that awareness of these pitfalls is itself a

17. See J. H. Randall, Jr., and George Haines, IV, "Controlling Assumptions in the Practice of American Historians," *A Report of the Committee on Historiography,* Social Science Research Council Bulletin 54, pp. 17-52; Herbert Butterfield, *The Whig Interpretation of History* (London: G. Bell and Sons, 1931); Ludwig Dehio, *The Precarious Balance* (New York: A. A. Knopf, 1962); Gerhard Ritter, "Scientific History, Contemporary History, Political Science," *History and Theory,* I, No. 3 (1961), 261-79, esp. pp. 275-76. Judgments of significance are often called interpretations of history. Both "significance" and "interpretation" are variously used, however, and we are not maintaining that concealed practical assumptions are involved in all so-called interpretations of history or all judgments about the significance of events.

18. E. H. Carr, *What is History?* (New York: A. A. Knopf, 1962), pp. 205 ff.

19. Karl Mannheim, *Ideology and Utopia* (London: Routledge and Kegan Paul, 1936), p. 180.

means toward achieving greater objectivity, and that a self-critical effort by an historian to suppress biases reflecting his current practical interests makes for more objective description and causal analysis. As for *use* of the past, the evidence merely indicates that *if* historical thinking is to serve practical reasoning, it can serve it best when the historian is fully aware of his intention, his practical principles, and his controlling assumptions, and when these are brought out into the open so that they can be scrutinized and criticized by those whose personal concerns are affected.

On the other side of this controversy, partisans of present-minded, pragmatic historiography have argued that thinking about the human past is deficient when it is not instrumental to rational action. Historical thinking, properly speaking, *is* practical thinking. What makes a history book history? asks Benedetto Croce:

> What constitutes history may be thus described: it is the act of comprehending and understanding induced by the requirements of practical life. These requirements cannot be satisfied by recourse to action unless first of all the phantoms and doubts and shadows by which one is beset have been dispelled through the statement and resolution of a problem—that is to say—by an act of thought. In the seriousness of some requirement of practical life lies the necessary condition for this effort. It may be a moral requirement, the requirement of understanding one's situation in order that inspiration and action and the good life may follow upon this. It may be a merely economic requirement, that of discernment of one's advantage. It may be an aesthetic requirement, like that of getting clear the meaning of a word, or an allusion, or a state of mind, in order fully to grasp and enjoy a poem; or again an intellectual requirement like that of solving a scientific question by correcting and amplifying information about its terms through lack of which one had been perplexed and doubtful. . . .
>
> Men with a gift for history (not to be confused with monks intent on compiling registers and chronicles, nor with the erudite who collect stories and documents, and by their industry produce reliable news, nor with scholarly compilers of historical manuals) have always been labourers in various fields, inclined to meditate upon situations which have arisen in order to overcome them and to assist others to overcome them by means of new activity. . . .[20]

According to this view, history is not the particular happenings of the human past and historical thinking is not simply the reconstruc-

20. Benedetto Croce, *History as the Story of Liberty* (London: Allen and Unwin, 1941), pp. 17-18, 44. See also Benedetto Croce, *History: Its Theory and Practice* (New York: Russell and Russell, 1960), chap. I.

tion of those happenings. History is the process of man's appropriating the past in making his future; historical thinking is the thinking that goes on in connection with this process or, rather, the thinking through which the process takes place. Similar ideas have been expressed in different terms and with different philosophical assumptions by, among others, Dilthey, Collingwood, Ortega y Gasset, and Aron: Instead of a nature, man has history; man is uniquely historical in his mode of being; only man makes or chooses himself in a process in which he passes from action to retrospective reflection, from reflection to new action, and so on. This is man's "historicity"—his making himself by historical thinking, consciously appropriating or rejecting the past, a developmental process altogether different from biological evolution.[21]

"Historical thinking proper" on our own part would presumably consist in our thinking about the past in the course of deciding what we should do. But what about our identifying understanding of another person's past practical thinking about his past: Would this understanding not also be historical thinking proper? There is considerable ambiguity in Croce's pronouncements as well as in statements by other partisans of the presentist-pragmatist thesis. Let us distinguish three possible conceptions: (1) Historical thinking, properly speaking, is restricted to thinking about the past from the standpoint of ourselves deliberating about what to do now. (2) Historical thinking, properly speaking, is restricted to thinking about the past from the standpoint of human agents—either of ourselves deliberating what to do now *or* of others living at that time, persons whose concerns, deliberations, and actions were directly involved in that past. (3) Historical thinking, properly speaking, is restricted to thinking about past rational actions of other persons from their standpoint, i.e., in terms of their concerns and circumstances at that time. Of these three, Croce sometimes appears to be espousing (1), at other times (2)—which combines (1) and (3)—but never merely (3).[22] In any case, it is (1) that

21. See the following: Wilhelm Dilthey, *Gesammelte Schriften* (Leipzig and Berlin: B. G. Teubner, 1942), VII, 135, 151, 276-78; R. G. Collingwood, *The Idea of History* (London: Oxford University Press, 1946), pp. 226-28; Ortega y Gasset, *Toward a Philosophy of History* (New York: W. W. Norton, 1941), p. 217; Raymond Aron, *Introduction to the Philosophy of History* (Boston: Beacon Press, 1961), pp. 37, 39.

22. It is interesting to see how William Dray in his account of historical thinking from the "standpoint of the agent" (in his sense) misses the point and the plausibility (with qualifications) of the Crocean assertion that "All history is contemporary history." See William Dray, *Laws and Explanation*

particularly interests us here. Obviously we can arbitrarily define "history" or "historical thinking" in such a way that (1) becomes trivially true, i.e., true by definition. But such a stipulation obscures rather than clarifies some of the ways in which we human beings can and do make particular happenings intelligible and, short of rendering it true in this trivial way, there appears to be no justification for the reduction of "history proper" to pragmatically oriented history.[23]

We can agree that a person's thinking about the past can be and often is involved in his choosing his future. Particular happenings of the past do acquire a special significance when they are viewed as illuminating what action we should take here and now. The intelligibility of the practical world, the world thought about by a person as living in the world and thought about with reference to his present concerns, does constitute one form of intelligibility. This form of intelligibility is involved in the historian's identifying understanding of the rational actions of others in the human past, where the personal reference is to their concerns *at that time.* It is likewise involved whenever any of us—including professional historians—is engaged in thinking about the past ultimately from the practical standpoint in reference to our present concerns: not in making past happenings intelligible by understanding how others thought of them but in making our situation here and now, our deciding upon a certain course of action, our engaging in that action, intelligible. For rational action involves making the world intelligible in terms of the reasonableness of what we are doing or are going to do. Even when we are still uncertain and deliberating, the world has an incipient intelligibility in relation to the ideal of appropriate rational action which we project upon unresolved situations; we know what line of questioning we are to follow even when we do not yet have the answers.

Granting the claims of this distinctive scheme of intelligibility,

---

in History (London: Oxford University Press, 1957), p. 140. Granting that Croce's position vacilitates between (1) and (2), we are surely misunderstanding him when we interpret that dictum, as Dray does, merely as an "exaggerated" or "paradoxical" endorsement of (3) (which approximates what we have called "identifying understanding"). Croce was certainly calling attention to the possibility and—in the case of some of his own historical studies—to the practice of thinking about past particulars in connection with formulating and deciding between *future* courses of action to be carried out *by the historian and his contemporary readers.*

23. Correspondingly, made true by definition, (2) would recommend itself only as being less restrictive, and so less gratuitous, than (1).

and recognizing that the personal reference can be to *our* present and prospective concerns in a situation calling for a decision among mutually exclusive courses of future conduct, what can justify the partisan claim that our thinking about past particulars is not *truly* historical thinking *unless* it is geared into the decision-making process by which we engage ourselves to preserve, reject, or modify the past? This would require showing that natural order intelligibility cannot be pursued for its own sake, that indeed there is no independent natural order line of questioning; but this cannot be done convincingly. Partisans of action-oriented historiography are obliged to distort or play down or restrict natural order questioning, treating analysis of particular pasts as *essentially* subordinate to decision-making. Secondly, it would have to be shown that identifying understanding of past rational actions is impossible or that it always turns out to be a disguised deliberation of our own about our present concerns. Neither of these countertheses bears up under scrutiny.

One defense of the partisan claim hinges on the definition of "understanding." Aron, for example, mistakenly supposing that he is able to overcome the first hurdle by establishing the possibility of an indefinite number of alternative natural order accounts of the same happening, attacks the second hurdle with the claim that all adequate understanding is essentially relative to the "interpreter" because "understanding always commits the interpreter." He, the interpreter, "is never like a physicist—he remains a man as well as a student. And he refuses to become pure scholar because understanding, beyond knowledge, aims at the *appropriation* of the past."[24] If one defines understanding as aiming at the appropriation of the past, then understanding does have relevance to the concerns of the interpreter built into it. But why *must* the interpreter aim at appropriating the past? It is more plausible to maintain that he can just as well aim at identifying understanding or at giving a natural order account, both cognitive ends in themselves. This or that segment of the world *can* be understood identifyingly or causally analyzed for the sake of ascertaining the thing to be done; *in such cases* that specific understanding or natural order knowledge does serve a cognitive end "beyond" itself. But this does not exclude the intelligibility of the world *for us* from the standpoint of *another* rational agent or from the impersonal natural order standpoint.

24. Aron, *Introduction*, p. 152 (italics in original).

A related argument for restricting "history proper" to presentist-pragmatic history consists in maintaining that either the historian's selection of a particular causal sequence for analysis and reconstruction is *arbitrary* or his selection must be guided by practical considerations pertaining to his present situation. More fully stated the argument is as follows: To select a particular causal sequence is to look upon past happenings as leading up to a certain outcome (e.g., Rostovtzeff wrote the history of Hellenistic empires as leading up to the Roman conquest). This selection constitutes a choice of focus on the part of the historian. *Any* focus "may be selected by the historian." He may select an outcome other than our present situation. "If one be content with such an arbitrary choice of focus . . . then reference to *our* present will not be called for. . . . But if the question be raised as to the justification for taking that particular past eventuation as the focus for historical investigation, then there must be and will be a reference to a still more 'ultimate' focus, in our present."[25] What is the nature of this justifying "reference"? It means that the historian who does not choose arbitrarily must either choose his present (as the outcome) or choose a past outcome that is significant to him in his present situation; choose it as *his* past, not merely as *the* past.[26] If the former, the selected causal sequence is also selected as *significant* to him in his present situation. "Significant to him in his present situation" is the criterion of selection. To be "significant to him," in turn, is to have consequences related to what he is trying to do, how he is going about it, what resources he has at his disposal, what limits and possibilities those materials have, and what he should be trying to do in the light of the foreseeable future.[27] In short, if the historian's selective account of a particular causal sequence is not to be arbitrary his selection must be guided by *practical* considerations pertaining to his *present* situation.

Let me comment on the preceding argument. Our question throughout this study has been: How are particular occurrences intelligible? Now it seems plausible to say that an occurrence becomes intelligible when we can give any natural order account of it. This at least is one mode of intelligibility, and it is of some importance to keep in mind the deterministic presumption of the natural order line of questioning. Any human occurrence can (in

25. J. H. Randall, Jr., *Historical Experience*, p. 50 (italics in original).
26. *Ibid.*, pp. 53-54.
27. *Ibid.*, pp. 57-58, 39-43.

principle) be made intelligible in this way. *No* natural order account *is* essentially subordinate to some more fundamental line of questioning. *Any* natural order account is a contribution to natural order intelligibility and, as such, is not "arbitrary." Objectivity in natural order historical knowledge does not presuppose criteria defining *the* appropriate focus.[28]

The question could still be raised: for what good reasons might the historian consider it appropriate on some particular occasion to ask the natural order question about just this occurrence rather than another; and why, of the possible alternative natural order accounts of the same occurrences, might he decide upon one of these rather than another—following out a certain causal sequence, utilizing one level of description rather than another, attending to remote rather than immediate conditions, and so on. Surely there are pertinent, legitimate reasons other than relevance to the historian's personal, present concerns from the standpoint of living in the world. The historian's choice—such as Rostovtzeff's selection of a focus—may be guided by considerations of ability, experience, available resources, or even the principle that in natural order inquiry one should ordinarily follow the promptings of one's intellectual curiosity.[29]

The claim that "genuine" history is based on a selection which presupposes a judgment or an effort to reach a judgment about the appropriateness of some present or contemplated action on the historian's part or on the part of his contemporary readers, obscures natural order thinking as an independent line of questioning and arbitrarily prescribes a categorical principle of action, a methodological master-principle to guide historians in the course of their work. This is not to deny that a strong practical case can be made against contemporary historians for their failure to come to grips with the "usable" past. And if a strong case can be made out—as Randall, Lynd, Carr, and others have maintained—then, indeed, the work of historians which displays indifference to present-day human problems is subject (from our standpoint as agents) to the charge of being misguided.[30]

Some historians try to steer a middle course between isolating

28. See *ibid.*, pp. 51 ff.
29. Cf. A. O. Lovejoy, "Present Standpoints and Past History," *The Journal of Philosophy*, XXXVI (1939), 481.
30. Robert S. Lynd, *Knowledge For What?: The Place of Social Science in American Culture* (Princeton, N. J.: Princeton University Press, 1939); Carr, *What is History?*, esp. chaps. V and VI.

historical thinking from present-day practical concerns and integrating historical thinking with rational action. This commonly takes the form of emphasizing the integrity of history and advocating that each of the disciplines dealing with man mind its own business. The business of the historian is impartial, objective reconstruction of past particulars. If generalizing social scientists (whether natural order thinkers, forecasters, or specialists in practical principles) can make use of historical reconstructions of the particular past, more power to them, but that is their business. If resultant generalizations are applied to present-day problem-solving that is the business of professional trouble-shooters and decision-makers. In neither case is this considered to be historical thinking, properly speaking.

Our earlier discussion of the interdependences involved in "using" the past, points up the vulnerability of this non-partisan, superficially sober and unassuming position. Generalizing from particulars and causal analysis of particulars are interdependent. Usable causal analyses of the relevant past are, for the most part, not produced inadvertently in the course of routine disinterested inquiry. Study of past particulars that is not consciously co-ordinated is likely to have at best a haphazard role in rational action. Exploitation of past experience for practical thinking entails closely integrated studies of past, present, and future, combining generalizing about what should be with specifying the ends and ideals involved in particular situations.

Consider the example of a writer who set out to learn from history about the best way of providing assistance to "underdeveloped countries" without generating undesirable political consequences. He explains why the results of his reading and study of history were largely negative or inconclusive. After mentioning first the limited number of countries available for study by historians, he continues:

> In the second place, it soon became evident . . . that the nature of the interrelations between political and economic changes is itself changing. It is doubtful how much we can learn about present and future relationships from experiences of fifty, one hundred, or two hundred years ago. . . .
> In the third place, I found that economic historians and historians in general, have for the most part not made their studies and written their reports in ways that answer the questions to which I needed answers. There has been little systematic attention to the political consequences and prerequisites of economic

development. What has been done is on a country-by-country basis and is not in a form that lends itself readily to cross-country comparisons. But without cross-country comparisons one is generalizing from single cases. It is often remarked that each generation has to rework history to bring the experience of the past to bear on its own problems. Today, the tremendous interest in economic development and the need for guidance not merely on its more narrow economic aspects but also on its political and cultural implications should send our historical experts back to their sources with some urgent new questions.[31]

Although available works of history in this case proved virtually useless, it was apparent that useful historical studies could be undertaken.

The past is "used" even when the professional historian does not lend a hand. Warrant for professional use of the past springs in part from the need to expose misconceptions perpetrated by pseudo-history; conceptions of history "of which everybody speaks and in which everyone believes" come "not from learned works of history, which have to be detailed in order to be sound and valuable, but from the catchwords of the journalism and publicity of the day."

Everyone knows how much the rigid and stubborn adherence of French diplomacy to antiquated concepts of hegemony in the twenties of our century contributed to preventing a reasonable reordering of Europe. Also well-known is the naivety with which many people in America believe that a united Europe must come about just as easily as once did the union of England's thirteen American colonies and that their democratic institutions can without further ado be carried over to the colored colonial peoples of all the world and operate just as wholesomely as in America. In this way, history can plainly narrow the width of the political horizon.[32]

If we are correct in maintaining that in serving rational action, generalizing judgments, judgments about particulars, causal analysis of particular pasts and current events, and predictions about the future are all logically interdependent, then much that historians—consciously or unwittingly mindful of present concerns—do with their subject matter can only be analyzed with reference to

31. Eugene Staley, *The Future of Underdeveloped Countries: Political Implications of Economic Development* (New York: Harper, 1954), pp. 80-81.

32. Gerhard Ritter, "Scientific History, Contemporary History, Political Science," *History and Theory*, I, No. 3 (1961), 269, 274.

their present situation and envisioned future. However we conceive of "history proper," we have to see the historian as living in the present and confronting the future if we are to understand the use of the past in practical reasoning. This awareness doubtless marks an advance in critical reflection; trouble begins when historical intelligibility is reduced to the terms of this insight.

5. RESPONSIBILITY AND INEVITABILITY

Pertinent to all conceptions of history are questions of the following sort: Is man's future inevitable? Do we, does any man—great or common—*choose* the future and, in choosing, forge his own destiny or that of mankind? Are we, any of us, *responsible* for what will come to pass in our careers or in world history? Although doctrines of historical inevitability and human responsibility are usually intended to apply to past as well as to present and future situations, the focus of the discussion in this section is our envisioned *future*.

In dealing with the alternatives which the above questions pose —man-made destiny *or* historical inevitability, human responsibility for what is to come *or* man's ultimate non-responsibility—we find that various positions and strategies have been adopted, none of them satisfactory. (a) One alternative is judged to be the correct view, the other erroneous. (b) We are told that both alternatives are true in their respective contexts, but we are not told precisely what these contexts are or how, if at all, they are related to one another. (c) The questions are side-stepped as "metaphysical" or "abstruse," something for philosophers to debate amongst themselves while plain men go about their business relying on common sense. Our own position is that plausible alternative *meanings* of "inevitable" and "responsible" correspond to different standpoints of human thinking, and that the truth or falsity of doctrines of historical inevitability and man's responsibility for the future can only be satisfactorily dealt with when the two standpoints—critically differentiated and refined—are kept in mind: the standpoint of natural order and the standpoint of rational agency.

To disentangle the issues involved in discussions of historical inevitability and man's responsibility for the future, we begin by asking what it might mean to say that we are responsible for the future. There are three relevant ideas which we shall formulate as necessary conditions. Responsibility for the future can be identified with *any one* of these, or all three may be regarded as necessary conditions of being responsible for the future. In stating these ideas we distinguish between our actions and their consequences and between intended consequences and actual consequences.

(1) *We are responsible for future occurrences if and only if our rational actions are among the necessary conditions of those occurrences.* ("Voluntary actions"—a broader concept—might be substituted for "rational actions," but this would needlessly complicate our discussion.) Correspondingly (and we shall refer to this as *the first conception of historical inevitability*), "historical inevitability" sometimes means that the future course of events (which is determined) will be entirely determined by causes other than our rational actions. We do not make history by our choices and decisions because our deliberate actions simply *do not affect the outcome.* This first conception of historical inevitability is tantamount to a denial of our responsibility for the future in sense (1).[33] There are many variations of this conception which need not be considered here in any detail: some or all future human events may be held to be "inevitable," and, if only some (e.g., only truly "historical" events or events of "broad human significance"), these are not always the same ones; it may be held that some of us are less ineffectual than others; it may be held that all of us by our actions can affect to some degree the *timing* of future developments, although *what* is going to happen sooner or later is beyond our control; what is envisioned as the inevitable future may be to our liking or horrendous; it may constitute the fulfilment of mankind or its annihilation; and so on. (The first conception of inevitability and the doctrine of man's *non*-responsibility in sense (1) *need not* be conjoined with the claim that a small number of transcendental, metaphysical, or abstractly conceived "forces" (such as God, Fate, Progress, Reason, *Geist*, etc.) determine what happens, for the number and variety of the determining conditions which *are* effective is immaterial; similarly they *need not* be conjoined with the claim that the course of human events, as a whole or in part, conforms to any "pattern"—linear, cyclical, morphological, etc. These observations apply also to the second and third conceptions of historical inevitability.)

(2) *We are responsible for the future if and only if in acting rationally, i.e., intending to do the appropriate thing, what we do*

33. See Ernest Nagel's example, *The Structure of Science* (New York: Harcourt, Brace and World, 1961), pp. 593 ff.

can reasonably be expected to affect the future so that actual consequences will conform to our intentions as agents. Correspondingly (and we shall refer to this as *the second conception of historical inevitability*), "historical inevitability" sometimes means that, even though our actions—including rational actions—*are* among the determining conditions of human events, the actual consequences of our actions do not conform to the intended consequences, i.e., we affect the course of events but we do not "control" it.[34]

(3) *We are responsible for the future if and only if, in choosing our actions and (thereby) the consequences of our actions, we confront genuine alternatives; only if, in other words, we "could do otherwise."* Correspondingly (and this we shall refer to as *the third conception of historical inevitability*), "historical inevitability" sometimes means that, even though future happenings (which are determined) are determined by our rational actions and even though the actual consequences of these actions conform with our intentions, our rational actions are themselves inevitable, together with their consequences. Our rational actions are inevitable in the sense that they have sufficient conditions over which we have no control: all things considered, we are not able to choose to act otherwise than we shall choose to act. This third conception of historical inevitability is tantamount to a denial of our responsibility for the future in sense (3), or at least to a denial of one interpretation of it, as we shall see.

As a condition of being responsible, (2) presupposes (1). (3), if it is recognized at all, is usually combined with (1) and (2) so that (1), (2), and (3) are all regarded as necessary conditions of being "responsible for the future." (Isaiah Berlin, for example, defends man's responsibility for the future in all three senses although it is responsibility in sense (3) that he is particularly concerned to affirm and, correspondingly, it is against the third conception of historical inevitability that his argument is principally directed.)[35]

34. We shall have little occasion to refer to this second conception of historical inevitability in the ensuing discussion. It is found, e.g., in C. Wright Mills's *The Causes of World War Three* (New York: Ballantine Books, 1958), pp. 26 ff., where he calls it the sociological conception of fate. Correspondingly, Mills speaks of responsibility in sense (2); men are responsible only for events which are not inevitable, i.e., which are consequences of rational actions, are foreseeable, and are not at variance with the intended consequences of those actions.

35. Isaiah Berlin, *Historical Inevitability* (London: Oxford University Press, 1954), *passim.*

Some insight into the confusion that pervades discussions of historical inevitability and human responsibility is obtained by noting that the first conception of historical inevitability is compatible with an indeterministic view of human decision and action,[36] whereas the third conception of historical inevitability presupposes a deterministic view of human decision and action. Moreover, *affirmation* of the third conception of historical inevitability (this affirmation often being tantamount to *denial* of our responsibility in sense (3)) is compatible with *denial* of the first conception of historical inevitability (this denial being tantamount to *affirmation* of responsibility in sense (1)). In other words, that causes beyond our control determine us to choose to act in a certain way is perfectly compatible with the view that deliberate acts are themselves efficacious. (It is also compatible with the affirmation that the actual consequences of our deliberate actions accord with our designs and intentions, i.e., with "responsibility" in sense (2).) Conversely, *denial* that our rational actions are efficacious and history-making is compatible with *affirming* that we "could do otherwise," provided that, as is commonly the case, efficacity is gauged by our influence upon *certain kinds* of events (e.g., large-scale events of "broad significance" such as military victories or defeats, socio-economic transformations, or the rise and fall of civilizations) or upon the future described in a *certain way* (e.g., with regard to long-term over-all trends). The actions that we do when we "could have done otherwise" will have consequences, thus will be—in a sense—efficacious, but they may not determine what are held to be the truly historical events. In short, the truth or falsity of either the first or the third conception of historical inevitability need not entail the truth or falsity, respectively, of the other.

Let us now consider historical inevitability and men's responsibility for the future in the light of our differentiation between standpoints of thinking.

From the standpoint of natural order the particular happenings of man's future are—like past happenings—plausibly presumed to be inevitable in the sense that, whatever the determining conditions, a deterministic (II) account could, in principle, be given of them. From the standpoint of natural order a person's choices of future courses of action, whether the choices are made by a throw

36. See, e.g., Berlin, *Inevitability*. This was discussed above, chap. VIII, sec. 5.

of the dice or by elaborate reasoning, are presumed to be manifestations of deterministic (II) relations. In principle they could
be predicted in terms of these deterministic (II) relations. More
particularly, it is plausible to presume that all human decisions and
actions are ultimately determined by causes none of which is accurately described as within the control of the agent. We presume
that, all things considered (and it is characteristic of natural order
questioning to persist in the search for determining conditions),
no rational agent could choose to act otherwise than he does. From
the natural order standpoint, therefore, *the third conception* of
historical inevitability *is tenable* and a person is not responsible
for any future action or any consequences thereof in sense (3).

From this same standpoint, our responsibility for the future
in senses (1) and (2) together with the tenability of *the first conception* of historical inevitability (which denies the efficacy of our
rational actions) are matters to be settled by empirical inquiry.
Even empirical inquiry will settle nothing unless it is made quite
clear which future occurrences are in question. It has been justly
remarked that "available evidence" does not support "the thesis
that [deliberate] individual or collective human effort never oper-
ates as a decisive factor in the transformations of society." More
positively expressed, the evidence warrants the judgment that
what transpires as a consequence of their efforts to shape their
destiny sometimes corresponds to or approximates the intentions
of some human agents; at least what transpires will occasionally
be less contrary to agents' intentions than would be the case were
no deliberate effort made on their part. This is not to deny that,
on the other hand, "in many historical situations individual choice
and effort may count for little or nothing, nor that there frequently
are ascertainable limits to human power for directing the course
of social changes—limits that may be set by facts of physics and
geography, by biological endowment, by modes of economic production and available technological skills, by tradition and political
organization, by human stupidity and ignorance, as well as by
various antecedent actions of men."[37]

To summarize, *from the standpoint of natural order thinking,
history is inevitable* (in the sense of *the third conception*) and
men are not responsible (in sense (3)) for what they do or bring
about, even by their rational actions. But we can expect that *we
shall be responsible* for some future occurrences in sense (1) and

37. Nagel, *Structure of Science,* pp. 593, 594.

that *we shall be responsible* for some future occurrences (although doubtless fewer) in sense (2), so that as a generalization about *all* future occurrences *the first conception of historical inevitability is not tenable.*

Turning to thinking *from the standpoint of agency* (i.e., living in the world), what we discovered earlier in our analysis of rational action from the standpoint of the agent applies to prospective actions of our own or of our contemporaries as well as to past actions of others. Our previous analysis, directed primarily at clarifying the nature of historical thinking about *past* happenings, thus stands us in good stead here in our consideration of man's outlook on his future. From the standpoint of rational agency, whether we ourselves are the agents deliberating about what to do or are identifying with our contemporaries who are engaged in like deliberations, the future is not inevitable, i.e., *not thought of as inevitable,* in the sense that we do not think of what we shall do and of the consequences thereof as manifestations of deterministic (II) relations, nor do we presume that, in principle, they can be made intelligible in that way. From this standpoint, therefore, the third conception of historical inevitability is not precisely "untenable" but it is "incongruous" or "out of the question." The questioning and the presuppositions of the questioning that could lead to an affirmation of the third conception of historical inevitability are not consonant with the questioning that goes on from the standpoint of rational agency. From the latter standpoint it is not a problem and we *do not ask* whether our choices are determined or not; accordingly, we do not judge that they are or are not, all things considered. Consequently, we neither affirm nor reject the third conception of historical inevitability with its notion that, all things considered, our choices and actions have sufficient conditions over which we have no control.

Whether we are responsible for the future in sense (3) has been supposed to depend upon rejection of the third conception of historical inevitability. If the latter is neither affirmed nor rejected from the standpoint of rational agency, does it follow that responsibility in sense (3) is also neither affirmed nor rejected? Do we not, as rational agents facing the future, definitely have genuine alternatives? Here again our earlier analysis is illuminating.[38] Sense (3) of responsibility, we must realize, is ambiguous. If "being able to do otherwise" (i.e., having genuine alternatives) is

38. Above, chap. VIII, sec. 5.

interpreted as presupposing that we *ultimately* control our choices —which implies indeterminism and which is *one* possible interpretation—then we are again raising the question as to the status of the third conception of inevitability from the standpoint of the agent: We neither affirm nor reject our "being able to do otherwise" when so interpreted. (*If* we affirmed our having genuine alternatives, interpreted as presupposing indeterminism, what we here affirm regarding the standpoint of rational agency *would be* incompatible with what we judge to be the case in thinking about our choices from the natural order standpoint.) But a more apposite analysis of our "being able to do otherwise" allows us to affirm that as rational agents we do have genuine alternatives, and it allows us to affirm this without presupposing indeterminism. The logic of deliberation requires that in deciding what course of action is appropriate we think of ourselves as able to carry out any of several mutually exclusive alternative acts. These acts are all thought of as feasible. They are not thought of as feasible all things considered, but then, as we saw, it is an essential characteristic of deliberation that the rational agent not think about certain things deterministically, namely, his decision-to-be-reached, his action-to-be-decided-upon, or the consequences thereof. The rational agent cannot ask: All things considered (i.e., considered *as* determining conditions), what shall I decide? what shall I be doing as a consequence of my decision? what will be happening as a consequence of my action?

Am I, then, responsible for my future? Are my contemporaries responsible for theirs—and perhaps mine too? Does our being responsible depend upon whether we are in positions of responsibility or not? The answer is that any person who is himself deliberating, or who thinks (identifyingly) of another—a contemporary—*as* a rational agent, thinks of himself or that other person as responsible for the future, as being able to make the future, in the sense of being able to make any of several decisions, carry out any one of several acts, determine any of several lines of consequences. Any such person is in a "position of responsibility" with respect to any of those future happenings which (according to the logic of deliberation) he cannot think about deterministically. To put this another way, *in thinking from the standpoint of rational agency* it is a natural order question about specific events whether we are responsible for them in sense (1) or sense (2), but it is not a natural order question whether we are or are not responsible in sense (3). Awareness of our responsibility in sense (3) as a distinctive presupposition of practical thinking is accomplished through critical reflection; it is a discovery *about the nature of human thinking about the world,* not a conclusion about the world as thought of from the natural order standpoint.

The sort of responsibility for the future that we discover to be an essential feature of thinking from the standpoint of rational agency is not that argued for by many critics of the idea of historical inevitability (e.g., Isaiah Berlin). It does not presuppose an *ultimately* self-controlled self. It does not impinge on the plausibility of a presumption of determinism in respect to the natural order line of questioning. Yet man's viewing the world as a *maker* of history, choosing among alternatives and responsible for the future—the idea that has inspired Berlin and others—is affirmed (with due refinement) by our analysis of the logic of rational action.

We particularly call attention to the inadequacy, as a defense of responsibility and a critique of historical inevitability, of the view that rational actions do after all take place, that a rational agent does after all exercise "control" over his actions and does have a greater or lesser "range of free choice." For it is usual, in conjunction with this view, either to maintain explicitly, without any differentiation of standpoints of thinking, that deterministic accounts of decisions actually reached could be given (at least, in principle), or else to leave unanalyzed the character of the "control" and "free choice." But to say that a deterministic account could be given is to endorse without qualification the third conception of historical inevitability, and thus to distort thinking from the standpoint of the agent. To leave unanalyzed the nature of the "genuine alternatives" and the "could do otherwise" is to leave the character and status of that same mode of historical thinking in obscurity.[39] By contrast, we have maintained that—and have shown why—deterministic accounts of rational actions *cannot* be given from the standpoint of the agent.

It remains to comment, still from the standpoint of rational agency, on senses (1) and (2) of "responsible for the future." Because our responsibility for the future in sense (2) (*conformity* of actual with intended consequences) presupposes sense (1) (our rational actions *do* condition the future), and because re-

---

39. These criticisms seem to me to apply, for example, to Nagel's remarks, in *Structure of Science,* pp. 592 ff., esp. pp. 598 and 602.

sponsibility in sense (1) depends directly upon history's *not* being inevitable according to the first conception of historical inevitability (rational actions conceived as having no effect upon the future course of events), we can deal with all the pertinent questions in the course of asking whether we are responsible for the future in sense (2). The plausibility of practical thinking and of its ideal of practical intelligibility (i.e., living in the world, engaged in action that is appropriate in reference to our concerns) does presuppose that we can *sometimes* act so as to contribute to effects, to differences in the world, which accord *to some extent* with our intentions. We can imagine a formulation of our non-responsibility for the future in sense (2), declaring that *all* our actions will fail *utterly* to produce their intended consequences. Such a formulation, if we could understand its meaning and if credible, *would* strike at the plausibility of deliberating about what we do in relation to what we care about. All that can be said is that, upon reflection, the ideal of practical intelligibility does not seem to be in jeopardy on such grounds. It *is* plausible for us to conceive of our future being, doing, and making in terms of mutually exclusive, feasible alternatives and to ask, in the light of past experience, "used" in all the ways it can be used in practical reasoning, which one of these alternatives is appropriate.

The issue that confronts us as rational agents is not whether our intention to act appropriately is naive but rather what feasible actions are appropriate. In so far as we consider future consequences of our actions we ask what effects specific feasible courses of action can be expected to have and which effects are preferable. If a person decides that he can "do nothing" about an unsatisfactory situation, no meliorating action being feasible, his deliberation does not issue in "ineffectual" or futile action; his action *is* his refraining from attempting the impossible. If I try to do or achieve what I cannot do or achieve, I am not doing what would be appropriate under the circumstances. The ineffectuality or unsuccessfulness of deliberate action, occasional or repeated, poses a challenge; it is an occasion for criticism, for learning from experience, or, it may be, for perseverance. Generalizations stating that what we are able to do can have little effect—or no effects *of a certain kind in certain areas*—can, in principle, be verified, and can serve as guidelines for practical reasoning: guidelines in choosing overt courses of action depending, e.g., upon *what* events cannot be controlled and *how much* or *how little* difference *of what sort* a certain course of action can be expected to make; guidelines, too, in deciding what attitudes toward the future, what habits of mind, are appropriate for ourselves, our contemporaries, our off-spring—in judging appropriate, for example, acceptance of what is inevitable and welcoming challenges to make the best of our abilities and resources, in lieu of longing for the impossible. Assuming that there are areas in which our rational actions can be expected to have no intended effect whatsoever, the reasonable thing, presumably, would be to expend one's energies and intelligence along other more constructive lines. Let there be uncontrollable events, let these be called "history" and history be declared "inevitable"; it still remains for us, living in the world, to do what we can in behalf of what we care about; to find the feasible alternatives in concrete situations and, choosing as wisely as we know how, to go on learning how to choose more wisely.

To summarize: *From the standpoint of rational agency, the inevitability of history* (in the sense of *the third conception*) *is not actually denied, but we do not think about our future decisions deterministically* (and therefore not as having sufficient conditions beyond our control). *We do think of ourselves as responsible in sense* (3), although not in a way that presupposes our having ultimate control over our decisions. As a generalization about all future occurrences *the first conception of historical inevitability is not tenable.* On the other hand, generalizations about our success or the lack of it, in specific areas, in achieving what we set out to do, are subject to empirical verification. Presumably, *some future occurrences are inevitable* (in the sense of *the first conception*); *for some others,* by contrast, *we shall be responsible in sense* (1), and *for a number of the latter, we shall be responsible in sense* (2).

The distinctions that we have made are glossed over in every-day life situations; this is as we might expect. It is of greater interest when we find them neglected or confused in thoughtful analyses of matters of general concern.

In his book *The Future as History,* Robert L. Heilbroner attempts to distinguish between future occurrences that will take place regardless of what we do and another class of events that is to some degree "within the scope of our control and responsibility."[40] The latter represent historical possibilities. "Freedom and necessity" co-exist in history, and freedom is correlated with possibility.

40. Robert L. Heilbroner, *The Future as History* (New York, 1959), pp. 181-83.

Heilbroner speaks of our "free decisions" and of events as amenable "to our wills." Nowhere does he define "free decision." The distinction between events within and not within our control, between the open future and the inevitable, is drawn with regard to what he calls "the living reality of history," "the experience of history itself." He contrasts this standpoint with that of "abstract thought," with its "classic dilemma" of "determinism versus historic freedom."

Heilbroner's distinctions are plausible enough, but they apply within only one standpoint of thinking. They are therefore vulnerable to critics who speak on behalf of natural order intelligibility and assume *it* to be the only form in which world happenings are truly intelligible to us. Heilbroner is mistaken in supposing that "abstract thought" is the only alternative to the standpoint of living in the world (i.e., "living reality"). From the latter standpoint, in confronting specific situations one of our problems is—as he correctly states—"to determine in the light of the actualities of the moment how much of history lies within our grasp and how much lies beyond."[41] To assist his American contemporaries of the 1960's in this task is the principal objective of his book. But to grasp its import clearly and correctly we must understand that another standpoint of thinking—natural order—by no means "abstract" and with its own distinctive presuppositions, is just as plausible and just as fundamental. From the latter standpoint we are *not* responsible for the future (according to one interpretation of the equivocal sense (3)) and (the third conception of) historical inevitability *is* tenable. The single-minded partisan of natural order intelligibility can therefore argue persuasively that "historical possibility" and "free decision" have no proper place in judgments accounting for what goes on in the world—past, present, or future. The "classic dilemma" is not as easily disposed of as Heilbroner supposes.

How is one to defend open possibilities, free decisions, and responsibility for the future against the plausibility of natural order determinism? Perhaps by defining freedom in terms of an absence of constraint? But do not reason-determined actions have sufficient conditions not under the agent's control? Are we responsible for any future occurrences if it is plausible to presume that, all things considered, we could not choose to act otherwise than we shall choose? The classic solutions *are* unconvincing.

41. *Ibid.*, p. 182.

We need a pluralistic conception of historical thinking and an analysis of the logic of each standpoint. In particular we need an analysis that shows how our thinking of decisions as "free," of alternative events as "possible," and of ourselves as "responsible" is rooted in the logic of deliberation, i.e., practical thinking from the standpoint of living in the world.

In *Uses of the Past* Herbert J. Muller distinguishes between "fatalism" and the view that human actions can and sometimes do make "a profound difference in history."[42] He makes out a strong case for rejecting the former and accepting the latter. In *our* terms, he affirms man's responsibility for the future in sense (1). He then goes on to speak about our "responsibility" for the future as though this were the same conception, opposed to fatalism, whose plausibility he had been maintaining. Actually it is not the same. It implies that human agents have "real alternatives" and therefore corresponds to what we distinguished as responsibility in sense (3). But to deny fatalism is not tantamount to affirming our responsibility for the future in sense (3); whether or not we have "real alternatives" (in any ordinary sense of this expression) is a matter quite independent of whether or not the actions we perform are efficacious.

Some other remarks of Muller's in support of our responsibility for the future *are* germane to the question whether we have "real alternatives" or not. Muller observes: "If everything that has happened is the only thing that could possibly have happened, we might as well close the book. The reason we don't is that even the determinists and fatalists are always implying that there were real alternatives, and that men made the wrong choice. Whatever we believe in theory, we continue in practice to think and act as if we were not puppets."[43]

This apparently means that the assumption we make, in practice, that we have "real alternatives"—"a wide range of choices," Muller says elsewhere[44]—presupposes that our decisions are ultimately within our control. That is to say, it presupposes indeterminism: We are responsible for the future in sense (3), *interpreted indeterministically*, and history is not inevitable (in the sense of the third conception of historical inevitability). Thus Muller appears

42. Muller, *Uses of the Past*, p. 37.
43. *Ibid.*
44. *Ibid.*, p. 69.

to affirm indeterminism.[45] Nowhere does he consider the case for the plausibility of the ideal of deterministic intelligibility, either to endorse it or to reject it. Yet the status of our "practical" assumption of "real alternatives" remains problematical—and controversial—until the implications of natural order questioning are squarely confronted. The plausibility of the ideal of deterministic intelligibility, confirmed by our analysis, invites attention to the contrasting assumptions of our thinking as agents. Once duly clarified, our responsibility for the future in sense (3) (i.e., having genuine alternatives) is disclosed not to be incompatible with the idea (which I rephrase so as to include the future) that Muller finds so menacing to our confrontation of the world caringly: everything that happens in history is the only thing that could possibly happen.

"The fact is that all human actions are both free and determined, according to the point of view from which one considers them. . . . Cause and moral responsibility are different categories." These remarks from E. H. Carr's *What is History?*[46] seem to promise insights into the differences between the standpoint of the agent and the standpoint of natural order. But Carr's discussion is disappointing in that respect. The standpoint of the agent is nowhere clearly described and differentiated from the standpoint of natural order. The obscurity of his position is all the more interesting because he is not only a respected historian but a man who has contributed to public debate over the social goals and policies appropriate to our present circumstances and future prospects. He has been concerned with making history as well as writing it. Not surprisingly, in his reflections about historical thinking he conceives the latter to embrace both reconstructing the past and shaping the future.

In a passage that happens to refer to reconstructing the past, we are told that *in practice* historians "frequently discuss alternative courses available to the actors in the story on the assumption that the option was open."[47] Presumably, when *we* are the actors, *we* assume in practice that there is an open option between alternatives. Is the historian serious when he makes this assumption? Is he naive if he is serious about it? Are *we* naive if we take it serious-

45. But, after serving notice that he is waiving "the metaphysical problem of free will," he defines freedom in terms of "the ability to do things in and to the world." If that is all there is to freedom, can we speak of men having "real alternatives"? See *ibid.*, p. 35n.

46. P. 124.

47. *Ibid.*, p. 125.

ly? Or are we and the historian merely thinking from one point of view? Supposing that we adopt this notion of a point of view, does the point of view here in question, i.e., that of human agents, imply that the agent's choice is not sufficiently determined by conditions beyond his control?

In so far as Carr has answered these questions at all his statements are vague or conflicting; in effect, he leaves the questions of our responsibility for the future and of the inevitability of history unresolved. Carr states, for example, that to assume "the option was open" is quite consistent with judging (as he says historians and ordinary men do) that the eventual decision could not have been otherwise, given "the antecedent causes"; or, prospectively, with judging that our future decisions and actions will be sufficiently determined by antecedent causes.[48] In other words, a deterministic (II) account of decisions is presumed to be possible in principle. Apparently then, the "openness" of an option, assumed by all of us ordinary men as agents, is consistent with the third conception of historical inevitability and implies the *denial* of the indeterministic interpretation of responsibility in sense (3). But other statements Carr has made identify "openness" with that same indeterministic interpretation of responsibility in sense (3), presupposing *denial* of the third conception of historical inevitability.

The human being is indissolubly bound, in both his actions and his judgments, by a chain of causation reaching far back into the past; *yet he has a qualified power to break the chain at a given point*—the present—and so alter the future. In common-sense language, he can decide and judge for himself, but only up to a certain point; for the past limits and determines his decision and his judgment in innumerable ways. To admit that our judgments are wholly and irrevocably conditioned is to plead moral and intellectual bankruptcy.[49]

In the quoted passage Carr clearly is not pleading "moral and intellectual bankruptcy." He is *affirming* the indeterministic interpretation of human responsibility in sense (3); i.e., that our responsibility for the future presupposes that deterministic (II) accounts cannot be given of our rational actions. Apparently, then, he both affirms and denies the plausibility of the third conception of historical inevitability and of our responsibility in sense (3).

It is also noteworthy that the so-called dilemma of determinism

48. *Ibid.*, pp. 125-26.
49. E. H. Carr, *The New Society* (Beacon Paperback ed.; Boston: Beacon Press, 1957), p. 14 (italics added).

and free will referred to in *The New Society*[50] is not the same dilemma as the "dilemma about free will and determinism" discussed in *What is History?*.[51] By differentiating voluntary action from action caused by compulsion, Carr easily resolves one dilemma (namely, how can one and the same action be both free and determined) and does so within the framework of determinism (i.e., natural order thinking). We are misled into believing that he has resolved a quite different dilemma: How can we think of ourselves as responsible for the future and as having genuine options among alternatives if our decisions result necessarily from antecedent causes beyond our control? We are misled because however plausible Carr's differentiation between voluntary and constrained action, it does not solve *this* dilemma. "Breaking the chain" of determinism—which is the solution proposed in the quotation from *The New Society*—would solve it; but unfortunately it is a solution at odds with the natural order presumption of determinism in human phenomena, a presumption Carr himself apparently deems plausible.

6. The Meaning of History

Is there a distinctive kind of historical thinking that takes the form of ascertaining "the meaning of history"? In this section we shall describe and comment upon conceptions of the meaning of history, taking special note of their relationship to thinking about particular occurrences from the two fundamental standpoints we have differentiated.[52]

Ideas about the meaning of history such as those held by Bossuet, Condorcet, Herder, Hegel, Comte, Spencer, certain Marxist thinkers, Spengler, Reinhold Niebuhr, and Toynbee are often incorporated in so-called philosophies of history. Our principal theses regarding "philosophies of history" and their claims as to the meaning of history are two: *first*, "philosophies of history" are uncritical in aiming at the intelligibility of history as a whole, without differentiating between schemes of intelligibility; *second*, once the two standpoints of thinking (natural order and living in the world)

50. *Ibid.*
51. P. 124.
52. Although natural order thinking about particular human occurrences sometimes takes the form of a claim about the meaning of history, our major conclusions regarding these claims presuppose as background our Part Two discussion of living in the world. For the sake of convenience, therefore, we have consolidated discussion of the topic here.

have been differentiated and refined, the plausibility—within limits
—of philosophy of history as the pursuit of unified intelligibility
can be duly recognized and appreciated.

We can distinguish two types of claims, both of which are found
in most "philosophies of history." Type (1): The claim that human
events follow one another in determinate sequence, the totality of
human events being either comprised in a single determinate sequence (e.g., world history) or distributed among a limited number
of very inclusive determinate sequences (e.g., the temporal careers
of Spengler's "cultures" or Toynbee's "civilizations"). In type (1)
claims, the characteristic form—or pattern—of the sequence as determinate (e.g., Herbert Spencer's "Law of Evolution") is itself
sometimes proposed as an ultimate explanatory principle, constituting the intelligibility of history. In this case the "meaning" of
an event is equivalent to its determinate place, date, and other
characteristics within the pattern. Or the sequence of events
(usually regarded as manifesting a pattern—*the* pattern of one
all-inclusive sequence; or patterns—one or more *general* patterns
exemplified in specific sequences) may be conceived of as determinate relative to certain factors or relations among factors.
(If the patterned character of the sequence is particularly emphasized, the "meaning" of an event may comprise *both* its place, date,
and other characteristics as determinate relative to the pattern of
the sequence *and* these characteristics as further determined relative to certain factors.) The factors may be causal agencies (such
as the will of God or the "will to power") or variables (such as
"forces of production" or climatic conditions). A "law of history"
associated with a type (1) claim may therefore take the form of
correlations between the course of events and causal factors; or it
may take the form of correlations between the patterned character
of the sequence and factors discriminated *within* the course of
events. In either case, type (1) claims usually postulate a small
number of patterns or basic factors, and the "meaning" of an event
is equivalent to its place, date, and other characteristics as determined by these. If more than one pattern or "law" is required to account for the course of events; if occurrences are not intelligible in
terms of "closed systems" (i.e., if the pattern or "law" allows of a
great many contingencies); if the pattern- or "law"-determined
events do not encompass a wide variety of human phenomena (e.g.,
social, political, economic, and cultural); or if the causal scheme is
complicated, then the formulation is not likely to be considered a

"philosophy of history" at all and is not held to disclose the meaning of history. Type (2): The claim that particular human events are intelligible in terms of a single axiological principle—a principle from which judgments follow as to what is "good" or "right."[53] In respect to type (2) claims, the "meaning" of any particular event depends ultimately on its having some positive status or function in relation to what is "good" or "right."

Corresponding to these two types of claims, the meaning of history can refer either to (1) the pattern or event-determining factors of the course of events, or (2) the axiological criterion of meaningfulness as realized or reflected in the course of events. Both types of claim have one point in common: they are supposed to make all of history intelligible. To be sure, philosophers of history usually have not dealt with the whole of history, but they characteristically hold out the promise of unified total intelligibility and their conception of historical subject matter is not supposed to be arbitrarily selective.

We have distinguished two types of claims; philosophers of history do not usually do so. We have differentiated a sense of the meaning of history corresponding to type (1) claims; but so characteristic of thinking about "history as a whole" has been the combination of type (1) and type (2) claims, that "the meaning of history" has an established association with intelligibility in terms of what is "good" or "right." In other words, a type (1) claim without a type (2) claim, a rare but perfectly conceivable phenomenon, would not usually be considered a proper "philosophy of history"; it would be scarcely thought to qualify as an attempt to reveal the meaning of history. A fundamental critical oversight is involved, however, in the tacit or explicit pursuit of the unified intelligibility of history—unified in the sense that the goal is a combined type (1) and type (2) claim. What is overlooked is that type (1) claims fall within the province of natural order questioning and type (2) claims within the province of thinking from the standpoint of living in the world.

We have already remarked that the differentiation and refinement of standpoints of thinking proceed interdependently. We have said that it is only retrospectively, from the vantage point of

53. The term "axiological principle" is used here instead of "principle of evaluation" because the principle in question can function as a "principle of action" as well as a "principle of evaluation" (in the special narrower sense in which we have been using the latter expression).

a certain critical sophistication, that we can judge a particular thinker to have combined judgments from different standpoints; it is only from this vantage point that we can judge him to have answered uncritically questions pertaining to one or another of these standpoints. The course of the development of man's thinking about history as a whole and of critical reflection regarding the quest for the unified intelligibility of history provides rich material for investigations into the nature of human thinking. We could deal with this material at considerable length, using it to corroborate our analysis or, applying our conclusions to it, assessing and comparing the critical sophistication revealed in the thinking of individual philosophers of history. Instead we shall assume that the differentiation and refinement of standpoints has been established by our previous discussion. Against the background of that discussion we make our distinction between the two types of claims and two senses of the meaning of history: a critically sophisticated distinction paralleling and reflecting that between the two standpoints of thinking. We shall further assume that even when a "philosophy of history" reveals no awareness of this distinction, it is still plausible to use the latter as an instrument of critical analysis. This could easily be substantiated by doing some comparative analyses of "philosophies of history." Before proceeding further, one point requires clarification and exemplification: our identification of type (2) claims with thinking from the standpoint of living in the world.

Elaborating first upon our description of the type (2) claim as to the meaningfulness of history, we note that not only the content of the various axiological principles set forth in such claims differs from one to the other, but also the way in which particular events are conceived to embody or realize "goodness" or "rightness." For purposes of analysis let us distinguish between (a) the asserted or assumed axiological principle that provides the criterion (or criteria) of meaningfulness and (b) the judgment that what has happened, is happening, and will happen satisfies the criterion (or criteria). Depending upon the criterion, this latter judgment may be to the effect that all particular human events are themselves "good" or "right," or that they are valuable as necessary conditions of the "good" or the "right," or that they are instances in which "goodness" or "rightness" are at stake. All type (2) claims as to the meaning of history include both (a) and (b).

Perhaps the simplest illustration of these components is provided by the conception of the course of human events as progressive, i.e., the view that there is an over-all trend in the direction of individual and social human perfection. A claim along these lines was made by Herbert Spencer and further developed by John Fiske. The criterion of meaningfulness, according to Spencer, is a notion of "fitness to the social state,"[54] and in Fiske's reformulation: the adjustment of "man's rules of action and emotional incentives" to "the requirements arising from the circumstances of their aggregation into communities."[55] The plausibility of this criterion is supposedly enhanced by these authors' disclosure of analogous tendencies toward "perfection" in *all* phenomena. Judged by the criterion, particular human phenomena are meaningful not only as embodying some degree of perfection, but more especially through the interrelatedness of events, as resultants of prior stages and as necessary conditions of subsequent higher levels of perfection. This conception of the meaningfulness of history extends to human lives, institutions, and societies of all times and places.

In other "philosophies of history," although strikingly different from those of Spencer and Fiske, we nonetheless find both (a) an axiological principle and (b) a judgment that events satisfy this principle.

According to Reinhold Niebuhr's version of the Biblical-Christian interpretation of history, "there are no observable facts of history which can not be interpreted" in the light of Christian faith.[56] "The process of history as a whole" is judged meaningful relative to the principle that anything taking place as part of God's overall plan is "right" or "good."[57] The lives of individuals and the rise and fall of cultures and civilizations are likewise meaningful, but in a different sense, namely, in relation to the idea that how we use our freedom—defying God or loving and obeying Him out of "humble recognition of the fragmentary character of our own wisdom, virtue and power"—is the ever-present and crucial moral issue during this our worldly pilgrimage.[58] In respect to this

54. Herbert Spencer, *Social Statics* (London: Williams and Norgate, 1868), p. 80.
55. John Fiske, *Outlines of Cosmic Philosophy* (8th ed.; Boston: Houghton, Mifflin, 1874), II, 208.
56. Reinhold Niebuhr, *Faith and History* (New York: Charles Scribner's Sons, 1951), p. 137.
57. Reinhold Niebuhr, *The Nature and Destiny of Man* (New York: Charles Scribner's Sons, 1941), II, 301.
58. Niebuhr, *Faith and History*, p. 234.

criterion, even sinful acts, i.e., those in opposition to God's goodness, are deemed meaningful.

In his lectures on "philosophy of history," Hegel declares that Reason is Good and that "the claim of the World-Spirit" (i.e., Reason as creative, producing the happenings of World History) "rises above all special claims." From this he infers that the "real import and value" (measured by the supreme criterion of meaningfulness) of individual deeds, organized societies, and their component institutions is their positive status and function as objectifications of Reason in the integral process of world-historical development. Inasmuch as Reason "governs the world,"[59] *all* of the particular actions and social-political institutions that comprise World History have a positive status and function (i.e., are meaningful) as partial realizations of freedom or self-consciousness, and as stages in a developmental process progressing gradually but inevitably toward complete freedom and self-consciousness. (Hegel's conception of world-historical events is more selective than that of many other philosophers of history. Entire peoples and civilizations are excluded from World History. Also, whereas Niebuhr, for example, views the meaningfulness of individual lives as involving a distinct mode of *historical* meaning, Hegel, although recognizing the intimate connection between Reason and individual morality and conceding that the latter has a share in Reason's "absolute claims," treats the "infinite worth" of individual morality as meaningful independently of World History. But there is no mistaking that Hegel considers his conception definitive: his version of world history is intended to be *the* biography of the World-Spirit; it is intended to disclose *the* meaning of history.)

In *The Decline of the West* Spengler argues that history is intelligible only when it is seen to consist of the careers of an indefinite number of distinct "cultures." (Spengler mentions some eight or ten of these.) The analysis of Western "culture" which gives the book its title comprises only a minor part of the evidence he cites in developing his claim. The outward manifestations of the various cultures are the product of as many unique vital principles or "souls." These vital principles come into being and, barring catastrophic interference from "outside," pass of necessity through a life-cycle of growth and decay comparable to that of physiological organisms. Although each unique cultural soul pro-

59. G. W. F. Hegel, *The Philosophy of History* (New York: Willey Book Co., 1944), pp. 36-37.

duces unique cultural manifestations, the pattern of growth and decay is the same. The axiological principle in Spengler's system is formulated in terms of "vitality": all activity that is an expression of a specific life-principle's creative potential has positive value—even activity during the terminal stage of cultural decrepitude. All manifestations of a given culture are *symbolically* meaningful in that they can be interpreted as expressions of their unique creative principle at different stages of its career. More to the point, however, once we know the nature of the origin of human history we know the true measure of *axiological* meaningfulness. Human phenomena are more or less axiologically meaningful in respect to their being more or less "vital." If history, by definition, comprises only realizations of the creative potentialities of individualized life-principles, then, even though particular human phenomena differ markedly in the *degree* of vitality they represent, Spengler's judgment on world history as a whole is unequivocal: measured by the appropriate criterion, *all* history is meaningful.

With these examples of type (2) claims in mind let us recall our description of the differentiated and refined standpoint of living in the world and of man's thinking from this standpoint. To confront the world from this standpoint is to confront it caringly. How the world is *matters*. To care is to presume that one or another alternative state of affairs is preferable. The world is intelligible to us as cared about when we think we know what is preferable. Judgments of preferability—evaluations and practical judgments—are intentionally objective judgments presupposing our thinking of alternative states of affairs as mutually exclusive possibilities. The concept of preferability—basic to thinking from the standpoint of living in the world—encompasses the traditional fundamental axiological categories, "good" and "right." We have seen that type (2) claims as to the meaning of history comprise (a) an axiological principle, which provides the criterion (or criteria) of meaningfulness, and (b) definitive judgments, utilizing this criterion, as to the meaningfulness of all historical events, i.e., judgments as to whether, in what respects, or to what extent these are "good" or "right." The orientation of these claims, we may say, then, is the standpoint of living in the world.

Assuming that type (1) claims fall within the province of natural order questioning and type (2) claims within the province of thinking from the standpoint of living in the world, let us now examine the logical flaw that discredits conceptions of the unified intelligibility of history—unified in the sense that a type (1) claim is combined with a type (2) claim. (The flaw is logical in the sense that it springs from a failure to observe the contrasting presuppositions of thinking from respective standpoints, not from misjudgment as to what is preferable or misjudgment as to the patterned or lawful character of human events.)

In our account of practical judgment, and more particularly in our remarks on causal analysis, we noted the subordinate but important function—within the over-all orientation of rational agency (and, therefore, of living in the world)—of judgments of natural order. The implication is clear: no logical flaw is involved in thinking about *some* occurrences deterministically in connection with practical thinking. But we also observed that in deciding which of two alternative courses of action is the thing to do, we cannot think deterministically about the course of action to be done. We can ask, *hypothetically,* what would necessarily (or what would probably) happen *if* we were to do one thing or the other. We can ask, *hypothetically,* whether it is likely that at the moment of acting such and such a course of action will be feasible. But if our thinking is to issue in a judgment of preferability we cannot ask what action we must do, *all determining conditions considered.* Any natural order thinking that we do in connection with practical thinking must allow us to think of alternative courses of action as possible.

The type (1) claims found in "philosophies of history" are, however, characteristically inclusive and necessitarian. They affirm that what *will* happen in our lives *must* happen; that what we *shall* do we *must* do; that what we *shall* choose to do we *must* choose to do. Among the occurrences conceived deterministically are rational actions, our own and others'. Now it is one thing to ask whether these type (1) claims *as such* are sound; i.e., whether a convincing case can be made out for a pattern or "law" in terms of which *all* events are intelligible as occurring in a necessary, determinate sequence. This question concerns natural order thinking alone. It is another thing to ask whether it is plausible to make such a type (1) claim, when rational actions are included among the "all events," *in combination with* the type (2) claim that "all events" are intelligible as satisfying a criterion of meaningfulness deriving from an axiological principle. The latter is our present query.

Although it is often difficult to discern how the conclusion has been reached, we do find philosophers of history asserting or assuming that what *must happen* is *preferable;* that there is an *interdependence* between what must happen in the course of future events (relative to pattern or "law") and the preferability (or meaningfulness) of what must happen, an interdependence such that one claim implies the other: Either (or both) (A) what must happen must happen *because* only thus will the course of events be preferable (i.e., meaningful), in which case the axiological principle doubles as a causal principle; or (B) what will happen is preferable (i.e., meaningful) *because* it is what must happen, in which case the pattern or "law" doubles as axiological principle. Included among the future events are either (or both) rational actions or consequences of rational actions.

As to (B), from our previous discussion of thinking from the standpoint of living in the world it is clear that a judgment about the preferability of a course of action (i.e., what is to happen) cannot be made on the ground that it (the action) must happen. Judgments of preferability—evaluations as well as practical judgments—*preclude* presupposing the necessity of the combination of particular circumstances about which the judgment is made. Of course, if it can be shown that a philosopher of history does not use "preferable" (or "good" or "right") as a category relating to our caring about the world, then his view of history does not even include a type (2) claim, properly speaking; he cannot then be accused of logically compromising his evaluational or practical thinking, but he also cannot be credited with illuminating the meaning of history from the standpoint of living in the world. Indeed, the propriety of considering him a "philosopher of history" would become doubtful.

As to (A)—the view that preferability implies inevitability—our previous analysis again points up the flaw. A judgment as to what must happen (natural order thinking) is not based on a judgment as to which future happening is preferable. It cannot be because judging preferability *precludes* thinking of the events, action, or situation about which the judgment is made, *as* necessary. The rational agent who says, "I must do x because x is the thing to do" is not and cannot be saying that he "must" do x in the sense that there are sufficient (natural order) conditions of doing x. (Unless, of course, "the thing to do" is not employed as a category relating to our caring about the world.)

Close scrutiny of the thinking of philosophers of history often reveals equivocation, obfuscation, and a fascinating vacillation between equally untenable positions in pursuit of the unattainable; namely, a unified type (1) *and* type (2) claim consistent with the contrasting presuppositions of natural order thinking, evaluation, and practical reasoning. For example: (a) While pretending to adopt the standpoint of living in the world, they warp the concept of rational action to fit the presuppositions of natural order intelligibility, viewing rational action as sufficiently determined. (b) Without any justification other than that it suits them to do so, they qualify their type (1) claim as to the "necessity" of history by making an exception of rational actions. (c) They give the impression that their type (1) and type (2) claims are aspects of the unified intelligibility of history, but never discuss rational action, responsibility, freedom, and determinism carefully enough to allow the difference in standpoints to become apparent. (d) Taking cognizance of problems raised by the apparent disparateness of standpoints they staunchly defend the idea of unified intelligibility, declaring that the solution of those problems is a mystery too deep for human minds to fathom.

A combined type (1) and type (2) claim is illogical—whether in form (A) or (B) or (A) and (B) together. We conclude then—and this was our first thesis—that there is a logical flaw in most "philosophies of history." It remains to consider the prospects for the unified intelligibility of history within the framework of each of the two standpoints *independently,* beginning with natural order thinking.

A type (1) claim characteristically not only affirms that all history is intelligible in terms of a single "law" or pattern, but also that the determinacy of the sequence of occurrences is necessary in some sense. The necessity predicated of an allegedly determinate inclusive sequence or sequences of events in a natural order judgment is not an absolute necessity. Even complete natural order accounts of occurrences only make these intelligible *relative* to the fact that certain conditions obtained: *under those conditions* the occurrences were bound to happen. As to unified intelligibility, the unity could conceivably be achieved by accounting for what happens either in terms of a small number of kinds of factors or in terms of inclusive closed systems within which occurrences exhibit the same sequential pattern. It would be arbitrary to rule out summarily the possibility of unification along either or both of these lines. No warrant for doing so can be derived from the fact that so many attempts at unification have been crude and arbitrary. The quest for broad patterns and inclusive laws of human events *is* perfectly plausible in principle, involving as it does the same kind of thinking as any natural order questioning about particular human events. The most that can be said by way of qualification is that up to the present, natural order inquiry into the course of human events has been most successful in formulating, not type (1) claims, but loose generalizations of restricted universality dealing for the most part with relatively restricted kinds of phenomena (economic development, political revolutions, migrations, the role of elites, etc.). For adventurous spirits who persist in the exciting quest for unifying nomological universals, experience suggests the value of familiarity with some of the devastating critiques that have been made of previous type (1) claims.

Passing to the standpoint of living in the world, let us recall that type (2) claims include (a) an axiological principle, and (b) a judgment to the effect that particular past, present, and future human events satisfy the criterion (or criteria) of meaningfulness provided by this principle. In the light of our previous remarks about principles of evaluation and principles of action, is it plausible to affirm, or even to inquire after, *the* meaning of history, i.e., unified intelligibility of the course of human events from the standpoint of living in the world?

We have noted that there are different ways in which meaningfulness can be conceived. Let us distinguish more formally between two principal ways. The particular events comprising history, considered discretely or in combinations (as coexistent or sequential), can be said to be meaningful either (I) if specified matters of human concern are judged to be *at stake* in these happenings (i.e., if specific "preferabilities" are involved), or (II), in a stronger sense, if these actual happenings, viewed in true perspective, are judged to be preferable ("good," "right," etc.) or to be positively related to the coming about of what is preferable (e.g., as necessary conditions of preferable outcomes or as manifesting a trend toward more preferable conditions). Obviously the second conception (II) presupposes the first (I), for it must be possible to specify what actual conditions or actions would be preferable if one is to judge that what happens is preferable or is positively related to the coming about of what is preferable. The implausibility of type (2) claims can be established, therefore, by showing that, in the first sense of meaningfulness, there is no unifying meaning of history. To show this, in turn, we need only challenge the plausibility of any and all unitary conceptions of man's concerns.

Conception (I) of meaningfulness reminds us of Niebuhr's notion that all incidents of human life—at least wherever human freedom is involved—have unity of meaning, in that all involve a "conflict between good and evil forces"[60] and the measure of good (and therefore of evil) is always the same: man's love of and obedience toward his creator. Similarly, it might be supposed, according to *our* account of the standpoint of living in the world, all events as thought of from this standpoint are meaningful in one and the same respect, i.e., all are meaningful in relation to some human concern. But whereas Niebuhr's unifying principle is substantive, ours is not; ours merely defines the standpoint of caring and does not imply *what* is at stake in our caring, let alone a *unitary* conception of what is at stake. When we do examine sound general principles of evaluation and action in search of a unifying substantive principle, we find none. The only universally applicable principle of judgment—a principle for reducing "indeterminacy"—is that what is objectively preferable for someone in a specific situation is to be ascertained by methodical inquiry pertinent to that situation and to that personal reference, utilizing as tools of analysis substantive and methodological principles based on experimental practice. But *this* "unifying" principle, of itself, also has no specific substantive import; it is purely methodological. In fact, there are three disunifying factors that effectively rule out a unitary substantive conception of human concerns.

We mentioned earlier the generalized principles of evaluation and action that issue from experimental practice. Some of these we can describe as substantive general formulations of kinds of conditions that are of universal concern to human beings: physical and mental health, maturity, creativity, etc. The first source of disunity is the character of these general principles: they are *not* systematically interrelated. More explicitly, what in general is to be preferred in accordance with these principles (conditions that in general make for satisfactoriness, and characteristics of actions that in general make for appropriateness of an action), cannot be thought of as modes or "organically" related constituents of a single desideratum. (Pseudo-unifications are common enough. But "happiness," "human welfare," "harmonious adjustment," "fulfilment of human potentialities," and comparable unifying concepts are, at best,

60. Niebuhr, *Faith and History*, p. 27.

labels for a number of diverse desiderata; more frequently they are simply vague.)

The concrete circumstances in which human beings find themselves are a second source of disunity. These make for *de facto* diversity, discreteness, opposition, and tension in specific human concerns. Circumstances, not a unitary concept of "the good" or "the right," determine what concerns are pertinent and which have priority. In other words, when the general principles referred to above, which are so many tools of analysis and do not of themselves systematically define *the* meaning of history, are brought to bear upon the multifarious actual circumstances encountered in the course of particular human lives, the result is not a unitary conception of "the satisfactory" and "the appropriate" embracing all situations of all persons. "The best under the circumstances," "the best that can (or could) be done," is not always substantively the same best, not even for the same person or identifiable group of persons at all times, in every situation. Thus, taking a synoptic view of all *actual* specific conditions and actions, even if it turned out that all *could* be characterized individually as "the best under the circumstances" or characterized collectively as manifesting patterns of progressive fulfilment, this would not overcome the pluralism of the modes of "best."

Disunity is further compromised by the pluralism of personal reference. The standpoint of living in the world is common to all men, but that standpoint involves self-centered reference. Each of us confronts the conditions and actions of his lifetime as a sequence of possibilities. We can identify with the standpoint of others, but their standpoint as living in the world is no less self-centered than our own. We can share concerns and pursue identical or interdependent goals co-operatively, but the pursuit, the successes achieved, the shared "consummatory experiences" have ultimate multiple *personal* reference. What constitutes a satisfactory state of affairs for me can be (in principle) objectively ascertained; what constitutes an appropriate action on my part can be (in principle) objectively ascertained; but the objective preferability in either case is a preferability *for me* as one human living in the world. Unified intelligibility cannot be grounded in the real unity of mankind or the human race, as though we were all components of a single entity with a single concern. In terms of the standpoint of living in the world, from which judgments of preferability are made, the only indubitable unity consists in the fact that all individual human beings confront the world from this standpoint; and this unity, as we have said, cannot sustain a type (2) claim as to the meaning of history.

With these sources of disunity before us, we reaffirm the implausibility of type (2) claims as to the unified intelligibility of history (in whichever of the two ways—(I) or (II)—meaningfulness is conceived). These claims presuppose a unitary substantive conception of what is at stake for human beings in the course of human events; no such conception is warranted.

To dismiss claims as to *the* meaning of history does not commit us, however, to a categorical denial of meaningfulness. To deny *unified* intelligibility is not to deny that there can be multiple, limited unified interpretations of the meaning of history from the standpoint of living in the world. It is true that, to some extent, our individual concerns are *un*like, and that, to some extent, unlike concerns are not harmonious or complementary. It is also true that some concerns of an individual are likely to clash with some concerns of other individuals; some shared concerns of groups of individuals are at odds with concerns of other individuals or groups; and some concerns of individuals and groups change, so that what is of concern today may bear no meaningful relation to yesterday's concerns or tomorrow's. A case in point is the disunity of the life-experience of successive generations within the same society—a disunity manifested in the disparity and discontinuity in the values at stake and in related practical principles. Nevertheless, specific criteria of preferability (applying to conditions or actions) with personal reference to one and the same individual human being are not utterly different from situation to situation, and do involve a structuring of "goods" and goals in terms of priorities and interdependence. The temporary viability of this framework of concern-identification and specification makes possible a unified interpretation of world happenings over a period of time with reference to that individual. Moreover, some components of this framework represent shared concerns; individual-referring frameworks interlock in complex fashion reflecting common interests and social roles. These shared components, including those representing elaborately institutionalized concerns and formalized activities of all sorts, may have considerable stability and continuity, permitting frameworks of interpretation which serve over long periods of time for making many virtually routine evaluations of specific situations and many routine practical judgments.

This stability and continuity together with the *shared* character of the concerns make possible unified interpretations of world happenings, which bear marked resemblances to "philosophies of history"—particularly the more primitive ones, where no conscious explicit emphasis is placed on the *unqualifiedly unitary* character of the framework and on its relevance to the *totality* of human events. When such a framework is implied or explicit in a wide-ranging survey of human events; when it is conjoined with appraisals of the satisfactoriness of conditions involving various matters of public concern—those of a nation, a civilization, or humanity at large; when it includes judgments as to what future conditions would be satisfactory, as to what are the general requirements for appropriate individual and group action for some time to come and for critical judgments of past conditions or past rational actions—then we have an even closer approximation to a "philosophy of history." Indeed, just such broad, yet limited, unified interpretations have sometimes been designated "philosophies of history."[61] The more consciously critical a formulation of this kind is, the more explicitly stated will be its limitations as an account of the meaningfulness of history. It is uncritical if the circumstantial (and therefore tentative) character of its structuring of "goods" and goals is lost sight of; it is uncritical if it is *assumed* that matters of public concern take precedence over matters of personal concern; it is uncritical if it hypostatizes any human collectivity or arbitrarily identifies the concerns of a portion of mankind throughout a certain period of time with those of humanity at large.[62]

It cannot be assumed that even a tentative unifying framework referring to inclusive public concerns is always possible. At certain times and among certain aggregations of human contemporaries shared concerns might be entirely absent. It has been pointed out, however, that the trend at present is away from diverse and conflicting human concerns, toward uniformity and interdependence. The method and achievements of scientific inquiry are becoming universally accepted and exploited in practical applications. Simi-

61. See Randall, *Historical Experience*, pp. 96, 210-12. Examples of "philosophies of history" in this sense are William H. McNeill, *Past and Future* (Chicago: University of Chicago Press, 1954), and Robert L. Heilbroner, *The Future as History* (New York: Harper and Brothers, 1959). Much of the discussion in sec. 2 of this chapter bears directly upon the thinking involved in working out and applying critical frameworks of concern-identification and specification relating to matters of public concern.

62. See Edel's relevant distinctions between a universal, local, and personal "valuation base," *Ethical Judgment*, pp. 297-339.

larities in the ways goods are produced, processed, and distributed become ever more striking, ideological differences notwithstanding. Economically and politically, the lives of men throughout the world become increasingly interdependent. A consequence of this universalization and integration in scientific, technical, and economic sectors is that contemporary human beings have more and more specific shared concerns. For the first time, circumstances are making possible a virtually universal "philosophy of history."[63]

Let us recall here that the particular events comprising history can be said to be meaningful either in the sense that specified matters of human concern are judged to be at stake (sense (I)) or in the stronger sense (II) that these happenings are themselves preferable or are positively related to the coming about of what is preferable. We have affirmed the possibility of interpretations of history affording limited unified intelligibility, i.e., possibilities for discerning meaningfulness *in the first sense*. We shall not undertake to assess the extent to which actual human conditions and actions are meaningful in the second sense, i.e., *are* (or have been or can be expected to be) preferable or conducive to what is preferable, measured by any of the multiple frameworks of interpretation. In terminating our critique of "philosophies of history" we can summarize our principal conclusions as follows: Attempts to integrate type (1) and type (2) claims as to the meaning of history run afoul of differences in the presuppositions—or schemes of intelligibility—of two standpoints from which human beings think about the world. The ascertainment of broad patterns and inclusive laws of human events is a task for differentiated and refined natural order thinking. It is impossible to establish a priori the limits and scope of unified natural order intelligibility. Finally, although disunifying factors rule out the definitive unified intelligibility of history as a whole from the standpoint of living in the world, more or less durable and inclusive unified interpretations of the meaning of history are possible.

63. See, e.g., Raymond Aron, *The Dawn of Universal History* (London: Weidenfeld and Nicolson, 1961).

Chapter X.

Conclusion

1. Historical Thinking and Philosophical Anthropology

Our analysis has stressed the fundamentally different ways in which human beings confront the world. We have taken note of the differentiated and refined lines of questioning and schemes of intelligibility corresponding to different confrontations. It is our contention that the differentiation and refinement referred to have been worked out in the course of critical reflection, i.e., through thinking about thinking. One field for critical reflection is the thinking men do about particular human events, and we have endeavored to take stock of the differentiation of standpoints as an outcome of reflection about thinking of this sort.

Although our conclusions have issued from an analysis of historical thinking, they are of general import. One of their most far-reaching implications pertains to the concept of man: In answering the question "What is it to be a human being?" we must take into account the two ways in which we confront the world, ask questions about it, and find it intelligible.

Critical reflection issues in a description of at least one facet of man's nature: being human comprises the possibility of thoughtful confrontations of the world in terms of natural order and in terms of the comparative preferability of alternative conditions and actions. Description, even when it issues from critical reflection, does not make anything intelligible. Intelligibility is relative to the lines of human questioning disclosed through critical reflection. Intelligibility is a function of standpoints of thinking. That there are standpoints of thinking is not itself intelligible; it is a fact.

We have described the schemes of intelligibility and sketched the requirements of adequate accounts of the world judged from the different standpoints. Implicit in each of these standpoints is a conception of human being. From the standpoint of natural order thinking we are a distinctive manifestation of natural order. From the standpoint of living in the world we are a center of caring, whose possible conditions and actions are matters of concern and therefore subject matter for evaluation and practical reasoning. These conceptions, like the standpoints they represent, are not incompatible but nonetheless cannot be unified. We conceive of ourselves in terms of two dissimilar schemes of intelligibility, neither more fundamental than the other. I can, in principle at least, take myself as caring and cared about, take my evaluating and the conditions I evaluate, take my practical reasoning and my actions all as subject matter for natural order inquiries. Or, I can, for example, evaluate my work as a specialist in natural order thinking and consider whether I might better have spent my time doing something completely different. Neither standpoint, however, can absolutely dominate or absorb the other. It is not possible for me reflectively to co-ordinate or integrate my conceptions of myself as deterministically intelligible and as a center of concern. Whatever further consequences our analysis may have for a theory of personal identity or conception of the self, we conclude that, at least, no unified concept of man, no unified self-knowledge, is possible.

2. HISTORICAL INTELLIGIBILITY

In our consideration of the nature of historical thinking we have tried to formulate a set of distinctions affording better understanding and positive appreciation of the *variety* of kinds of histories, as well as insight into *unifying* presuppositions of historical thinking (i.e., fundamental schemes of intelligibility).

We have approached the questions "What is history?" and "What is historical thinking?" by examining the judgments men make about particular human events. Our conclusions discredit claims to the effect that there is only one way, or one intrinsically pre-eminent way, in which particular human occurrences become intelligible. The distinction we have established between standpoints of thinking is the basis for a pluralistic conception of the intelligibility of particular human occurrences.

We have maintained, among other things, that this distinction affords insight into the tension that exists in historical practice between two directions of historical inquiry. Simply as affording alternative possibilities for specialization, the differentiated standpoints invite inquirers to engage in the single-minded pursuit of one or another of two lines of questioning; they invite judgments about particular occurrences in which one or another of two schemes of intelligibility completely dominates the construction of the historical world. A critical awareness of the basis for this tension exposes the groundlessness of controversy between partisans of scientific history (at least in one sense of the term) and those who insist that the essential or proper task of the historian is to evaluate and to criticize—to make judgments, of one sort or another, that reflect or illuminate vital concerns of our own, of our contemporaries, or of mankind in general.

At various points in our discussion we have noted the opportunities that abound for varied and complementary treatments of the same human happenings. We distinguished description of happenings from judgments that make happenings intelligible. Using the concept of descriptive understanding we have shown how formulations of distinctively human meanings as well as formal-logical meanings belong neither essentially to natural order thinking nor essentially to thinking from the standpoint of living in the world. Our analysis has disclosed possibilities of multiple accounts of the same happenings *within* each of the two standpoints of thinking, a multiplicity which does not jeopardize objectivity. We have already taken note of these explicitly in the case of natural order. As for accounts from the standpoint of living in the world, it is obvious from our discussion in Part Two that the number of possible objective accounts making the same events intelligible is legion. Judgments from this standpoint have personal reference, and since various concerns of any number of persons can be involved in any one event or chain of events, there is virtually no limit to the evaluative or action-oriented accounts that can be given.

Conventional conceptions of history leave much to be desired as clues to the intelligibility of particular human events. In this regard we have remarked upon a number of allegedly defining characteristics of the subject matter of historical thinking: pastness, uniqueness, social significance, purposive activity, objectified experienced meaning of any kind, etc. We have also discussed various characteristics supposed to set historical thinking apart as a distinctive way of making occurrences intelligible: narrative reconstruction of sequences of events; evaluational interpretation with present-practical import; disclosure of the meaning of events; explanation in terms of the intentions and reasons of purposive agents. Our delineation of standpoints of thinking has disclosed the status and significance of these various traits. As a result it becomes possible to ascertain whether any proposed concept of history or historical thinking is clear and coherent; whether it is arbitrary or circumspectly grounded in critical insight into the nature of man's thinking about the world. For example, we have exposed the untenability of the thesis that the historian's distinctive task is to make unique events intelligible, and we have exposed the arbitrariness of the conventional restriction of historical subject matter to *past* events or to events of *social* significance.

Some of Clio's champions, therefore, perform a disservice in projecting or perpetuating the image of "history proper" as an essentially pure, well-defined, individual discipline, one that has become differentiated and perfected through centuries of historiographical endeavor and finds near perfect, if perhaps never completely perfect, realization in the works of the "great" historians, paragons who excel both in literary artistry *and* in mastery of facts. Whatever kind of thing an historian does can be done well; the best historians are not necessarily all engaged in the same kind of undertaking.

Besides insisting on the importance of a theory of historical thinking that does justice to differences in the way in which particular human events can be treated and can be made intelligible, we have called attention to the co-presence of diverse judgments *within* individual historical accounts. It is not unusual to find that an historian combines many undertakings in one and does so as a matter of course. We refer here not to undertakings that are logically interdependent; not, for example, to a combination of causal analysis with evaluation or practical reasoning, where the former is logically involved in the latter. Often the historian simply combines different kinds of judgments, not integrating them within any one dominant line of questioning. Indeed, although they may relate vaguely to the same theme or topic, are presented under one title, and come to us assembled between the covers of one book, we may wonder whether there is any cognitive unity or significance, any logical coherence at all to the judgments the historian has made and assembled for us in his *"History of Such and Such."* With only piecemeal logical linkage, he may combine descriptive understanding, identifying understanding, natural order explanation, multiple specific criticisms of diverse sorts having diverse personal reference, multiple over-all interpretations of the same course of events employing various frameworks for determining significance, and so on.

Awareness of the dis-integral character of many historical works destroys the assumption that every competent historian has as his objective a single, simple mode of intelligibility, which he attains by working apparently loose strands and odd fragments into a coherent tableau. It exposes the naiveté of the quest—usually undertaken by philosophers—for the identity of this remarkable type of intelligibility. Scrutinized logically, historians' tableaus are often just not coherent. Therein lies the aptness of the frequently made comparison of the historian's standpoint with that of everyday life. Both in the questions some historians ask and answer about past particular human events and in the way they depict men of the past viewing the world about them, we find reflected the motley, disordered questioning and answering, in short the incoherence, of everyday experience. In our awareness of and thinking about the world, we proceed much as the historian often proceeds: sometimes simply noting facts; sometimes working them into a scheme of intelligibility—but rarely thoroughly; sometimes viewing the world from the standpoint of our own concerns; sometimes identifying with the concerns of others—sometimes only identifying and sometimes criticizing as well; sometimes disinterestedly curious about natural order as a distinct kind of intelligibility; sometimes interested in natural order and predictability as bearing on the ascertainment of what is "good" or "right"; sometimes engaging in critical reflection directed towards differentiating and refining standpoints of thinking; sometimes seeking general insights into our own human condition or that of man in general—searching for and testing criteria of meaningfulness; sometimes interested in the past quite apart from present and future considerations and at other times interested in it because of problems confronting us here and now or looming on the horizon of our practical world. Little wonder that we are not discomfited by dis-integrated works of history; they have the familiar feel of the *dis*-order of everyday experience.

On the basis of our analysis of historical thinking, specialization in the study of particular human events is to be expected: some historians will focus their efforts on giving natural order accounts on the plausible assumption that particular human events can be accounted for deterministically, and others will concentrate on making judgments from the standpoint of living in the world. But still others can be expected to eschew either sort of specialization; to cultivate the multiplicity of perspectives, the very casualness and ambiguity of judgment characteristic of man's ordinary, every-day, unspecialized thinking. The latter kind of history might appropriately be called "ordinary history." Ordinary history, so conceived, has profound philosophical import. Whether the ordinary historian realizes it or not, the vision of the world that moulds his work mirrors concretely the pluralism painstakingly discerned and articulated through critical reflection. The critical philosopher of history at least will have a special appreciation for these ordinary histories, reconstructions of human experience which evoke so vividly and forcefully his own complex vision of the historical world; a vision that includes not only man's often tragic ignorance —his not knowing all the answers—but also the fundamentally pluralistic character of the questions themselves, the pluralistic intelligibility of human events.

INDEX

Rostovtzeff, M., 232, 233
Rostow, W. W., 220
Russell, Bertrand, 33-34
Ryle, Gilbert, 21-23, 81

S

Science, unity of xii, 46, 62, 113, 122,
124, 126, 133; objectives of, 36-40;
predictive, 39-40, 66, 75, 211, 216;
historiography of, 94
Scientific explanation, logicians' model
questioned, 43-44, 113-14
Scriven, Michael, 119-22
Sorokin, Pitirim, 87
Specific past, 211-25 passim
Spencer, Herbert, 250-51, 254
Spengler, Oswald, 87, 250-51, 255-56
Staley, Eugene, 234-35
Standpoint of the agent, xiii, 46, 95,
100, 106, 174-88, 190-92, 197-200,
202-5, 241-49
Standpoints of thinking, xi, xiii, 85, 94,
147-48, 268-69; differences between,
152, 153-54, 155-56, 170-72, 179-
82, 186, 188, 208, 252-53, 257-59;
rational development of, 90, 92, 93-
94, 209-10. See also Attitudes,
Natural order, Standpoint of the
agent
State of affairs, 7n
Statistical accounts, 17-19
Statistical laws, 17, 75, 119
Strout, Cushing, 70n
Sufficient conditions, 6, 10, 121, 168
Sweezy, Paul, 56n
Systems, deterministic, 27-29, 34;
closed, 29, 49, 136-37; "neutral
meaning," 86, 92; cultural, 90, 97,
98; elementary, 133-37 passim;
composite, 136; heterogeneous, 136,
138; homogeneous, 136

T

Theory, as systematization of laws,

not an essential requirement of na-
tural order, 75-76
Thinking. See Intelligibility, Stand-
points
Tilly, Charles, 124
Toynbee, Arnold, 250-51
Traits, 7n; identifying function of, 26
Trevelyan, G. M., 4
Triviality, alleged of nomological as-
sertions, 32-34
Truisms, 119-21

U

Understanding, 70n, 231; as method,
96. See also Descriptive understanding, Identifying understanding
Unified intelligibility, combining both
standpoints, 250-59; from the standpoint of natural order, 259-60; from
the standpoint of living in the world,
260-65
Uniqueness, of historical occurrences,
7-9, 52, 59-63, 114, 124-27, 226,
227
Universal conditionals, differentiated
from nomological universals, 10
Universals of fact, 11, 14, 76
Unrestricted universality, 7, 12-14, 23-
27, 53, 65-69
Useful history, 225-36

V

Ventris, Michael, 91
Verifiability of natural order accounts,
33, 34-35
Vianna, Eremildo Luis, 222-23

W

White, Morton, 20n
White, Theodore H., 97-98
Working generalizations, 117-33 pas-
sim, 213, 215
Wright, Quincy, 219